*An American Chef*

*Redefines the Food Styles*

*of Two Cultures*

# *by Ken Hom*

*Wine Notes by Ron Batori and Darrell Corti*

*Photography by Victor Budnik*

# Ken Hom's East Meets West Cuisine

*SIMON AND SCHUSTER* New York

Parts of this book appeared originally in slightly different form in *Bon Appétit, The New York Times Sunday Magazine, Food & Wine, California Living, Washington Post, The Boston Globe, Image, Chicago Tribune, A La Carte* [London], *Taste Magazine* [London], *Australian Gourmet, Epicurean* [Australia], *House & Garden* and *The Home Journal* [Hong Kong].

Simon & Schuster, Inc., would like to thank the following for the loan of accessories and services for the photographs: Sherry Phelan, Surfaces; Annie Glass, Dishes; Dianne McKenzie
Designed by Karolina Harris
Food by Gordon Wing and Todd Koons
Styling by Karen Hazarin
Manufactured in the United States of America
10  9  8  7  6  5  4  3  2  1
Library of Congress Cataloging in Publication Data
Hom, Ken.
        Ken Hom's East meets West cuisine.

        Includes index.
        1. Cookery, American.    2. Cookery, Chinese.
    I. Title.    II. Title: East meets West cuisine.
TX715.H758   1987       641.5951       87-9433
ISBN: 0-671-47086-8

# ACKNOWLEDGMENTS

My life has been blessed throughout with wonderful people who have helped me to learn and grow. Their relentless hard work and love make the success of any book I work on theirs as well.

First and foremost among them is Gordon Wing, my associate chef, friend, and colleague, whose wit and unerring good taste were essential to the success of the recipes in this book. I owe an immense debt to Gerry Cavanaugh, whose editorial grasp of words and research helped clarify my thoughts into a coherent and flowing text. I am grateful for the editorial skills of Mimi Luebbermann and Issac Cronin, and to Todd Koons, who is always there when his chef's skills are needed.

This book would not have been possible without the guidance and care of Carole Lalli, my editor at Simon and Schuster. Her interest in the subject combined with her formidable background in food made Carole an author's dream come true.

I owe thanks to Dan Green, former publisher of Simon and Schuster, who first saw the potential of this book and championed it.

Thank you to Victor Budnik and his team—Karen Hazarian, Caroline Cory, and Dianne McKenzie—for making the food come alive in his beautiful photographs.

My sincere appreciation to Bob Anthony for his lovely cover design and to Karolina Harris for the book design; thanks as well to Frank Metz and Eve Metz for their overview of the book's look and consultation on photography.

The wine notes that accompany the individual recipes and menus add great dimension to East-West cookery; I thank two experts, my good friends Ron Batori and Darrell Corti, for them.

I am very lucky to have the counsel of Martha Casselman, my literary agent, and Ted Lyman, my international agent.

And finally, special thanks to Carol Field, whose inspired article in *Bon Appétit* magazine many years ago gave birth to the concept for this book. Her encouragement through the years has not been forgotten.

To my Chinese mother
and my French family

*A ma mère chinoise
et ma famille Taurines*

# CONTENTS

# *Introduction*

**CHINA AND CHICAGO**

The meeting of East and West has been a major theme in my life, although I did not fully perceive it until I was a young man. I was born in Tucson, Arizona, in 1949, of Chinese parents—what could be more Eastern or more Western? My father died when I was only eight months old, and my mother took me to Chicago. It was there that I grew up, learning, as all good Chicagoans do, that the city is "Hog Butcher for the World . . . Stacker of Wheat, City of the Big Shoulders." It was not those shoulders, however, that bore me up, but my mother's bosom, her traditional Chinese cookery, and the close-knit ties of kinship that characterize the Chinese extended family. Although my mother never remarried, she and I had family enough. We were welcomed into the warm circle of our relatives who were already established in Chicago's minuscule Chinatown.

Thus, I spent my childhood and youth among Chinese kin, following Chinese customs. My mother and my relatives spoke only Chinese to me. I attended a Chinese school in the afternoons after public school. I was immersed in Chinese culture, folklore, and habits. In those days that culture was mainly Cantonese; until very recently the overwhelming majority of Chinese-Americans came from the Canton area of China. The "Judaic-Christian" ethic was not mine; I was reared according to the principles of the unique Chinese amalgam of Confucianism, Taoism, and Buddhism, which emphasized respect for and harmony with nature, and reverence for the family, including one's ancestors. Only gradually and by degrees, as I ventured out into the public schools and streets, did I become a true—that is, a hyphenated—American.

As Americanized as I became, I was, like all second-generation Americans, a creature of two cultures, and my traditional Chinese roots were deep and quick. Nowhere was this more apparent than in my absorption of the Chinese attitude toward food: its various tastes, textures, and colors; the techniques of its preparation; and its significance beyond mere nutrition. In no other culture, with the possible exception of the French and Italian, are the preparation and service of food of such central importance. For my mother, aunts, and uncles—indeed, all of my Chinese elders —food was the favorite topic of discussion. I remember as a child listening in on endless conversations around the table and in the kitchen concerning what food was to be bought, how it was to be prepared, what favorite dishes were to be selected, what the appropriate menu was for the time of year or holiday or other special occasion. This concern or obsession with food is manifest in the very structure of the Chinese language: The phrase *Chi fan le mei you* literally means: Have you eaten yet? In fact, it is close to the English greeting How are you? and is, as well, a wish for one's health and happiness. This all seemed perfectly natural to me at the time. Only later, as I moved out into the larger American society, did I learn that such discussions were less than typical. It was not until I visited France as a young man that I found a culture in which food was a serious and delightful topic of conversation.

My appreciation of Chinese food was nurtured not only at my mother's table but also at my uncle's restaurant, where I began working part-time at the age of eleven. It was there, during long hours after school and on weekends, that I learned in the best and hardest way about Chinese food preparations and techniques. In those early days I was allotted all the onerous, drab, routine but essential jobs. It was some years later before I understood the semantic difference between a galley slave and a kitchen drudge—in practice, there is very little. To really appreciate the subtle delicacy of prawns one should spend hours peeling hundreds of pounds of them. I performed that tedious and painful chore many times. But I still love prawns just as I love conch (sea snails), even though every Thursday I cleaned hundreds, scooping them, still alive, out of huge, wet, sea-smelling burlap bags.

While learning the theory and practice of Chinese food preparation I became aware that the restaurant was also a place of warmth, wonderful aromas, and bright colors. My uncle served not only foods that were familiar to me because my mother prepared them at home, but also "Chinese'" foods that were unfamiliar to me. I learned what the anthropologists now call the "cultural determinants" of eating. Chinese restaurants in those days often had two separate menus: one for ethnic Chinese that listed traditional dishes and the other for "Americans" of all other ethnic origins. These dishes sounded and looked foreign but were reassuringly familiar in taste and texture. Chop suey and chow mein, which sound so Chinese, are as American as vichyssoise and cioppino, those equally exotic dishes invented in America.

It is worth noting that Chinese restaurants today have opened their secret menus in response to customer demand. Americans are more sophisticated about food in general than they were a generation ago and are much more familiar with Chinese dishes that are truly representative of the classic cuisine. The same is true of the menus in the Japanese and Southeast Asian restaurants, which have become increasingly more common in American metropolitan centers. This willingness, even eagerness, to learn, to experience, to enjoy the cuisine of other cultures is one of the outstanding characteristics of the American food scene today. It is true that "American cooking" has from the beginning been based on and derived from foods and recipes brought over by immigrants. What is different about the contemporary adoption of "foreign" foods and techniques is the conscious awareness, the thoughtfulness, that characterizes the process. In most cases the innovations have proved deliciously worthwhile. It seems to me that in America today there are more people than ever before who care about good food and seek meals that are nutritious, fresh, balanced, well prepared, and served with care and imagination. On balance, the results have enriched our social existence in the most palatable ways.

But things were not so years ago, in my uncle's restaurant. In learning of the "two menus" at a very early age, I understood the economic sense of it: Serve the customers what they want. I did not fully grasp the culinary necessity, however, because I myself had shifted easily from Chinese cuisine to the various American foods available to me outside my family circle. My mother had insulated herself within the Chinese community, but I was very much part of the larger "American" society, if only because I attended the public school and walked the Chicago streets. As I grew older, my culture continued to be heavily Chinese, but my social lessons and experiences were increasingly American.

I believe that this journey to ethnic identity, or, rather, toward the easy acceptance of a dual identity, was facilitated by my growing up in Chicago, arguably the most "ethnic" and most ethnically segregated city in America. In this it was but a sharper image of the "country of immigrants." America is not truly a "melting pot," however much we insist upon it; it is more like a stew pot, a ratatouille, in which, generally, all the ethnic components retain their characteristics but also manage to exist at least in comity if not in outright amity. To pursue the metaphor, as with the ratatouille, the test of success lies in the sauce, in the reduction of all the flavors of the separate ingredients into something new and delightful. By that test the American ratatouille certainly *vaut le voyage*—it is worth a special journey. I'm proud to be a part of this particular ragout.

Admittedly, I often wondered at some of the foods eaten by my non-Chinese friends—turkey, for example. I found it unbelievably dry and tasteless, as it often is when roasted to an overcooked stage, American-style. On the other hand, I remember distinctly how much I enjoyed other American staples such as corn, in almost any form, and mashed potatoes. Because the Chinese believe in hot meals, my mother used to place hot rice with Chinese sausages in a thermos for my school lunches. My class-mates were fascinated by such exotic treats. Some of them tasted them and loved them. So I traded my tasty lunch—for cold bologna sandwiches! Could this have been a presage of my future? At least it demonstrates the potential of cultural-culinary exchange. (And I hasten to point out that bologna in the good old days was richer and tastier than today's commercial product; moreover, in Chicago it was traditionally sandwiched between thick slices of ethnic rye or pumpernickel—real bread!)

So, my childhood and adolescence were, in their own way, typically American: two cultures clashing and blending, inhibiting and revealing. With a little bit of luck one may have the best of both worlds. I was lucky. For one thing, even as I was gaining some proficiency as a chef of Chinese cuisine, I saw myself more and more as an American. As such, I was open to other influences, which were emphatically more Western than Eastern. The fruits of that openness were to come later. As a young man not yet twenty, I made a typically American decision to follow Horace Greeley's advice: I moved to California.

**CALIFORNIA AND EUROPE**  In the late 1960s, San Francisco and Berkeley, like many parts of the country, were in a state of intellectual and social ferment. The Vietnam War was in full swing, inspiring as much controversy and protest in the Bay area as anywhere else. This was also a time of rising ethnic consciousness. Black Americans had initiated it all, with their civil rights movements in the 1950s and '60s. But ethnicity was a general phenomenon and, along with many others, I was touched by it.

By the late 1960s and '70s, San Francisco and Berkeley had become perhaps the most tolerant and congenial places in the country for Asian-Americans and other minorities. I certainly found them so, despite lingering and subtle manifestations of racial discrimination. Moreover, the entire area was culturally and cross-culturally alive, innovative, accepting of new ideas, and respectful of ethnic and cultural differences.

Perhaps the tolerance of the Bay area came about because it had already expressed its bile toward minorities and worked the poison out of its system. Clearly, California's proximity to Mexico and Latin America and its openness to Asian-Pacific influences helped to create a climate conducive to the acceptance of ethnic diversity. The opening of China in 1972 had perhaps the greatest impact on the American consciousness. Ever since then, Chinese history, society, and culture have been legitimate and fascinating subjects of both scholarly and popular interest. The cuisine of China, in all of its rich variety, received new attention and drew immediate accolades. This reception of Chinese cookery was enormously assisted by the relatively sudden emergence in America of the full range of Chinese culinary tradition. Heretofore, Cantonese-style cooking had dominated. And with reason: In my opinion it is the richest, most varied, most innovative of the regional cuisines. But in the 1960s, slowly, and in the 1970s, with increasing rapidity, restaurants featuring Sichuan, Shanghai, Hunan, Fujian, and other regional cuisines of the brilliant Chinese culinary spectrum were established and won acceptance.

What was perhaps most impressive to me about the San Francisco Bay area scene in the 1970s was its restaurants. Though I came from a food-conscious and restaurateur background, I was unprepared for their sheer numbers, quality, and ethnic diversity. Even today the area has the highest per capita ratio of restaurants to residents of any American metropolis.

There is another aspect of the California environment that cannot be overemphasized: the year-round abundance and variety of vegetables, fruit, herbs, spices, nuts, meats, and seafood. California does have seasons, but they are less dramatically different from elsewhere. In many ways, parts of the state do constitute an Eden. Luther Burbank decided that the area around Santa Rosa, forty miles north of San Francisco, was the ideal garden spot in America and perhaps in the world.

But again, only in such a wonderful place can one always find fresh fruits and vegetables in season. A comparable place, believe it or not, is in South China, the area radiating inland from Canton, my family's region.

Canton's climate is very similar to that of the Bay area and of southern Europe, mild enough to allow people to sit outdoors almost all year-round and to support a growing season that permits two or three crops a year. I need only to quote from the scholars' account:

> The food of contemporary southern China is, in the opinion of many, the finest in the world. It combines quality, variety, and a nutritional effectiveness that allows it to sustain more people per acre than any other diet on earth. . . . South China may well cultivate more crops, at least on a commercial scale, than any other comparable region. . . . It has the most diverse flora of any region outside the wet tropics. A complexly faulted and folded landscape blessed with abundant rain and warmth encouraged tremendous diversity, and the human inhabitants of the region were not slow to make use of this. Indeed they increased it, by borrowing every easily adaptable crop from every major region on earth.[*]

Would anyone be surprised to learn, then, that my heart stirred when I arrived in this northern California that is so reminiscent of my ancestral lands in climate?

I had no idea that northern California was anything like it turned out to be. I had come west to complete my formal education at Berkeley, and my student days were extremely happy and busy ones. I enjoyed my studies, especially those that dealt with European culture. I remember with particular clarity and appreciation a course on the social history of France through the eighteenth century and the French Revolution. It aided in inspiring me to visit the source, which I did as soon as I could.

Europe was another liberating experience to me. In those days, student flights were relatively cheap, and over the next few years I made several trips and stayed for months at a time. One could live in Europe on ten dollars a day, and I usually managed on less than that. I had become a rather good photographer, and part of my European expenses were paid for by the sale of color slides I made of artworks and architecture in France and Italy.

One aspect of Europe that immediately caught my attention and imagination was the food of the various regions, particularly France and Italy. In most places I had previously visited, one had to expend much time and energy finding a good meal; it seemed to me that in these countries the same time and energy would be required to find a poor meal! And so I

*E. N. Anderson, Jr., and Marja L. Anderson, in* Food in Chinese Culture reveled in my enjoyment of French and Italian breads and pastries, cheeses, fresh fruit, yogurts (which up to then I had not liked), sauces, stews made with the freshest vegetables, and herbs right out of the gardens of Provence. I was captivated by the smells, sights, and sounds of the marketplaces; I enjoyed wonderful and inexpensive meals in the most unlikely places, as I explored the countryside and towns by train. I knew a few things about cooking, but I learned a great deal more because I loved to eat and was not too inhibited to observe and ask questions. And I let my senses take full flight.

People in France and Italy were always extraordinarily gracious to me. I felt this was at least partly because to them I represented not America but China, and particularly its culinary traditions. Such are the advantages of being a cultural hybrid.

My stays in Europe were of incalculable importance to my development as a cook. To be sure, at this time of my life I was not yet certain of my profession, but, in retrospect I believe this allowed me a beneficial flexibility when I confronted the French and Italian cuisines. I readily perceived the possibility, the desirability, of blending ingredients and techniques. Without any culinary defensiveness I immediately saw that Western pastries, based on butter, were lighter and tastier than the lard-based pastries of Eastern culture. On the other hand, Chinese and Japanese mushrooms, with their rich, smoky flavor, are often preferable to the more delicate, subtle Western varieties. Chinese roast duck is the best in the world, but it is even better with Western herbs instead of the traditional ginger and scallions. Herbs, in fact, are perhaps the one food ingredient in which China is relatively deficient, since most Chinese herbs are used for medicinal purposes. The French, I discovered, cooked turkey in a way that enabled me for the first time in my life to enjoy it, but still, why not steam the bird à la chinoise and guarantee its flavor and moistness? And in lieu of bread-chestnut stuffing and cranberry sauce, why not jazz up the old bird with a Chinese sweet rice and Chinese spice stuffing and Chinese plum-apple sauce?

I began preparing dishes around such insights or speculations in the early 1970s, experimenting on my friends, to their palates' delight and to my professional encouragement. By 1975 I realized my apprenticeship, unselfconsciously served, was over; my deliberate journey toward professionalism began in earnest. I knew then what I wanted: to be a cook and to prove that the twain can and should meet. As I undertook the task of combining hitherto discrete techniques and ingredients, I felt no sense of incongruity, no betrayal of the culinary traditions of either East or West.

Nor do I feel any today, after a decade of continued learning, teaching, and practice in the blending of East and West. Let me not to the marriage of true cuisines admit impediments! It only remains to describe in more detail the meeting of those different ways and of what the meeting consists. I have loved the journey; it has been delicious fun all the way.

<table>
<tr><td>

**WE ARE WHAT WE EAT, AND HOW**

</td><td>

Why the fuss about food? Aside from sustaining our lives, bonding us together, giving deep meaning to our rituals, bolstering our egos, defining our identities, and bringing us pleasure and contentment, what good is it?

</td></tr>
</table>

To ask the question is to answer it. A moment's thought suffices to explain why food is perennially a subject of study, why cookbooks are popular far beyond the capabilities of our kitchens, and why so many people derive pleasure from reading the literary efforts of professional cooks and the accounts of the "peregrinations of epicures," as Joseph Wechsberg called them. To all of us, both as individuals and as a species, food is as vital a matter as sex; moreover, according to the Marquis de Sade and the Kamasutra, our appetites and needs—and our ability to improve upon and enrich our natural capacities—are even greater in regard to food than to sex. Whether we are "virtuous" or not, there shall be more cakes and ale!

Such thoughts as these did not inform my days or disturb my dreams as I began my professional career in the mid-1970s. I was aware, however, that things were happening in the world of food selection, preparation, and service. What was happening was both generally important socially, and specifically influential on me as an aspiring chef and a lover of good food.

It was the dawn of a new age of health awareness, with particular reference to wholesome food. At the end of his stimulating book *Culture and Cuisine,* Jean-François Revel concludes that the one safe judgment we can make concerning food trends today is the "back to nature" theme. By this he means "the accent [is] on the natural food, its freshness, its authenticity. Hence, mixtures in which natural flavors and odors cancel each other out are banished, as are added spices (beginning with salt), which destroy them by brutally overwhelming them. Subtle, imperceptible, or nonexistent aromas."

One may differ with M. Revel in detail, but his emphasis on the trend (or return) to the fresh and the natural is certainly correct. It is a characteristic that profoundly shapes both the so-called nouvelle cuisine and the California cuisine, about which more later. In the 1970s California chefs, food writers, and consultants were among the leaders of the movement. It is true that California has a "food fad" reputation. Much fun has been poked at the avocado-bean sprouts-nuts-and-yogurt cults that allegedly flourish there.

But there are fundamental differences between the contemporary emphasis and direction and mere food faddishness. There is, for example, a quantitative difference. A very significant proportion of the general population has created the demand for "natural foods"; that is, for fresh, unprocessed foods, or, if processed, for foods without added salt, sugar, synthetic colors, or other additives. When the giant commercial canners begin producing and the supermarkets begin showcasing unsweetened fruits and unsalted vegetables, you may be sure they are not responding to food faddists or even to scientific studies. Rather, they are cashing in on a broad-based consumer demand.

In part, the predilection for the fresh and the natural may have been a rebellion against the Establishment, this time in the guise of "agribusiness" and corporate food processors. The idea, as I often heard it expressed, was to circumvent the "system"; to go directly to the farmer or even to grow your own; to establish "alternative, organic markets"; to adopt a "holistic" approach to food, one that fed the soul as well as the body. Not all of this was nonsense, and some of it proved successful, turning a nice profit without too many compromises with one's principles. On the whole the impulse and results were beneficial in terms of both our health and the quality of our food.

In another part, the desire for the fresh and the natural was no doubt prompted by nostalgia (often misplaced) for the rapidly disappearing traditional regional foods. The emergence of network television and the effective completion of the interstate highway system in the early 1970s constitute perhaps the last stage of the process of obliterating true regionalism. Friends have told me that when they drove and hitchhiked back and forth across the country in the 1940s and '50s they actually experienced regional styles of cooking that have since disappeared. These local and regional cuisines have been overcome by perhaps cheaper and more convenient, but also characterless, homogeneous, processed, and pre-packaged, "national brands."

Whatever the varied reasons for the new directions in food preferences, there was undoubtedly a growing consciousness among masses of people not only in California but also in the rest of the country that eating means more than merely ingesting edible matter. No doubt, without most of them knowing it, people were adopting and living out the truth of M. F. K. Fisher's lapidary expression, "There is a communion of more than bodies when bread is broken and wine drunk." Food, the sharing and serving of it, means caring for others as well as for oneself. It means taking a little time to shop and directing your attention to the preparation and the savoring, the enjoyment of food, not only as a necessary end in itself but also as an essential means of social contact and affection.

Now, as I turn to the specific elements that inform my blending of the cuisines of East and West, I must acknowledge other great influences on me: the contributions of Craig Claiborne and Julia Child. Beginning in the 1960s but growing to prominence in the 1970s, they moved from being known only among a relatively small group of food enthusiasts to the status of national celebrities. And justifiably. They were instrumental in educating the public taste and in introducing Americans to the cooking of other cultures. They encouraged others to take food seriously and unselfconsciously, demonstrating how the preparation of food is at once a necessity and an occasion for the most significant human and humane interaction. I believe that much of the social history of America in the past two decades may be discovered in their writings. Their influence will be as lasting as it has been beneficial.

**CHINESE AND OTHER ORIENTATIONS**  I have already indicated that in no other culture does food play so central and pervasive a role as in China. Historians, anthropologists, poets, and novelists have expatiated upon that role without exhausting its rich meanings. In my own life, my mother and my family impressed its varied significances upon me long before I was able to fully understand them. I do remember quite clearly when I was a child one of my uncles pointed to a whole steamed fish on the table and admonished me never to eat the cheek meat and to leave the tail portion to my mother. The cheek meat, of course, is a delicacy, and filial piety required that my mother receive the choicest morsels.

Thus, among Chinese families, the preparation and consumption of food is an exercise in tradition, in esthetics, in mutual caring and, often, in moral lessons. This tradition is normally followed unselfconsciously, taken for granted. But circumstances can make the tradition come alive, as it were. For example, the immigrant generation elders in my family did not assimilate into the American culture. They clung tenaciously to their Chinese language, culture and, especially, cuisine. As we all know, food has a psychological dimension, and this dimension was accentuated for me when the elders around the table fondly recalled the dishes they had customarily enjoyed in China. I read recently that the human olfactory sense is unique in that its sensations are transmitted directly to the emotional and memory portions of the brain, bypassing the cognitive functions. This helps explain the common human experience of a smell, odor, or fragrance immediately evoking the clearest memories of long-past events.

Certainly, among the elders in my family—exiles all, and no doubt in their dreams still living in China—great effort was made to re-create the fragrance, taste, texture, and appearance of the old favorites. Traditional techniques were applied and rituals were followed, authentic ingredients or their closest substitutes were sought, experiments were made, adaptations were thoughtfully introduced—*à la recherche du goût perdu.*

In the attempt to recapture the tastes of the past, nothing helped my family so much as the marvelous adaptability of Chinese cooking. It is one of its sterling attributes. Chinese cooks have served throughout the world, and Chinese cuisine has been remarkably well received everywhere. This is largely because Chinese cookery lends itself to the use of new and different ingredients. Only those foods that were basically incompatible with Chinese geography or cultural traditions were not adopted—for example, dairy products. Thus, the Chinese have readily accepted new foods into their diet; most recently, corn, tomatoes, and asparagus.

Chinese cooking technique, however, with its logical principles and simple equipment, has been relatively unvarying for thousands of years. And here I must quote from Marcella Hazan's superb work, *The Classic Italian Cookbook:* "The character of a cuisine is determined more by basic approach than by ingredients. Ingredients come and go, depending on popular taste and the changing patterns of commerce. . . . This is not said to encourage indifference but rather to discourage an exaggerated dependence upon them." The same words may be applied to Chinese cuisine.

This may be contrasted with the close dependence of the great Japanese cuisine on traditional ingredients. As Shizuo Tsuji writes: "The greatest barrier to learning Japanese cooking is not so much cooking techniques as ingredients. Simmering, steaming, grilling, and the like are the same or similar in other cuisines, but unfamiliar ingredients and their combinations are another matter." This reliance on the traditional ingredients has its perils. Tsuji sorrowfully concludes: "I am sorry to say, our own cuisine is no longer authentic. It has been polluted with frozen foods, which are freely used in heedless ignorance of tradition. Japan must be the only country in the world where the everyday fare is such a hodgepodge [of Western, Japanese, and Chinese food], and whose people know so little about their own traditional cuisine that they do not try to preserve its authenticity." One sympathizes with this great chef's regret at the passing of the traditional cuisine following Japan's entry into the world's commercial mainstream with its new and exotic ingredients. Technique and approach, however, are timeless and trans-historical, and it is only through them that the "traditional" may be maintained.

Thus, it is their philosophical approach and traditional technique, rather than the availability of bok choy or Sichuan peppercorns, that allow the overseas Chinese to create authentic Chinese dishes and to recapture their past, their homeland. The Chinese cook in a foreign kitchen will take whatever is at hand and create a distinctively Chinese menu. This trait, by the way, provides the basis for the origins of chop suey: rough and tough forty-niners demanding "Chinese food" from a hapless restaurateur who was almost out of provisions. He steamed some rice, chopped and roll-cut whatever he had on hand that could pass for a vegetable, stir-fried it with some pieces of spiced leftover chicken, and voilà! Technique gave rise to an apparently authentic Chinese dish, or at least to a reasonable facsimile thereof.

The basic principles of Chinese cooking technique are universal in their applicability. The various slicing, chopping, dicing, mincing, and other preparations; steaming, steeping, and braising; deep-frying, shallow-frying, and stir-frying—all these techniques of Chinese cooking are readily learned and applied. Woks and cleavers are the preferred implements, but knives and skillets serve well enough. The essence of the technique lies in its simplicity. Stir-frying offers a good example of this. All that is required is a little oil, a hot wok or pan, and a rapid stirring of chopped and sliced food. This produces what is generally regarded as the tastiest of cooked vegetables. And it works equally well with meat, poultry, and seafood.

For a variety of reasons—the high price of firewood, the cost of ovens, the lack of kitchen space—roasting never became a popular cooking technique in China (or in Japan or India, for that matter). Commercial ovens were available for use on ceremonial or religious occasions. But since there is more than one way to cook one's goose, the Chinese rely on techniques involving cut-up parts of the whole that are easily and quickly cooked and that involve relatively more efficient use of fuel. The wok's design concentrates heat; a bit of oil suffices to cook the food. Steaming is more efficient than roasting; boiled water retains its heat much longer than dry air, and the food remains moist, tender, and naturally flavorsome in the bargain.

Such techniques were fashioned by the experience of thousands of years. (One study of food in ancient China begins at 5000 B.C.) It would be surprising if simple, practical, and common-sensical techniques did not evolve out of those millennia of kitchen labor.

Ingredients may be substituted for each other in Chinese cooking; the age-old techniques may be similar to those found in other cultures. What is unique to China is its philosophy, the fundamental understanding of food and its multifarious relationship to cultural life. Food in Chinese culture has for thousands of years signified much more than mere sustenance. Throughout most of their history the Chinese people were poor and were always threatened with scarcity, and yet in normal times they were well fed. While they enjoyed the blessing of having food beyond the mere subsistence level, they also experienced the necessity of making the most of whatever edibles were available.

Experience, serious and playful, led the Chinese to their wholesome attitude toward food and to their view that good cooking is essential to good eating. This in turn required them to learn the qualities of each ingredient and to understand how different cooking techniques can dramatically affect foods in different ways. (For a homely example of this, someday compare a steamed and a roasted turkey.) This situation, over thousands of years, led to inventiveness and creativity in food preparation; it also encouraged the fullest exploitation of local ingredients and the deepest receptivity of foreign foods.

What prevented this inventiveness and receptivity from creating a hodgepodge cuisine was the maintenance of certain invariable relationships that are peculiar to the Chinese cuisine. The most important of these is the fan-t'sai divisions. One thousand years ago a Chinese food critic reported that "the things that people cannot do without every day are firewood, rice, oil, salt, soybean sauce, vinegar, and tea." Of the "seven essentials," notice that only one is a substantial food: rice. Rice is the epitome of "fan" foods, which also include grains, noodles, and dumplings. The other foods, the t'sai, include vegetables, meat, poultry, and seafood. Linguistically, these latter foods were known as "hsia fan," or food to help get the rice down. Clearly, fan foods were primary, just as "bread is the staff of life" in the West.

Moreover, the fan-t'sai are never mixed together. They may be closely juxtaposed, as in Chinese dumplings, but never confused. Each retains its proper proportion and distinctiveness; rice is always served in a separate bowl.

But always the aim was for a balanced meal, which by definition consisted of the proper proportions of both food groups, each prepared in appropriate ways. And, what is very important, the meal is accompanied by a soup, usually of vegetables. The Chinese consider soup not as a separate course but as a beverage to be consumed throughout the meal.

In the preparation of t'sai dishes, multiple ingredients and a blend of flavors is the rule. This means that the ingredients must be cut up, sliced, diced, chopped, shredded, ground (but never pureed, for textures must be preserved), and the appropriate spices and seasonings added. The combination of ingredients so prepared and flavored produces dishes of an almost infinite variety of shapes, flavors, tastes, aromas, and colors. The great eleven-volume compendium of *The Famous Dishes of China* credibly maintains that "there are over 5,000 well-known and well-defined Chinese dishes, each commanding its own distinctive color, flavor, aroma, and texture, which are appealing to the human palate." Such a number is made possible by the approach and the technique, not the ingredients. Age has not withered nor custom staled that infinite variety.

One other philosophical tenet has for centuries guided the Chinese approach to food: the belief that the varieties and amounts of food consumed are directly and intimately related to one's physical and spiritual well-being. Food is thus regarded not only as essential to life but as a physical restorative, at times as an actual medicine. Chicken soup is one such medicine, as we in the West agree. It is the most universal cure-all and, as recent research indicates, for practical, not only psychological reasons. But food in China is also a spiritual support, a way of maintaining harmony with society, nature, and the cosmos.

This emphasis on harmony shapes the entire Chinese approach to food. In the ancient Chinese philosophy, harmony within both the body and the cosmos consisted of the proper relationship among the five essential elements—metal, wood, water, fire, and earth—and the appropriate balance between heat and cold. Why five elements? The Chinese appear to prefer that number. Thus, there are also five tastes—bitter, sweet, salt, sour, and hot—and these are linked in theory to the five elements. And then on to the five vital organs—heart, liver, lungs, kidneys, and stomach—and beyond.

At this point the yin and the yang of food comes into play. All foods fall into one of three groups. Yin foods are "cold" and include crustaceans, especially crab; vegetables, such as cabbage; and certain beans. Yang foods include fatty meats, oily plant foods, such as peanuts, and smoked fish. Yin-yang foods, such as rice and wheat, are neutral. All this is similar to the ancient Western belief in the "humors"—blood, phlegm, bile, and choler—which were supposed to determine both a person's qualities and disposition as well as the attributes of nature.

The Chinese are much too adaptable, however, to lock themselves into any rigid system. The appropriate cooking techniques can compensate, if need be, for any yin-yang imbalances; moreover, the individual's bodily or personality makeup may require more or less yin or yang. The logic of all this is not immediately apparent to outsiders (or to critical insiders, for that matter!). In matters of the yin-yang of food, the essential thing for the Chinese is to attain a harmonious blend of taste, texture, color, and fragrance, and the right balance of fan and t'sai foods.

A Chinese meal, then, is an essay in concord. Generally, along with the fan there are four t'sai dishes—seafood, poultry, meat, and vegetable. Appropriate cooking techniques applied to the various foods and the judicious application of spices and seasonings assure the contrast and balance of textures, colors, shapes, sizes, aromas, and flavors.

Thus, harmony, wholesomeness, esthetics, flexibility, and inventiveness characterize the Chinese approach to food, to eating. Such traits are appropriate to a culture in which almost every partaking of food is also a social exchange. Chinese cuisine may or may not be the greatest in the world, but what is undeniable is that Chinese culture is the most strikingly oriented toward and around food. The only other cultures I know that are worth comparing in this regard are in France and in Italy, where, writes Marcella Hazan, "eating is one more manifestation of the Italian's age-old gift of making art out of life." And it was those two European culinary traditions that most impressed me and influenced my own professional development.

**THE NEW AMERICAN COOKING AND EAST MEETS WEST**

In writing this book on the blending of Eastern and Western cuisines, I had no intention of changing anyone's food habits and preferences. Even the Chinese do not accept every new food. And the most recent surveys of the eating habits of Americans show that, despite intense public interest in food and the relationship between health and nutrition, the typical American diet has changed little over the past decade. This is not surprising. It is as children that we learn what and how to eat, and it is difficult to change habits and preferences so ingrained in us. Moreover, eating is an emotional and psychological act; in support of this I will simply note that people will both starve and eat themselves to death, and in between surround themselves with a host of food taboos, inexplicable to others.

And yet, fortunately for my efforts here, in recent years people have been changing their eating habits. To say that the "typical" American diet has not changed much does not rule out significant movement. When I first arrived in the Bay area fifteen years ago, there were indeed many restaurants. But in Berkeley, for example, it was almost impossible to find a bagel, to say nothing of a quiche, and the Chinese restaurants preserved the tradition of stereotypical and unrepresentative Chinese foods. There were, to be quite frank, few good restaurants of any cuisine. Today, Berkeley alone has a number of superb and justifiably acclaimed restaurants, along with excellent charcuteries, cheese stores, bakeries, and delicatessens. Nor is this merely the Bay area scene. Throughout America, in every metropolitan center, foods are now common that once were either unheard of or available only through specialty gourmet shops. Thus, I find that I am not attempting to initiate any great or profound changes in people's eating habits. I am in fact following a process that has been under way for some time.

That process may be said to have begun with the introduction of the French nouvelle cuisine. This new style of cooking first stole upon an unsuspecting world around 1965, during that time of innovation and radical movements. A few years later the food critics Henri Gault and Christian Millau "discovered," baptized, confirmed, and then broadcast its virtues to the world. Gault and Millau "defined the outlines" of a new type of cooking perfected by a group of younger French chefs, among them Roger Vergé, Paul Bocuse, Jean Troisgros, Swiss chef Fredy Girardet, Michel Guérard, and Alain Senderens. It cannot be overemphasized that all of these master chefs had been thoroughly schooled in the great traditions of Escoffier and the classical French style. Successful revolutionaries know in their hearts and souls what they are rebelling against; they launch their movement from a solid foundation of real background.

The essential elements of the new style of cooking include shortened cooking times ("as in Chinese food," Gault and Millau wrote, while Bocuse noted the influence of Japanese apprentice cooks in the 1970s); an emphasis on fresh and an avoidance of processed foods: "Make do with what the modern world has not yet ruined," Gault and Millau wrote; lightness of dishes and menus, which follows from "the recognition of the idiotic pretension and the mediocrity of rich, heavy sauces . . . which have massacred so many innocent livers and covered up so much insipid flesh." This led to the banishment of flour as a thickener; reduced heavy cream or crème fraîche and reduced stocks took its place. The use of modern techniques was encouraged whenever appropriate (electric blenders, food processors). Above all, inventiveness was encouraged and revered. Craig Claiborne has written that "the soul of the new cuisine depends on the inspiration and improvisations of a cook or chef. Nouvelle cuisine is not . . . doctrinaire." Gault and Millau wrote, "There are still thousands of dishes to be invented—and probably a hundred of them will be memorable. [The new cooks] don't disdain special condiments, products, and recipes from the East. Bocuse brings saffron from Iran for his mussel soup; Oliver is learning to lacquer ducks; Guérard mixes together duck and grapefruit." If one is to stay with the fresh, which by definition means the local, one must be inventive, finding new ways to prepare the necessarily fewer local foods. The nouvelle cuisine at its best, which was uncommonly often, meant delicious fresh foods, new dishes, and new tastes and combinations, prepared and served with flair and color.

In my own cooking, the new cuisine has been both a liberating influence and a confirmation of many of my own beliefs and practices. Clearly, one must be well versed in the basic cooking techniques and practices. This does not mean simply studying them but applying them on the job. Peel

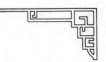

those shrimp! Breathe some life into that soufflé! Baste it, don't bathe it! Fresh foods are the sine qua non of Chinese cooking, so this aspect of the "nouvelle" was immediately to my liking. The receptiveness to new foods and other ingredients was also congenial to my taste and proclivity, as was the emphasis on balance, lightness and color, and the blending of textures and aromas in the preparation and serving of the various dishes —Chinese characteristics all. In a very meaningful way, the nouvelle cuisine allowed me to be myself, to move beyond my Chinese cooking without being a rebel against it. Once more, the best of both worlds.

By now, the nouvelle is no longer novel. It has been around for so long, as we moderns measure time, that there are "classic" dishes in its repertoire: To endure, inventiveness must be codified. In the nature of things, a reaction had to occur—nothing fails like success. The approach and techniques of the cuisine were so widely adopted that one could foresee the results of what Mimi Sheraton observed, namely, "The same principles that bring out the best in certain chefs bring out the worst in others." Those principles were mimed by many practitioners who were less able, less well trained, less well rooted in the old methods and philosophy than the masters they were imitating.

This was to be expected. All such developments are open to misuse, to gourmet-chic exploitation; they may easily degenerate into preciosity or into manifestations of elite conspicuous consumption. We have already witnessed the arrival and departure of a number of nouvelle fads. There have been "in" dishes, there are "out" dishes. Snobbery and one-upmanship are always with us, to our misfortune. However, there is not, or ought not to be, anything pretentious or exotic about using the best and the freshest ingredients available, or in applying new and different, even "foreign," spices and herbs to familiar foods, or in trying out a new technique.

So simple a message may well be lost in the flush of success, and the success of the nouvelle cuisine brought with it a certain reaction. When it came, the reaction was led in part by some of its originators. For example, Guérard now seeks an "equilibrium" between old and new "classics." It is time, he says, "to give a few glances at the past." Bocuse has turned, or returned, to regional classics and to what he perceives as the basis of the French cuisine: wine, cream, cheese, and bread. Earlier I spoke of revolutionaries who must know intimately that which they seek to overthrow; one may say in this context that rebellious children must finally have the courage to admit that their parents were not always wrong.

While the crest of the nouvelle vague is past, the new cuisine is by no means passé. Its enduring virtues comprise elements that must be present in all good cooking: freshness of ingredients; undercooking (or, more precisely, avoidance of overcooking); respect for but not blind adulation of the past masters and approaches; inventiveness, innovation, imagination.

For these reasons, and because of the undeniable deliciousness and satisfying nature of the foods prepared according to its principles, the influence of the nouvelle cuisine is here to stay. In the judgment of Craig Claiborne, writing in 1983, "nouvelle cuisine is the greatest innovation in the world of food since the food processor and, like that machine, it has opened up and broadened horizons in the world of cooking that slightly more than a decade ago were unthinkable." That stands as the final word on the matter—and it is certainly no epitaph.

All of the best features of nouvelle cuisine are manifest in what has come to be known variously as the New American Cuisine or, in regional form, California Cuisine. As I noted earlier, the desire to escape from overly processed foods, to return to the "natural," to regain a simpler, more authentic life-style was a dominant theme in many people's lives during the 1960s. The theme was carried over to cooking in America. It was marked throughout the country by a great ferment of ideas and innovations.

Craig Claiborne, Julia Child, and James Beard were, in their different ways, the heralds, explicators, and exponents of the movement. Alice Waters, of Chez Panisse, was one of the earliest and certainly among the most famous American practitioners of the new cookery. As with every such social-cultural development, definitions prove elusive. However, in discussing James Beard's "crucial role in guiding and refining the nation's growing culinary sophistication," Raymond Sokolov captured much of the essence of the new cuisine:

Had Beard been present [at this benefit feast], he surely would have been struck by two things: the emphasis on regional or ethnic specialties and the readiness to combine ideas and ingredients that had never been mixed before. . . . None of this would have escaped Beard, who had so lovingly wallowed in classic American cookery and watched it coalesce into a cuisine. . . . By [1980], a generation of Americans had lived through the so-called culinary revolution. They had been to Europe and had learned firsthand what traditional cuisines were and how to cook them. They had also observed how the most famous French and Italian restaurants

prided themselves on keeping regional foods and ideas alive on their tables. . . .
[Concurrently] the nouvelle cuisine reveled in exotic ingredients and bizarre food
combinations. . . . French nouvelle cuisine restaurants had opened in this country on both coasts. But at the same time, Americans well grounded in French
ideas combined the new European grammar with an American vocabulary. Especially in California, this meant mixing ingredients with a historical abandon and
putting special emphasis on ingredients of a markedly local and recherché sort
—wild mushrooms, native chestnuts, fiddlehead ferns. . . . It is the approach
that matters.

What made the new cuisine so readily adaptable into a "California
cuisine" was California's natural endowments of climate, agricultural re-
sources, and vineyards. Just as the South China area is blessed by a
geography and climate conducive to the growing of good foods and to the
presence of game and seafood—with the result that the Cantonese were
able to develop a great cuisine—so too the California chef has at his or
her disposal a marvelous bounty with which to experiment and to create.
Similarly, it is no accident that Michelin stars cluster around the vicinity
of Lyons. As Joseph Wechsberg noted years ago, Lyons, "the gastronomical
capital of France . . . is strategically located between the vineyards of
Burgundy, Beaujolais, and the Côtes du Rhône, the fish, game, meat,
sausages, and cheese treasures of the Auvergne, Dauphiné, Franche-
Comté, and Savoie, and the poultry area of Bresse. . . . Lyon—one of the
richest food cities in France—has contributed to French cooking more
regional specialties than any other French city."

Northern California was my "fat city." It afforded me both generous
acceptance as a newcomer and an abundant field in which to ply my
cookery. I entered that field at a most propitious time. The new or California cuisine movement was characterized by an openness to innovation, a
receptivity to different tastes and textures, an almost unprecedented readiness to assimilate many aspects of other cultures, but especially their
cuisines. It was a time of rapid change. The idea took hold that eating
means caring for others as well as for oneself; it means taking a little time
and directing some attention to the preparation and the savoring of food
in a socially and personally and interrelating manner.

I am well aware of a paradoxical and troubling dualism in the "culinary"
development in our society during these same years: The emergence and
growth of a new appreciation of "good" food—fresh, natural, carefully
prepared and served—coincided with the explosion of "fast foods"—

processed, frozen, artificial, and untouched by human hands. There is a class and education factor involved here. But I know that natural or relatively unprocessed fresh foods are superior in taste and nutrition to the processed, the synthetic, and the machine-made, and I know that economics is not always the determining factor—what is better can be the cheaper or at least competitive.

As an American I believe in equality and democracy, even in the democratization of good taste. One of the underlying themes of my work is that good food and good taste are not functions of social class. Education cannot by itself change dietary habits—especially in the face of agribusiness and advertising forces—but as a first step the alternatives must be offered to people. And it helps if the alternatives are both delicious and easy to prepare, as my recipes are.

My cooking, to repeat, does not pretend to be a new California or American or Franco-American cuisine. As I see it, I am continuing a long tradition in a number of ways. In the first place, as Richard Olney has noted, "good and honest cooking and good and honest French cooking are the same thing." This holds true for all serious-playful cooking. It is a standard I always strive to maintain. In the second place, leaving aside some Native American dishes, American cooking has always been a changing amalgam of foreign influences. It is true that the dominant (and, some would add, unfortunate) strain is Anglo-German—a relatively heavy, unimaginative cuisine. Nevertheless, Americans, who in their own way are the most cosmopolitan of people, have always been open to new ideas, new foods. The "new cuisine" is the most recent example of this openness, and my East Meets West contribution is but an aspect of that process.

East Meets West is basically an unforced, natural blending of ingredients and techniques borrowed mainly from China, France, and America. On occasion ideas from Japanese, Italian, and Mexican cuisine also come into play. I recommend local and fresh ingredients, but imported foods inevitably have a role. The point is that I neither imitate Chinese, French or American dishes, nor do I try to disguise them. I simply respect them while I explore their possibilities and extend their potentialities. My view is that a recipe is not a rigid formula. I believe that cooking is an art, not a science, imitative as well as creative, and more play than work. Experiment and use your imagination. It has been my experience that such loving playfulness results in dishes that are both familiar and exotic, and delightfully satisfying as well.

In the recipes that follow I discuss how I came to choose a particular combination and why I believe it works. I note the characteristics of foods, spices, herbs, and seasonings, and the advantages and limitations of the various techniques. I appreciate the historical, social, and mythical aspects of cooking, and I include materials I find relevant and interesting. My goal is to accentuate the best of both East and West, and to assist in the creation of new and palatable foods. I have loved it all.

# Glossary
## of East-West Terms

# COOKING TECHNIQUES
# AND EQUIPMENT

**GRILLING**       Grilling uses high heat, often in conjunction with basting, to seal juices in and give a rich flavor with a crisp outside and a deliciously moist-textured taste within. Meat, fish, vegetables, and even fruits can be grilled. Large cuts of meat in particular should rest for fifteen minutes before carving; cut-up chicken, steaks, chops, and fish can go to the table in five to ten minutes.

**STEAMING**       Steaming is gentle cooking with moist hot vapors. Have the water one inch below the food. This method does not dry out foods; it preserves the flavors of delicate foods and helps to retain many of their nutrients. Several dishes can be cooked at the same time in a steamer, but be sure to leave room along the sides for the steam to circulate. Replenish the water in the steamer as needed, but try not to uncover it more than absolutely necessary.

**STIR-FRYING**    This famous Chinese cooking method depends on having all the ingredients of a dish ready and uniformly cut to be cooked over very high heat. This is one of the healthiest ways of cooking because little oil is used, and stir-fried foods retain their color, shape, and texture during rapid cooking. A wok, especially designed for stir-frying, is best for this technique, but slope-sided skillets also work very well.

**DEEP-FRYING**    Deep-frying in hot oil seals food but allows it to cook within. The temperature of the oil is critical; the food must cook through inside but not be burned outside. Chinese cooks deep-fry in the wok because it takes considerably less oil than a Western pot. It is important to test the heat of the oil before starting—a haze forms over the surface and a small piece of food bubbles all around when the oil is sufficiently hot. Do not overcrowd foods you are frying; each piece of food as it is added causes the temperature of the oil to drop. Dry the food carefully before dropping it into the oil to avoid splatters. Carefully strained oil can be reused three times, but always keep oil in which fish has been fried separate from oil used to fry meat or other food.

**BRAISING**    This technique is used for some vegetables and tougher cuts of meat. First browning and then simmering for an extended time in stock improves the flavor and the tenderness of the ingredients. Braised dishes freeze well, so you can make large quantities for later use. The braising sauce also can be reused, and the flavor improves.

**ROASTING**    This technique allows the hot, dry air of the oven to circulate around the food to give it a crisp outer skin and a moist interior. Allow the meat to rest before carving.

**STEEPING**    Steeping is immersing food in a simmering liquid, covering the pan, and then turning off the heat. This slow, moist cooking brings out very delicate flavors and smooth textures.

# INGREDIENTS

**BASIL**

There are Asian, French, and Italian varieties of basil, and although the tastes are subtly different, they are interchangeable. I find the Asian variety stronger and more pungent. The anise flavor of this herb is delicious, and I use it a great deal in my East-West cooking. Washed and dried leaves should be stored in good olive oil; the leaves turn dark easily. Use only fresh basil; dried basil is a poor substitute.

**BEAN SAUCE**
*(Brown Bean Sauce, Brown Bean Paste, Yellow Bean Sauce)*

This comes whole or crushed, in bottles or tins. I prefer the whole bean sauce, which is less salty. Made from soybeans, flour, salt, and water, the sauce adds richness to braised dishes with a subtle bean taste. Transfer any tinned bean sauce to a glass jar and keep it in the refrigerator, where it should keep almost indefinitely.

**BEAN THREAD NOODLES**
*(Cellophane or Transparent Noodles)*

Made from green soybeans, starch, and water, they come dried and look like thin, brittle, opaque threads. They add bulk to fillings such as spring rolls and are used in soups.

**BEANS, FERMENTED BLACK**

These small soybeans are fermented and preserved with salt and spices. Their strong, pungent essence is often combined with garlic and ginger, adding a distinct "Chinese" flavor to dishes. They can be purchased in bottles, in plastic bags, and in cans, but avoid the canned ones because they have a tinny taste. There is no need to rinse the beans, but add salt to the dish very carefully if at all. Use fermented black beans moderately; too much can easily overwhelm a dish. They must be coarsely chopped to bring out their unique taste and aroma. They will keep indefinitely at room temperature, but keep them tightly covered to preserve their aroma.

BOK CHOY — A member of the cabbage family, it is native to southern China. The stalks are crisp and sweet. The leaves are mild and spinachlike. I like to use the flowering variety which is younger and less fibrous. To prepare, cut the leaves and peel the stalks. Cut the stalks into thin slices crosswise. Wash well.

BUTTER — I like to use the best quality of unsalted butter available. When recipes in this book list butter, it means good-quality unsalted butter, which has a more delicate flavor than salted butter and gives a beautiful sheen and rich taste to sauces. Butter can be stored tightly wrapped in the freezer and defrosted as needed.

CAUL FAT — This thin covering of the lower part of a pig's intestine looks like a lacy sheet of marbled skin. It can be found in Chinese, French, and Italian meat markets or is specially ordered from your local butcher. Caul fat is widely used in Chinese and European cooking to wrap food, to keep it moist while it cooks. It freezes very well when tightly wrapped.

CHILI BEAN PASTE — Chili paste is made from chili peppers and salt, often combined with black beans or soybeans, garlic, or other ingredients. (Recipes specify which variety to use.) Refrigerate in tightly sealed glass jars.

CHILI PEPPERS — The most commonly used chili pepper in Chinese cooking is small, dried, about two inches long, and fiery hot; it is used to flavor sauces or oil used in stir-fried dishes. You can buy chili oil in Chinese supermarkets or make your own by cooking a few chopped dried red peppers in a cup of oil at a moderate temperature (325 degrees) for about five minutes. Let the peppers cool in the oil, then strain the oil into a glass jar. The number of peppers used gives a flavor ranging from mild to very hot. Supermarkets carry ground chili powder or chili flakes. The test for the fullest flavor is a strong, rich smell. Among the fresh chilies are jalapeño, Thai, and serrano. To use, cut them in one-half-inch lengths and discard the seeds. Wear rubber gloves and keep your hands away from your eyes when preparing hot peppers.

CHINESE SEASONED SALT — This is a seasoning I have adapted from traditional Chinese cooking and applied with great success to Western dishes, especially to grilled recipes or roasts (Roast Pork with Chinese Spices, page 174, is one example) and foods that call for some sparkling additive (such as Steamed Scallops, page 110). Chinese seasoned salt includes Sichuan peppercorns, which are rather biting with a slight spicy, hot aftertaste that stings ever so lightly, like the Sichuan cuisine itself. To me, the fragrance recalls coriander seeds mixed with lavender from the south of France. No substitute for Sichuan peppercorns really is adequate, but they are widely available in specialty and gourmet shops and by mail order. In my many travels around the country I have also noticed their appearance on spice racks in some supermarkets.

Here is the formula for Chinese seasoned salt:

*4 tablespoons Sichuan peppercorns*
*2 tablespoons coarse salt*

Heat the Sichuan peppercorns and the salt over medium heat in a wok or medium-sized skillet. Turn the heat down to low and stir for one minute, or until the peppercorns begin to darken—don't let them burn. Remove from the wok and cool. Coarsely grind in a blender. Place in a tightly sealed jar until ready to use. Makes about one-third cup.

**CORIANDER**
*(Cilantro, Chinese Parsley)*

Fresh coriander can be found easily in Asian and Latin markets, but it is also becoming more available in supermarkets. Look for bright green unwilted leaves. To store, wash and dry the leaves and leave them on the stems. Store the leaves wrapped in damp paper towels inside a plastic bag in the refrigerator. People either love the pungent musky flavor of fresh coriander or dislike it intensely.

**CREAM**

This is not normally used in Chinese cooking, but in some of the East Meets West recipes it adds an overtone of richness to the flavors. Use heavy (whipping) cream.

**CRÈME FRAÎCHE**

Crème fraîche, with its wonderful tangy flavor, adds another dimension of tangy richness to sauces. Available in gourmet and cheese stores, it also is easy to make at home. Here is a simple recipe:

*1 cup heavy cream*
*1 tablespoon buttermilk*

Combine the cream and buttermilk in a small stainless steel or glass bowl. Cover and place in an unheated oven or a warm place overnight. The crème fraîche should be thickened to the consistency of thin yogurt. Refrigerate, covered, for up to one week. Makes about one cup.

**FIVE-SPICE POWDER**  This distinctive Chinese spice is a blend of star anise, Sichuan peppercorns, fennel or anise seed, clove, and Chinese cinnamon. Purchase it in powdered form, checking that it is still fragrant. It is wonderful for marinades, but use it sparingly because it is very strong. It will keep indefinitely in an airtight container.

**GARLIC SHOOTS**  These are the young, tender scallionlike shoots of the garlic plant before it forms a bulb. Use with delicate-tasting foods as a substitute for chives.

**GINGER**  This knobby rhizome is now widely available in its fresh forms. Young ginger is a pale pinkish brown with a smooth skin that does not need to be peeled. Older ginger should feel firm, the skin should not be wrinkled, and it should be peeled before using. Ginger stored unpeeled in the vegetable bin of the refrigerator will keep for up to two weeks. To keep it longer, peel and cut it into chunks. Cover the pieces with rice wine and store, in a covered jar, in the refrigerator. Ginger is used like lemon with fish and shellfish; it is also used to flavor oils and to season many Sichuan dishes. It can confront bitter vegetables, adding a hot, spicy taste, and it is wonderfully pungent in marinades.

**GOAT CHEESE**  Fresh, young goat cheese has a soft cream cheese texture. As it ages it develops a stronger taste and firmer texture. Mild goat cheese is called for in the wonton soup on page 98. American goat cheeses tend to be milder than the imported varieties and do not dominate the taste of the recipes.

**HOISIN SAUCE** *(Duck Sauce, Red Seasoning Sauce)*  This sweet, piquant sauce, made from soybean flour, red beans, chili, sugar, salt, garlic, and spices, has a thick jamlike consistency. It is often sold in cans but once opened should be stored in a glass jar in the refrigerator, where it will keep indefinitely. It is wonderful in marinades and as a dip or a condiment for many dishes.

**KUMQUATS**  Kumquats are a small one- to one-and-one-half-inch citrus fruit with a tart orangelike flavor. The whole fruit, including the peel, is edible.

**LEMON SAUCE**  This thick, jamlike, ready-made sauce of lemons, salt, and sugar, not unlike an Indian chutney, is used in Cantonese cooking, especially with braised dishes. Chinese lemon sauce comes in jars and should be kept in the refrigerator once opened.

**LEMONGRASS**  Lemongrass is an aromatic tropical grass that adds a distinctive flavor to foods; it is far more commonly used in Southeast Asian foods and so can be found fresh in Southeast Asian markets. Use the lower part, up to the first branch of the stalk, and only the white underlayer. Discard the loose leaves and crush lightly before slicing to release more flavor. Store in a plastic bag in the vegetable bin for four to six weeks. Lemongrass can be fibrous and should be finely chopped. Lemongrass is available frozen, dried, and powdered, but in this book only fresh lemongrass is recommended.

**MUSHROOMS, Black**  Dried black mushrooms have a meaty texture and a dark, earthy flavor. To use them, the mushrooms must be soaked in hot water until they become soft, and then the tough stems removed and discarded. Rinse well, watching for sand. Kept dried in a tightly sealed jar, they will keep forever. The less expensive, smaller mushrooms are fine for dishes in which they are served chopped or shredded. The expensive ''flower'' mushrooms have thick fissured caps and are white or light-colored. When rehydrated, they are thick and have a velvety texture, and they add to the appearance of a dish when served whole. Both types are usually sold in cellophane bags in four-, eight-, and sixteen-ounce sizes.

**MUSHROOMS, Fresh**  Enokitake mushrooms are becoming more widely available in supermarkets as well as specialty produce stores. Rinse off, cut off, and discard the stem bottoms, and store the mushrooms in the vegetable bin of the refrigerator wrapped in paper towels inside a plastic bag.

Oyster mushrooms have a mild, fresh taste. Store them in the refrigerator as you would Enokitake.

Shiitake mushrooms can be bought fresh or dried. The fresh mushrooms have a nice but more delicate taste than dried ones.

**NOODLES, Rice**  Rice noodles are made from rice flour, and when soaked for fifteen minutes they become soft and pliable. To store them after they have softened, toss them lightly with sesame oil and keep them in the refrigerator.

**OIL, Olive**   The best olive oil is first press, cold press, unfiltered extra-virgin olive oil, which must have less than one percent acidity. The flavor is mild but fruity. Store olive oil capped or corked in a cool place.

**OIL, Peanut**   The Chinese prefer peanut oil for stir-frying and deep-frying because of its flavor and its high burning temperature. Corn oil is less expensive and high in polyunsaturated fats; other acceptable oils are soy and sunflower. Store oil in a cool dry place.

**OIL, Sesame**   Rich-flavored sesame oil is made from the toasted seeds and is used as a seasoning, not as a cooking oil. Dark and thick, it burns easily and so is added at the last moment of cooking to finish a dish. It is often added to soups just before serving. The strong, distinctive flavor of sesame is a wonderful ingredient for marinades if used lightly; diluted with other vegetable oils, it makes a wonderful dressing for salads and cold pasta dishes. The light-colored variety is not a suitable substitute because it imparts no flavor.

**OYSTER SAUCE**   This sauce from southern China is made from oysters cooked together with salt and spices. The most expensive brands tend to be the best. Good oyster sauce has a rich, almost beefy flavor. Store in the refrigerator.

**PEPPERCORNS, Sichuan**   Not true pepper, these are reddish brown dry berries with a strong, pungent odor, which distinguishes them from the hotter black peppercorns. Roast them briefly in a moderate oven or sauté in a dry skillet. Grind in a blender and store in a jar until ready to use.

**PLUM SAUCE**   This traditional jamlike Chinese condiment is widely available in cans and jars. Usually served in Chinese restaurants as an accompaniment to duck dishes, it also can be diluted with a lighter preserve and used as a dip for spring rolls, meat balls, fried wontons, or other appetizers. Made with plums, preserved ginger, chili, vinegar, and sugar, it is spicy and assertive and can be delicious used with a braising sauce.

**RICE**   Many varieties of rice are becoming available, but there are really two main types: long-grain (not converted) and short-grain. While it used to be necessary to wash rice, processing now makes this unnecessary. Short-grain Oriental rice is labeled Pearl Rice or Japanese Rose Brand and can be substituted for long-grain. Glutinous rice is short and pearl-shaped, and is usually used in stuffings and desserts.

**RICE PAPER**  This kind of noodle wrapper is lighter and crisper than the type made with wheat flour. Made from ground rice flour, rice paper keeps indefinitely unrefrigerated. Soften the rice papers in warm water until flexible and ready to use. Buy the Banh Trang brand or variety, which comes in small and large rounds. I found it to be excellent.

**RICE WINE**  Shaoxing, or rice wine, is made from fermented rice. Golden brown in color, it has a rich, sweet, mellow flavor. Dry sherry can be substituted, but not sake or mirin. Pagoda is an excellent brand. Store opened bottles at room temperature.

**SALT**  Kosher salt, available in supermarkets, is coarse in texture but pure and mild-tasting. Sea salt is stronger, with a more distinctive taste, so use less than the recipe calls for.

**SAUSAGE,**  Chinese sausage is made from pork, beef, or duck liver, but pork is the
**Chinese**  most common. Sweet and mild, it is delicious by itself and is a perfect complement to vegetables. Stir-fry or, if you prefer, blanch until the fat becomes translucent and the sausage is tender. Blanching makes the sausage less fatty. Refrigerate if you plan to use the sausage within two weeks; wrap well and freeze for longer storage. Sometimes sold in strings of two, Chinese sausage also comes in one-pound packages. A delicious one-course meal can be made by steaming the sausage on top of rice as it is cooking. The sausage cooks perfectly and flavors the rice.

**SCALLIONS**  As one of the three most important ingredients in Chinese cooking, along
*(Green*  with ginger and garlic, scallions, or green onions, provide an essential and
*Onions,*  distinctive flavor. To prepare them, peel off the outer layer of the onion
*Spring*  and trim the green tops. The white ends can be finely chopped or cut in
*Onions)*  long strips for garnishes. The green tips are also used and add color as well as flavor.

**SHALLOTS**  This member of the onion family is widely used in European and Chinese cooking. They are found in most supermarkets and are stored like onions.

**SOY SAUCE**     Soy sauce is the result of the aged fermentation of soybeans, wheat, and water. There are two main types of soy sauce, light and dark. Light soy is saltier and excellent for cooking; it is sold under the name of Superior Soy. Dark soy is darker, thicker, and has a deeper aroma; it is used mainly for braised dishes and for dipping. Japanese soy sauce is sweeter than Chinese soy. Mushroom soy is between dark and light soy, and has been made with the addition of straw mushrooms. All soys keep well when stored at room temperature.

**STAR ANISE**     This eight-pointed, star-shaped seed is an ingredient of five-spice powder, but when used by itself whole, it contributes a rich licorice flavor in braised dishes. Sold in plastic packs, it should be stored in a tightly covered jar in a cool dry place.

**SUGAR**     Sugar has been used in Chinese cooking to balance hot and salty flavors. There are several forms of sugar—rock or yellow lump, brown sugar slabs, and maltose or malt sugar—all available in Chinese groceries. Break the lumps into smaller pieces by covering them with a lint-free cloth and using a wooden mallet or hammer. White sugar may be substituted.

**TOMATOES,**     Imported or domestic, these pungent, tangy, dried tomatoes are sold as
**Sun-Dried**     they are or packed in olive oil. Keep them in a cool dark place or in the refrigerator.

**VINEGAR**     Chinese vinegars are made from rice and come in a range of subtle flavors, from slightly tart to sweet and pungent. All can be bought in Chinese grocery stores and will keep indefinitely. Cider vinegar is an acceptable substitute.

White rice vinegar is clear and mild in flavor but has a fuller flavor than the harsher white vinegar. It is excellent in sweet-and-sour dishes. The Japanese variety, Marukan, may be used as a substitute.

Black rice vinegar has a dark, rich color that belies its mild taste. It is excellent in braised dishes or dipping sauces. Chikiang vinegar is named after the province where it developed and is similar to balsamic.

Red rice vinegar is sweet and spicy in taste, and is usually used as a dipping sauce for seafood.

**WATER CHESTNUTS**

These misnamed edible roots are about the size of a walnut and, when fresh, are sweet, crunchy, and delicious. Fresh water chestnuts have tight skins and should feel firm. Stored in a paper bag in the refrigerator, unpeeled water chestnuts keep for about two weeks. Peeled chestnuts can be stored, covered with water, in the refrigerator. Canned water chestnuts, sold in most supermarkets, have little taste. Rinse them in cold water before using them; stored in water that is changed daily, they will keep for several days. Jicama may be substituted for canned water chestnuts.

# How to Use This Book

This book is a natural development of my own cultural experiences and elective affinities. The blending of Eastern and Western foods, seasonings, and techniques offered here derives from my family life, my professional career, my travels, and my experiences with the preparation and enjoyment of food. I learned to cook without the use or assistance of recipes; I watched professionals at work, followed their orders, and developed or absorbed the "sense" of rightness, of compatibility, of simplicity, of doneness that is the basis of all good cooking. My exposure to two cultures opened up possibilities to me that I exploited, however unselfconsciously at first. Later, in my travels to distant and foreign places, I realized the advantages of such bicultural openness to what is new and strange: I had perhaps fewer prejudices than most people and was thus better able to adapt to and even adopt as my own the customs and manners of others. This is, in any case, a particularly valuable gift; in the matter of the appreciation and enjoyment of food—as culture-bound and psychologically determined as it is—my adaptability and openness was a rich and delectable blessing.

As I say, I learned to cook without recipes. So do we all. In the beginning we follow someone's directions and mimic his or her actions. Eventually, if we are fortunate, we escape this tutelage and begin to cook for ourselves, in the sense of creating our own dishes, our own combinations of ingredients. The point is that, while recipes may be the heart of any cookbook, the soul that informs good cooking must be provided by the cook. As American folklore would have it, "Better a crust of bread in a joyful home than the stalled ox in a palace of discord." Not so much does the recipe matter—although of course it does—as the care, thought, and affection that goes into the preparation of food. Cooking is always a very personal act. It is also an ideal act of communion with others in ways that are at once very psychological and sensuous: human interaction at a fundamental biological and social level. It involves sharing, giving and receiving, touching, tasting, sensing, and enjoying. In homes filled with affection and harmony, all meals, however plain, are satisfying and palatable. There is no such thing as a good meal, however baroquely complex, without caring about others at more than a superficial level.

Recipes, then, are the letter of the law, but the spirit giveth life. The recipes in this book have all been "truth-tested" by me and, more persuasively, by my friends, and they reflect my preferences in food and cooking. Almost all of the recipes are simple, demanding little that is fancy or complex or grand. Use these recipes as your introduction to some delicious meals, but more than that, use them as points of departure for your own experiments and flights of fancy. Try the recipes but never be imprisoned by them. You are free to elaborate, change, and modify to suit your own taste, to create and, above all, to enjoy.

The book is organized in the traditional cookbook manner. There are few sauces and only the basic master stocks. Fish, shellfish, poultry, and meats are emphasized because these foods were in my experience most warmly and naturally receptive to the marriage of different cuisines. To some tastes, a decidedly Eastern flavor may predominate in the recipes, although I myself do not detect a tilt to the East except perhaps in poultry, where my mother's spirit is powerfully evident. In any event, this is cooking for the home, everyday food, if you will, that is at once innovative and traditional.

It is clear that the American diet, food habits, and preferences are receptive today to new and exotic influences. The emphasis on what is fresh or locally grown; the introduction of new cooking techniques; a renewed awareness of the relationship of diet to health; the steadily increasing acceptance of foreign cuisines, especially those of the East (our metropolitan area supermarkets now stock Oriental foods and ingredients as a matter of course)—all indicate that the philosophy and recipes in this book are not so much breakthroughs as they are a recognition that we as a people are already blending our cuisines. The book is, among other things, an explanation of how best to use the new foods and techniques in the most sensible and palatable ways.

In the menu section of the book I elaborate on the ideas that underlie my approach to cooking. The menus illustrate the harmonious unity of styles I seek. My theories about cooking led me to expect that the blending of East and West would result in savory and nutritious dishes; my experience confirmed my theories. Now you must move on to the proof of the pudding. Use my experiences to enrich your own. Do not be timid—take the recipes and run with them. Do it with love and gusto, and you will find, as I did, that it is delectable enjoyment.

# A Note on the
# Wine Suggestions

I have often had the pleasure of sampling Ken Hom's cooking over the past eight years, and during that time I have been impressed by the extraordinary versatility of his dishes; they can be paired with a wide variety of wines. With his meals we have enjoyed some of the world's greatest wines, as well as some of the simplest. Above all we have discovered that wine is an integral part of the complete enjoyment of the recipes in this book.

Knowing Ken's own preferences, it is difficult to resist suggesting a light, fresh red wine as an accompaniment to every dish. We have discovered over the years that a Beaujolais-style wine from France, California, or Italy is extremely well suited to all but a very few of the recipes. But I have attempted here to offer some variety in order to explore some unique combinations, even some daring ones. In selecting the wines for individual dishes I have applied some conventional wisdom, but I have also tried to look beyond for that combination which adds even more to their unique East-West character.

There is little chance of making too grievous an error in selecting wines that one feels instinctively work with these dishes. To that extent it is really not necessary to try to be too specific, too narrow, or too dogmatic in the wine selections. What I have learned over the years is that an easy harmony exists between the complex flavors found in these unique recipes and the composition of sugar, acid, tannin, and alcohol that defines the flavor spectrum of wine.

Darrell Corti provides some excellent counsel in his section on selecting wines for the seven menus found at the end of the book. I have been cognizant of the direction he suggests but have found that in a few cases my own ideas are not wholly consistent with his. Still, little harm can come from following one's own inclinations.

Given a choice, I can think of no more exciting prospect than being challenged every day to match Ken's food with the contents of my cellar. I have had little hesitation in pulling out my most prized bottles to serve with the kaleidoscope of duck, game, rice, and pasta dishes that Ken has invented. And as it has turned out, at least one interesting choice could be found for each of the recipes in this collection. There are only a few— mostly among the desserts—that totally frustrated my wine-matching ability.

It would be nice to finally lay to rest all the agonizing we have done over matching our Western beverage—wine—with dishes having a distinctive Oriental character. The wine is simply one more ingredient, one more seasoning. In trained hands it can lift the dish to even greater heights. I have tried to suggest earthy and fresh; mature and young; fruity and dry; spicy and soft; as well as red, white, and rosé—in much the same way that Ken uses a pinch of salt, a spoonful of ginger, and a sprig of basil.

*Ron Batori*

# ADDITIONAL WINE SUGGESTIONS

Most of these recipes are for light, savory dishes. Accompanying wines should be light and savory. With aromatic dishes, the wine should be less aromatic and flavorful: sort of yin-yang in notion. Ken says that the dishes have "colors, texture, tastes, and contrasts." Wines should play their part in the scheme.

Dishes with black beans need red wines, even if they garnish fish. Young Beaujolais or other similar wines are best.

In dishes with light sauces whose composition is intensified by reduction, wines can be fuller in body and heavier.

Dishes using crème fraîche will take a full- or very full-bodied white wine.

Ken writes, "Simplicity is a desirable character in cooking." Wines should also be simple if the food is complex, complex if the food is simple.

*Darrell Corti*

# The Recipes

---

*with Wine Suggestions by Ron Batori*

# STOCKS AND SAUCES

---

*Give me the proper stock, and I will move the world to the table.*
Archimedes to his friend Apicius, ca. 79 A.D.

*What is sauce for the goose is sauce for the gander, but it may not work as well.*
Lévi-Strauss

*Wild duck with Vatel sauce—wine vinegar, egg yolk, tomato paste, butter, cream, salt and pepper, shallots, tarragon, chervil, and peppercorns. Is any of those distasteful to you?*
Nero Wolfe (Rex Stout)

**STOCKS**

Stock is at once a cooking medium, a seasoning, and a congenial facilitator and liaison for other foods. It is the basis of any good cooking. In France, for example, this is literally true, for the French phrase for stock, *fonds de cuisine,* indicates the importance of stock in cooking. The word *fond* means, variously, the basis or foundation, capital or principal. A good stock in the kitchen, then, is a foundation waiting to be built on; it is like money in the bank—always ready to use and producing dividends.

Every great cuisine, East and West, emphasizes the importance of stock. In Japan, dashi, the stock derived from bonito and kelp, gives to Japanese cuisine its characteristic flavor: It is used in all but chicken dishes. Japanese master chefs maintain that the success or failure of a dish is decided by the quality of the dashi that seasons it. In Chinese cuisine, meat stock made from pork is featured in some recipes, but chicken stock is over-whelmingly favored. Sometimes, as in the recipe for Roast Pork with Chinese Spices (page 174), pork and chicken stock are combined. Stock is essential in almost all Chinese recipes and is a natural but quite differ-ent concomitant to soup, which is indispensable to Chinese cuisine. (See Basic Chicken Stock, page 67.)

Incidentally, bouillon, consommé, broth, and stock are terms that are often interchanged, but they are not quite the same things. Bouillon (from the French *bouillir,* to boil) is any liquid in which meats or vegetables have been cooked. It is, then, a broth produced as a by-product; when it is clarified (made clear and sparkling), it is called a consommé. Bouillons, broths, and consommés are treats meant to be consumed directly—they are themselves dividends, as it were, produced by a boiled dinner. Stock, however, is capital, to pursue my metaphor. It produces dividends of what might ordinarily amount to waste: The traditional stockpot transforms the redundant carcasses of stewing hens, odd leftover parts and bones of chickens or ducks, carrot ends and pieces, and many other bits of bones and vegetables into a zestful basis for sauces, gravies, aspics, and soups.

A few caveats are in order in regard to the preparation of stocks. Starchy vegetables, such as potatoes and beans, should be avoided because they affect the clarity of the stock. Cabbage, turnips, and other strongly fla-vored vegetables should likewise be left out because they impart their tastes to the cooking liquid and tend to dominate any stock. Fish and shellfish remains make delicious stock but must be made and used sepa-rately. (See Fish Stock, page 68.) Raw bones provide too much gelatin and generally should not be used; on occasion they can be combined with cooked bones. Never boil stock or it will cloud up. Skimming is a vitally important part of the stock-making process, essential in obtaining a clear and flavorful stock.

By observing these guidelines you will be doing much to protect your capital, and its rich dividends will flow. So, stock up and keep the treasure in the freezer—it is the one frozen asset I know of in which liquidity is no problem.

The stocks I have included here are designed to provide the substantial basis for a variety of soups and dishes and to complement and enhance the flavor of the foods they serve.

Let me list a few key elements to remember when making stock:

1. The basic stock should never come to a boil. It should remain at a

low simmer at all times, preferably uncovered; with the cover on you run the risk of overheating the stock.

2. The most important task in making stock is the skimming, and it is one of the most tedious. Skimming the stock keeps it clean and clear, gives the stock its clarity of flavor, and is a small price to pay for the rich results. Use a large, flat spoon to skim the scum as it rises to the top.

3. Add the mirepoix, (vegetables, seasonings and herbs) after the initial skimming.

4. Remember never to stir the stock either at the beginning or during the cooking process. Agitation causes the liquid to cloud.

5. Decant the stock as you would wine. By carefully ladling the stock, many of the unpleasant sediments can be left behind. I usually strain the stock through at least four layers of linen cheesecloth.

6. Let the stock rest in a cool place, then take off all the fat and place the stock in smaller containers. Store in the freezer.

7. Finally, a word about the chicken. Here we have an exception to the general rule of always using the best and most tender meat and fowl. For chicken stock (as with soup) old chickens are best. Use an old hen or stewing chicken, including, if obtainable, the feet (washed and without the claws); they add, as the Chinese say in their inimitable manner, a certain *je ne sais quoi* to the stock.

My basic chicken stock suffices as a delicious all-purpose stock, and I utilize it in recipes throughout this book. Why chicken stock? Because it is a delicious base, it is very light, its chief ingredient is cheap and plentiful, it has versatility and is adaptable, and it is easier to make than veal or beef stock. Chicken stock is the base for most Eastern cuisine and is used throughout Western cuisine, too. Beef stock, however, is much too robust for the Chinese palate (and sense of smell). I rely on chicken stock heavily in my recipes; I also use it to make a quick demiglace and as a glazing finish for sautéed dishes (such as Chicken Breasts with Red Peppers and Bok Choy in Cream Sauce, p. 162) and for soups.

SAUCES All cuisines worthy of the name feature a variety of sauces: aillade and vinaigrette, ponzu and yakitori, balsamella and salsa rossa, bean paste and hoisin. In Anglo-American cooking, sauces are often confused with gravy, which is, technically speaking, a sauce made from the juices expressed by cooked meat. The essential difference between the two is that gravies overpower or dominate the flavor of whatever they are poured on

—a result that is acceptable in the case of mashed potatoes—while sauces must not overwhelm a dish. Sauces are designed to enhance, to offer contrasts, to complement and highlight other flavors.

The French, influenced by the artful Italians of the Renaissance, initiated the classic Western sauces. Beginning with La Varenne (ca. 1650), improving under the genius of Carême (ca. 1830), and culminating with Escoffier (ca. 1900), French sauces evolved into mellow, velvety graces that lent themselves to a delightful variety of delicious applications. Escoffier included almost two hundred different sauces in his *Guide Culinaire* (1902), and he wrote: "The sauces represent the *partie capitale* of the cuisine. It is they which have created and maintained to this day the universal preponderance of French cuisine."

Indian, Japanese, and Chinese cuisines are noted for their imaginative and flavorful sauces, which are distinguishable from Western sauces by the absence of starch and eggs, the ingredients that are the basis of the two main Western types. (Nouvelle cuisine innovators, incidentally, in their search for lightness and smoothness, banished flour [the traditional roux thickener] from their sauces and instead used stock reductions, butter, and cream. It is now being used again, however, because despite its drawbacks, it does add body to a sauce.) Eastern cooks tend to think that Westerners drown their foods in sauces, masking the true flavors. Certainly, in the East it is preferable to keep the sauces separate from the foods; one dips food into the sauce to the extent individual taste dictates. There is something to this view, but in fact a classic French sauce is misused if it drowns a dish. We can have it both ways.

Sauces in Eastern cuisines rely upon the manipulation of spices and seasonings and upon blends of vegetable oils, stock, and wine. They can be ambrosial, pungent, sharp, mild, sweet, spicy, sour, subtle, or all of the above at once. Whatever the combination, however, Eastern sauces are identical in function to their Western cousins: They are meant to enhance, extend, and deepen the flavor of the dishes they accompany.

The sauces I have included here represent the results of my experiments in blending Eastern and Western concepts and flavors. For example, Ginger-Scallion Mayonnaise (page 72) introduces two traditional and popular Chinese dipping-sauce flavorings to mayonnaise (which Eastern cooking does not use). All of the sauces manifest the delicacy and congenial flavors that the *partie capitale* should have.

# Basic Chicken Stock

Your basic chicken stock is only as good as the material you begin with, so all your ingredients (even the old hen!) should be as fresh as for any recipe you would prepare.

One 5-pound hen or roasting chicken
    7 pounds chicken bones (such as
      backs and feet)
    8 quarts cold water
    2 pounds carrots, peeled and
      coarsely chopped
    1 pound small yellow onions, peeled
    1 tablespoon coarse salt

2 tablespoons whole black
    peppercorns
2 whole cloves
3 bay leaves
3 heads garlic
4 fresh thyme branches, or 2
    teaspoons dried thyme

Place the chicken and bones in a large stockpot. Add the cold water and bring slowly to a simmer. Skim the stock frequently until the surface is clear. Add the vegetables, herbs, and spices. Simmer slowly for 5 or 6 hours, skimming as necessary.

*Yields 7 to 7½ quarts*

Remove the chicken, bones, and vegetables with a large slotted spoon. Ladle the stock through a cheesecloth-lined strainer. Allow the stock to cool. Refrigerate, skim the fat, and freeze in small containers.

# *Fish Stock*

Since fish stock is not used in Chinese cooking, it was not a part of my tradition. I discovered its virtues, however, when I lived in France. It is appropriate for seafood recipes and sauces, and is easier and requires less time to make than chicken stock, even though the same principles are applied to its preparation. For example, it should never be boiled. Once made and then frozen, it keeps well and is readily available for those dishes compatible with its use. If the following recipe will leave you with too much stock on hand, simply reduce all the ingredients by half.

*9 pounds fish bones from any firm-*
*fleshed white fish, such as sea bass,*
*rockfish, and halibut*
*4 quarts water*
*8 ounces yellow onions, coarsely*
*chopped*
*1 pound carrots, coarsely chopped*
*4 ounces shallots, coarsely chopped*
*1 cup coarsely chopped leeks, white*
*part only*

*¼ cup parsley, loosely packed*
*4 sprigs fresh thyme, or ½ tablespoon*
*dried thyme*
*2 whole imported bay leaves*
*4 garlic cloves, lightly crushed and left*
*unpeeled*
*1 tablespoon whole black peppercorns*
*Salt to taste*

*Makes 4 quarts*

Rinse the fish bones well under cold running water. Place the bones in a large stockpot, cover with water, and bring the mixture to a simmer. Cook for 10 minutes, skimming frequently. Add the rest of the ingredients and simmer for 1 hour. Remove the fish bones and vegetables with a slotted spoon. Strain the stock through a cheesecloth-lined strainer. Allow to cool and skim the surface. Divide in small containers and freeze for future use.

# Rich Turkey and Chicken Stock

This is definitely not your basic everyday stock. It is more expensive to make than Basic Chicken Stock (page 67), but it has an exceptionally rich flavor and provides the necessary foundation for a sumptuous holiday dinner. You may cut some corners by substituting extra chicken bones or parts for the whole chickens, but chicken must be used because the stock produced by a turkey carcass does not have enough substance to hold up against a dressing as rich as Rice and Herb Stuffing (page 143).

Follow the same principles and steps as outlined in the recipe for Basic Chicken Stock (page 67). The result will be a marvelous base for sauces and gravies and for a clear consommé as well. For a richer sauce, such as for the Boned Stuffed Turkey (page 141), simply reduce the stock, thereby concentrating its flavor; no binder such as flour or cornstarch is needed.

The stock by itself makes a wonderful hearty broth.

This stock needs to be prepared at least a day in advance. Any leftover stock can be frozen for future use.

| | |
|---|---|
| 1 turkey carcass | 3 leeks, white part only, washed |
| Three 3-pound chickens | thoroughly |
| 2 pounds chicken necks, back, feet, | 4 heads garlic |
| or wings | 2 teaspoons whole black peppercorns |
| 8 quarts cold water | 8 sprigs fresh thyme, or 2 teaspoons |
| 2½ pounds carrots, peeled and halved | dried thyme |
| 4 medium-sized yellow onions, | 3 bay leaves |
| peeled and halved | 1 teaspoon coarse salt |

*Yields 7 quarts*

In a large stockpot, place the turkey carcass, chickens, chicken parts, and water, and bring to a simmer. Skim the stock frequently until the surface is clear. Add the vegetables, herbs, and spices. Simmer slowly for 7 hours, skimming as necessary. Remove the turkey carcass, chicken, and vegetables with a large slotted spoon. Ladle the stock through a cheesecloth-lined strainer. Allow the stock to cool. Refrigerate, skim the fat, and freeze in small containers.

# Tomato Concassé

Concassé means broken in French. What we have are broken tomatoes, peeled, seeded, and dusted with a little granulated sugar to "sweat" their excess water. This leaves the essence of the tomato flavor. Don't waste any of the tomato in this process: The excess juice can be added to broth, and the peels can go into your stockpot.

This basic recipe upon which many sauces can be built has many applications. It can serve as a source for Cold Tomato Cubes Tossed in Tarragon and Sesame Oil (page 92), as a salsa with Crispy Whole Fish with Tomatoes (page 112), as an accompaniment or garnish with Steamed Scallops (page 110). It is also a zesty sauce for pasta and cheese. A sauce for all seasons.

*1½ to 2 pounds fresh ripe tomatoes, peeled, seeded, and coarsely chopped*
*1 tablespoon sugar*

*2 tablespoons butter*
*Salt and freshly ground black pepper to taste*

Dust the chopped tomatoes with the sugar. Let the tomatoes drain in a stainless steel colander for 20 to 25 minutes. Blot the tomatoes with paper towels to remove all excess moisture. To prepare hot tomato concassé, melt the butter in a medium-sized skillet. Add the tomatoes and cook them for 2 minutes over medium heat. Add salt and pepper to taste and serve.

*Makes 2 cups*

# Ginger Salsa Sauce

One of the benefits of California living is Hispanic or Mexican cooking and ingredients. Here, a traditional fresh tomato salsa sauce has been given the added dimension and sweet bite of ginger. This salsa works especially well with fried foods because it cleans and balances their rich taste while affording a nice contrast to their crunchiness; serve it with Crispy Whole Fish with Tomatoes (page 112) or Shrimp Tortillas (page 79).

*2 cups Tomato Concassé, page 70*
*2 teaspoons finely chopped ginger*
*2 tablespoons finely chopped scallions*
*1 tablespoon finely chopped fresh hot*
*  red chilies*

*2 tablespoons finely chopped fresh*
*  coriander*
*2 tablespoons fresh lemon juice*
*  Salt and freshly ground black pepper*
*  to taste*

*Makes 2½ cups*

Mix all the ingredients together in a medium-sized bowl. Refrigerate for 1 hour. Serve cold or at room temperature.

# Ginger-Scallion Mayonnaise

Mayonnaise is perhaps the first French word American children learn, which is not a bad beginning. Mayonnaise is rightfully a favorite condiment, but it is also splendid in combination with other foods. The basic ingredients, eggs and oil, blend well with many flavors, from anchovy to fresh herbs. The possible combinations are limited only by your imagination, good taste, and the demands of the dish the mayonnaise is to grace.

This ginger and scallion mayonnaise is really a blend of two concepts: In Eastern cuisine ginger and scallions are popular flavorings in dipping sauces, but there is no such thing as mayonnaise in traditional Eastern cooking.

The pungency of the ginger and the sharpness of the scallion make a mayonnaise perfect for chicken, pork and, especially, seafood (see Grilled Crab and Lobster, page 109). I use an olive oil-peanut oil mix because olive oil alone would overwhelm the ginger-scallion taste. For an even nuttier flavor, use ¾ cup of peanut oil combined with 2 tablespoons of sesame oil.

Mayonnaise should be kept in the refrigerator for no more than 2 weeks.

For an unusual and different flavor, fold into the mayonnaise 2 tablespoons of finely chopped fresh coriander.

| | |
|---|---|
| *3 large egg yolks* | *½ teaspoon ginger juice* |
| *1 teaspoon coarse salt* | *2 tablespoons finely chopped scallions* |
| *½ teaspoon freshly ground white pepper* | *¼ cup olive oil* |
| | *½ cup peanut oil* |

Have all ingredients at room temperature. In a food processor, blender, or bowl, beat the egg yolks with the salt and pepper. Add the ginger juice and finely chopped scallions. Add the olive oil in a very slow steady stream until it is thoroughly blended with the egg yolk mixture. Add the peanut oil and beat consistently until the mayonnaise is thick. Seal tightly and refrigerate until ready to use.

*Makes about 1 cup*

*Note:*

The technique for making mayonnaise is simple and almost foolproof. However, if the mayonnaise "turns" or "breaks" (which happens when too much oil is added at once, overpowering the capacity of the egg yolks to emulsify with it), don't despair. Simply mix 1 tablespoon of warm water with 1 tablespoon of the mayonnaise and begin again, beating the broken mayonnaise in a little at a time. This will repair the mayonnaise.

# Apple and Plum Sauce

This combination is as American as apple sauce and as Chinese as plum sauce. Plum sauce is a traditional Chinese cooking ingredient, combining plums, apricots, vinegar, chili, and sugar. It is both spicy and thick, with a strong tart quality reminiscent of Western bittersweet jams. Plum sauce most often is canned, and preserving does not seem to affect its flavor. The two sauces blend together nicely—the apple bringing lightness and smoothness, the plum bringing zest and a heavier, biting texture.

The sauce may be prepared well in advance and then refrigerated until ready to use. It should be paired with dishes such as pork—Roast Pork with Chinese Spices (page 174) and Boned Stuffed Turkey (page 141); in fact, any dish where a fruity tart condiment would be appropriate. Trust your own taste, and experiment.

I use Golden Delicious apples because of their availability and reliability —they are excellent for most cooking purposes.

*2 pounds (about 4) Golden Delicious*
*  apples, peeled, cored, and cut into*
*  1-inch cubes*
*1 teaspoon fresh lemon juice*

*1 tablespoon sugar*
*  Water*
*½ cup Chinese plum sauce*

*Makes about*
*1½ cups*

Place the apples and lemon juice in a medium-sized saucepan. Add the sugar and enough water to cover the apples. Simmer, uncovered, for 10 minutes. Drain the apples in a colander and allow to cool to room temperature. Puree the apples and plum sauce in a blender or food processor. Refrigerate until ready to use.

# Garlic-Hot Pepper-Sichuan Peppercorn Mayonnaise

This mayonnaise was inspired by the legendary "rouille" that originated, some say, in Martigues, the Venice of Provence. It accompanies the area's bouillabaisse and, I believe, is the secret of that fish stew's deliciousness. It is remarkable for its burnt orange color (*rouille* means rusty) and for its hot spices—local convention holds that the sauce sets the bouillabaisse afire in one's mouth. Legend also has it that bouillabaisse is an aphrodisiac whose potency is increased one hundred-fold by the addition of rouille. Its aphrodisiac properties were discovered, the story goes, when a handsome but poor fisherman lost the ravishingly beautiful love of his life to a rich sea captain. As the unforgettable beauty sailed off with the wealthy swain, she spied her erstwhile lover languishing hopelessly on shore. Pitying him, she tossed him a fish liver which, in the fashion of Martigues, he proceeded to mince, lace with garlic and oil, and season with hot red peppers. He consumed the dish on the spot and not only forgot his love immediately but ever after found all women beautiful and reciprocally attracted to him. Such are the aphrodisiac qualities of rouille! Here is a more potent version of this traditional mayonnaise—one with Sichuan peppercorns, which add more spice and an exotic, almost lavenderlike flavor to the sauce. It goes well with Ginger Fish Stew (page 113) and Ginger-Steeped Fish Fillets (page 114).

| | |
|---|---|
| *4 ounces fresh hot red chilies* | *Salt and freshly ground white pepper* |
| *2 medium-sized egg yolks* | *to taste* |
| *1 tablespoon finely chopped garlic* | *2 tablespoons fresh orange juice* |
| *1 teaspoon Chinese Seasoned Salt,* | *½ cup olive oil* |
| *page 42* | *½ cup peanut oil* |

Roast the peppers over a gas or electric burner until the skin is charred on all sides. Place the peppers in a plastic bag and close tightly. Allow the peppers to steam for 15 minutes. Cut the peppers in half lengthwise. Peel the skin and remove the seeds. Finely chop the peppers and set aside.

Combine the peppers, egg yolks, garlic, Chinese seasoned salt, salt,

*Makes about
1 cup*

pepper, and orange juice in a mortar or food processor. Mix until the ingredients form a thick paste. Add the olive oil and then the peanut oil in a slow steady stream, whisking until the oil is fully incorporated. The final result will not be as thick as most mayonnaise.

# Garlic-Sesame Seed Mayonnaise

Garlic mayonnaise is an addiction I formed during my stay in the south of France. Invoking my Eastern heritage, I lace it with sesame and rice vinegar. The result is a mayonnaise with textural bite that adds zest to foods without overpowering them.

*2 medium-sized egg yolks
1 tablespoon finely chopped garlic
2 teaspoons Chinese white rice vinegar
  Salt and freshly ground white pepper
  to taste*

*1 tablespoon sesame oil
½ cup olive oil
½ cup peanut oil
¼ cup very finely chopped scallions
1 tablespoon sesame seeds, roasted*

*Makes about
1 cup*

In a food processor, blender, or bowl, beat the egg yolks, garlic, white rice vinegar, salt, and pepper. Combine the oils in a medium-sized bowl and add them in a slow steady stream until fully incorporated. Add the chopped scallions. Transfer the mayonnaise to a bowl and gently fold in the roasted sesame seeds.

# Ginger-Tomato Sauce

Tomatoes, especially vine-ripened ones, simmered down to the right consistency and flavored with ginger, onions, scallions, butter, and garlic, are the simple basic ingredients of a sauce that will prove a delight with any pasta—such as Chinese Greens-Stuffed Ravioli (page 220)—or with a dish such as Scallion-Corn Soufflé (page 204).

This can be prepared well in advance, covered, and kept refrigerated. It also freezes well when properly wrapped and stored.

*3 tablespoons butter*
*½ cup finely chopped yellow onions*
*¼ cup finely chopped scallions*
*1 tablespoon finely chopped ginger*
*4 cups Tomato Concassé, page 70*

*3 garlic cloves, peeled and lightly*
  *crushed*
*Salt and freshly ground black pepper*
  *to taste*

Melt the butter in a medium-sized saucepan. Add the onions, scallions, and ginger. Turn down the heat to low and cook until the onions are translucent. Add the tomato concassé, garlic, salt, and pepper. Simmer, uncovered, for 25 minutes. Remove the garlic with a slotted spoon and discard.

*Makes 4 cups*

# APPETIZERS AND SALADS

Fresh Garden Salad with
  Chicken Crackling in
  Orange Sesame Oil
Crispy Shrimp Tortillas
Chicken Sun-Dried Tomato
  Spring Rolls
Chinese-Style Dumplings
  with Fresh Herbs

Fresh Crab and Lemongrass
  Quiche
Broiled Oysters with Three
  Sauces
Steamed Seafood Packages
Chopped Chicken Liver
  with Asian Flavors
Stuffed Chicken Wings

Chicken-Asparagus-Sesame
  Salad
Asian-Flavored Duck Salad
Fresh Tuna Salad
Cold Tomato Cubes Tossed
  in Tarragon and Sesame
  Oil
Tomato Salad with Ginger-
  Scallion Vinaigrette

*Hunger is the best appetizer.*                                                    Proverb

*Ho! 'Tis the time of salads!*                                            Laurence Stern

Western-style appetizers and salads are unknown in Eastern cuisines. It is not thought necessary to create or sharpen one's appetite for dining, nor is the concept of "cocktail food," which the late James Beard maintained is synonymous with "appetizer," congenial to the Eastern temper. There are salads of sorts: "vinegared" or "dressed" foods in Japan and China, pickled and salted foods in China. But the Western version made of garden greens is unknown.

Nevertheless, there are many delicious Eastern foods and flavorings that easily adapt themselves to the role of appetizer: for example, Shrimp Tortillas (page 79) and Stuffed Chicken Wings (page 88), finger foods par excellence, and Broiled Oysters with Three Sauces (page 84). Similarly, our fresh garden salad takes on new meanings when we dress it with chicken in orange-sesame oil.

The appetizers and salads offered here demonstrate that while the concepts may be strange to one culture, the foods and seasonings nevertheless know no boundaries.

# Fresh Garden Salad with Chicken Crackling in Orange Sesame Oil

Here, I preserve the essence of our home garden variety fresh greens, crisp, clean, and delicately flavored, by using orange juice, only slightly acidic, instead of vinegar. The peanut and sesame oil mixture completes a dressing whose mild nutty flavor overwhelms neither the tang of the orange nor the subtle taste of the greens. Chicken skin strips, slowly rendered into cracklings and then lightly salted, add a contrasting relish and crunchiness to the salad. The recipe is simplicity itself and may readily be doubled or tripled as the occasion warrants.

*The skin of one chicken breast*
*1 tablespoon peanut oil*
*2 cups young salad greens*
*2 tablespoons fresh orange juice*

*Salt and freshly ground black pepper*
*to taste*
*1 teaspoon sesame oil*
*1 tablespoon peanut oil*

Cut the chicken skins into 2-inch by ¼-inch strips. Heat a small frying pan and add the oil. When the oil is hot, add the skins and slowly render them over low heat until the skins are crispy. Blot off any excess oil with paper towels.

Wash and thoroughly dry the salad greens. In a medium-sized bowl, combine the orange juice, salt, and pepper. Slowly beat in the sesame and peanut oils. Add the greens and toss thoroughly. Top with the cracklings and serve.

*Serves 2*

*Wine Suggestion:* an off-dry Riesling from Germany or California, or a similarly styled California Chenin Blanc, young and fresh.

# Crispy Shrimp Tortillas

The original inspiration for this dish is the southern Chinese assortment of snacks known as dim sum where the shrimp is wrapped in a light egg crepe and deep-fried. In this version, the shrimp is marinated in the Chinese mode with a touch of lemon juice and then wrapped in corn tortillas. I find this a delicious variation because the stronger flavor and texture of the tortillas go so well with the distinctive taste of both the shrimp and the marinade.

The ginger and lemon juices give the marinade a bite that offsets the richness of the deep-frying process. I like to serve these shrimp rolls with Ginger Salsa Sauce (page 71). Much of the work here can be done ahead of time; the deep-frying, of course, must be done at the last minute.

*1 pound (about 10) large prawns or*
*   shrimp, peeled and split in half*
*   lengthwise*

MARINADE
*1 tablespoon fresh ginger juice*          *1 tablespoon fresh lemon juice*
*1 tablespoon light soy sauce*             *Salt and freshly ground pepper to*
*2 tablespoons finely chopped scallions*   *   taste*
*1 tablespoon rice wine*

*3 or 4 cups peanut oil*                   *20 toothpicks*
*10 fresh corn tortillas, cut in half*     *Ginger Salsa Sauce, page 71*

Split the prawns and wash them in cold running water. Drain and blot them dry with paper towels.

Combine the marinade ingredients, stirring them well, and add the prawns. Marinate for about 1 hour. Drain the liquid and discard it. Dry the prawns on paper towels.

Heat the peanut oil in a wok or deep-frying pan until it is moderately hot, about 300 degrees. Dip the corn tortillas in the oil to soften them. Do no more than 2 at a time and leave them in the oil for just a few seconds. Remove the tortillas immediately and drain on paper towels.

Lay 1 marinated prawn half on 1 end of the tortilla half and roll it up completely. Then put the toothpick through the center of both the tortilla and the shrimp to hold it together. Continue until you have rolled all the shrimp and tortillas.

Heat the oil in the wok or pan until it is quite hot, about 375 degrees, and fry the shrimp rolls until they are brown and crispy. This should take no more than a few minutes for each shrimp roll. Serve with the ginger salsa sauce on the side.

*Makes about*
*20 shrimp rolls*

*Wine Suggestion:* a rich California Chardonnay, 3 to 5 years old; a white Burgundy from Meursault; or, for interest, a white Rhône—such as Condrieu or Hermitage.

# Chicken Sun-Dried Tomato Spring Rolls

My first experience with Vietnamese rice paper wrappers convinced me that they were more interesting in taste and texture than the Chinese flour versions I knew. They are lighter, crisper, and have a more delicate parchmentlike quality, which I love. I find Vietnamese wrappers most suitable for this dish in which I combine Western herbs, sun-dried tomatoes, chicken, and distinctively Asian bean thread noodles. The noodles, which are made from soybeans, add substance without heaviness.

This version makes a wonderful appetizer, and much of the work can be done ahead of time.

*2 ounces bean thread noodles*
*8 ounces boneless chicken breasts,*
*  cut into thin strips about 3 inches*
*  long*
*  Salt and freshly ground pepper to*
*  taste*
*2 teaspoons olive oil*
*1 tablespoon finely chopped fresh*
*  marjoram, or 2 teaspoons dried*
*  marjoram*

*2 tablespoons finely chopped fresh*
*  chives*
*2 tablespoons finely chopped sun-*
*  dried tomatoes*
*One 1-pound package Banh Trang rice*
*  paper rounds*
*2 or 3 cups peanut oil*

Soak the bean thread noodles in warm water for about 15 minutes, or until they are soft. Drain them in a colander and cut them into thirds. Squeeze out any excess moisture in a linen towel.

Meanwhile, in a medium-sized bowl, combine the chicken strips with the salt, pepper, olive oil, marjoram, chives, and sun-dried tomatoes. Add the noodles, mix well, and let the mixture sit in the refrigerator for about 1 hour, covered with plastic wrap.

When you are ready to make the spring rolls, fill a large bowl with warm water. Dip a rice paper round in the water and let it soften a few seconds. Remove and drain it on a linen towel.

Place about 2 to 2½ tablespoons of the chicken mixture on the edge of the rice paper. Roll the edge over the mixture once, fold up both ends of the rice paper, and continue to roll to the end. The roll should be compact and tight, rather like a short, thick finger cigar about 3 inches long. Set it on a clean plate and continue the process until you have used up all the mixture.

(The spring rolls can be made ahead to this point; cover with plastic wrap and refrigerate for up to 4 hours.)

Heat the peanut oil in a wok or deep-frying pan until it is moderately hot, about 350 degrees, and deep-fry the spring rolls a few at a time. They have a tendency to stick to one another at the beginning of the frying, so

*Makes 35 to 40 spring rolls*   do only a few at a time.

Drain the spring rolls on paper towels and serve at once.

*Wine Suggestion:*  an earthy California Sauvignon Blanc, a Pouilly-Fumé, or Sancerre, 2 to 3 years old.

# Chinese-Style Dumplings with Fresh Herbs

We all had favorite foods in our childhood whose scents and tastes today evoke sweet memories. One such favorite of mine is steamed dumplings. The Eastern method of steaming preserves the most delicate flavors and textures of food. This is especially important when it involves meat wrapped with pasta. Employing this traditional Chinese technique, I combine in this recipe some popular Eastern flavors, soy sauce and rice wine, with robust herbs commonly used in the West. The result is a blend of seasonings that creates a delicious dumpling, traditional in one sense but quite different in another. The dumplings need no accompaniment, but I like to serve them with Ginger-Tomato Sauce (page 76) as a first course.

1 pound ground pork
1 teaspoon finely chopped fresh or
   dried rosemary
1 tablespoon finely chopped fresh or
   dried thyme
1 tablespoon finely chopped fresh or
   dried marjoram
2 tablespoons finely chopped
   scallions

1 tablespoon light soy sauce
1 tablespoon Chinese rice wine
One 12-ounce package thin wonton
   skins
   Ginger-Tomato Sauce, page 76
   Parmesan cheese

Mix the pork, herbs, scallions, soy sauce, and rice wine together in a large bowl.

Place about 3 tablespoons of the pork mixture in the center of each wonton skin. Lift the 4 sides and pinch them together. Continue to fill the wonton skins until the pork mixture is used up.

Put a rack or trivet in a wok or deep casserole. Add 2 inches of water and bring to a boil. Place the dumplings on a heat-proof plate or platter. Put this on top of the rack or trivet. Cover and steam for 20 to 25 minutes. They are done when firm to the touch. Dumplings can also be steamed in a bamboo steamer that has been lined with damp cheesecloth.

*Makes 25 to 30 dumplings*

Serve with the ginger-tomato sauce and Parmesan cheese.

*Wine Suggestion:* a snappy Alsatian Gewürztraminer or a dry California equivalent.

# Fresh Crab and Lemongrass Quiche

One of my most treasured discoveries, as I explored popular French cooking, was the quiche. Although the dish has recently fallen out of fashion, I retain my high regard for this simple creation—a pastry filled with a light custard and flavorings—because it lends itself so successfully to so many delicious variations. Here, I employ the quiche concept to blend fresh crab with lemongrass and ginger, two Eastern delights. Both spices work nicely with the delicate flavor of the crab, and the result is a new twist to the old quiche. The special taste of the lemongrass makes the search well worthwhile.

PASTRY
*1 cup flour*
*4 tablespoons butter*
*½ teaspoon salt*

*2 tablespoons very cold water*
*2 tablespoons heavy cream*

EGG FILLING MIXTURE
*3 medium-sized eggs*
*1 cup heavy cream*
   *Salt and freshly ground white pepper*
   *to taste*
*1 teaspoon finely chopped fresh ginger*
*2 tablespoons finely chopped fresh*
   *lemongrass*

*1 tablespoon finely chopped scallions*
*2 teaspoons finely chopped fresh*
   *chives*
*1 cup fresh crab meat*

*3 tablespoons freshly grated Parmesan*
   *cheese*

Mix all the pastry ingredients together in a bowl. Roll the dough into a ball on a lightly floured board. Cover with plastic wrap and refrigerate for about 30 minutes.

Preheat the oven to 350 degrees.

Roll out the pastry until it is about ⅛ inch thick and press it into a 12-inch tart pan. Place a sheet of foil over the surface of the pastry and put about 2 cups of dried beans on the foil to weigh it down. Bake the pastry in the oven for about 12 minutes. Remove the beans and the foil from the tart pan. Lightly pierce the pastry surface with a fork, return it to the oven, and bake 10 minutes more. Cool to room temperature.

*Yields a 12-inch tart*

Combine all the ingredients for the filling and pour into the shell. Sprinkle the top with the Parmesan cheese and turn up the oven temperature to 400 degrees. Bake for about 25 minutes, or until the egg has set.

*Wine Suggestion:* a dry California Riesling, Chenin Blanc, or a Vouvray sec.

# Broiled Oysters with Three Sauces

I prefer fresh shucked oysters, eaten simply with lemon and no other embellishment. Nevertheless, there are times that I enjoy these seafood savories when they have been enhanced with a light, tasty, and worthy sauce. In this recipe I follow a Western example by broiling the oysters and using, variously, three different sauces, all of which smack of Eastern flavorings. The result is contrast in light tastes and varied colors, a nouvelle cuisine look that is not a cliché.

These oysters make a notable first course for any meal. Much of the work can be done in advance because the broiling is merely to warm the oysters and brown the top of the dish.

*1 dozen oysters, shucked (save the shells and their liquor)*

*1 cup Fish Stock, page 68*
*4 cups rock salt*

SAFFRON SAUCE
*¼ teaspoon saffron threads*
*1 tablespoon rice wine*

*2 tablespoons Crème Fraîche, page 43*

SPINACH SAUCE
*4 ounces (about ½ bunch) spinach leaves*

*1 tablespoon finely chopped scallions*
*2 tablespoons Crème Fraîche, page 43*

TOMATO SAUCE
*2 tablespoons Tomato Concassé, page 70*
*1 teaspoon very finely chopped fresh ginger*

*2 tablespoons Crème Fraîche, page 43*

Preheat the broiler.

In a small saucepan, combine the oyster liquor and fish stock. Bring to a simmer and add the oysters. Cook them for just 2 minutes to "plump" them. Drain immediately. Depending on the type of oyster, you should have about 1¼ to 1½ cups of liquid.

Spread the rock salt evenly in an oval or round gratin pan. Place the dozen oyster shells in the salt and place 1 drained oyster in each shell.

Divide the oyster liquor-fish stock liquid into 3 equal parts and place in 3 small pans. In one pan, combine the ingredients for the saffron sauce with the stock and bring to a simmer. Cook for about 5 minutes.

Blanch the spinach and press out all the liquid in a colander using a wooden spoon or squeezing with your hands. Add to a blender with the scallions, crème fraîche, and the stock. Puree until it is liquid, return to the pan, and simmer for 2 minutes.

Combine the tomato sauce ingredients together with the stock in a blender and puree until liquid. Return it to the pan and simmer for 2 minutes.

Ladle each sauce over 4 of the oysters. When you are ready to serve, place the gratin dish under the broiler for a few minutes, until the sauce and oysters are hot. Serve at once.

*Serves 4*

*Wine Suggestion:* a rich Champagne or a full-bodied California Blanc de Noir sparkling wine.

# *Steamed Seafood Packages*

In this recipe I borrow the Chinese dim sum practice of parchment wrapping; however, instead of parchment I use the more fragile and subtle rice papers popularized by the Vietnamese. Once steamed, the seafood packages become transparent, exposing the delicacies within. Moreover, because the rice wrappers are edible there is no need to unwrap the packages —the whole ensemble may be enjoyed.

Once the packages have been assembled, the steaming takes minutes. Other fresh herbs, such as marjoram, chives, or parsley, may be substituted for the basil. These steamed treats make an attractive and savory opener for any meal.

MARINADE

| | |
|---|---|
| 2 teaspoons fresh lemon juice | Salt and freshly ground white |
| 1 tablespoon rice wine | pepper to taste |
| 1 tablespoon light soy sauce | 1/4 teaspoon cumin powder |
| | |
| 8 ounces (about 9) large prawns, shelled and cut in half lengthwise | 18 shreds (about 2 small ones) fresh hot red chilies |
| 8 ounces sea scallops, cut into 18 slices | 18 small fresh basil leaves, washed and dried |
| One 1-pound package Banh Trang rice paper rounds | Ginger-Tomato Sauce, page 76 (optional) |
| Zest from 1 lemon | |

Combine the marinade ingredients in a medium-sized bowl. Add the prawns and scallops to the marinade and leave, covered, for 1 hour in the refrigerator.

Fill a large bowl with warm water. Dip each rice paper round in the water and let it soften a few seconds. Remove and drain on a linen towel.

Drain the prawns and scallops. Blot with paper towels.

In the center of a rice paper round, place 1 of each ingredient in the following order: lemon zest, red pepper shred, scallop slice, basil leaf, and finally a prawn piece.

Make an envelope by folding the edge of rice paper nearest you over the ingredients and two-thirds of the way to the opposite side. Fold the 2 sides toward the center so they meet. Fold the bottom edge over halfway to the top. Fold the top edge over and tuck it in underneath the top layer of rice paper.

*Yields 18 packages*

Put about 2 inches of hot water and a trivet in the bottom of a steamer. Place the seafood packages on a plate on the trivet and steam for about 15 minutes. They can be served straight from the steamer with the ginger-tomato sauce, if desired.

*Wine Suggestion:* a crisp California Sauvignon, or Fumé Blanc, or a French Sancerre, 2 to 3 years old.

# Chopped Chicken Liver with Asian Flavors

I have always been struck by the many cultural affinities shared by the Chinese and Jewish cultures. The overlapping of tastes and styles, however, is not total. Many of my Jewish friends love Chinese food, but Jewish cuisine has won few Chinese converts. There is, however, one traditional Jewish dish that has won my heart and palate: chopped chicken liver. Drawing upon that affinity, in this recipe I blend aspects of the two traditions by brightening chicken livers with Eastern flavors and textures: ginger, rice wine, and water chestnuts. The result is a delicious variant, perhaps not better than the traditional version but certainly different. It is a simple dish to prepare, but remember not to overcook the liver. This is a delightful appetizer for large gatherings and should be served with crackers.

*1 teaspoon peanut oil*
*1 tablespoon butter*
*1 pound chicken livers*
*3 tablespoons chopped shallots*
*¼ cup finely chopped scallions*
*2 teaspoons chopped fresh ginger*
*Salt and freshly ground black pepper*
  *to taste*

*2 tablespoons rice wine*
*2 teaspoons ground cumin*
*2 tablespoons heavy cream*
*2 tablespoons finely chopped fresh*
  *water chestnuts*
*Fresh coriander leaves for garnish*

Heat the oil and butter in a frying pan over a medium-high flame and add the chicken livers. Sauté for 1 minute, until they begin to brown, then add the shallots, scallions, ginger, salt, and pepper. Sauté for 1 minute, then add the rice wine, cumin, and heavy cream. Continue to cook 4 or 5 minutes more, until the livers are cooked but still slightly pink inside. Stir in the water chestnuts and take the pan off the heat. Cool to room temperature. Process the mixture in a food processor until smooth. Serve in a bowl garnished with the coriander leaves.

*Serves 12*

*Wine Suggestion:* an off-dry Chenin Blanc or Vouvray, or a sweeter-style Spätlese Moselle from Germany.

# Stuffed Chicken Wings

Chicken wings, fried or braised with black beans, garlic, and ginger, have been a favorite in my family ever since I can remember. This is easy to understand—chicken wings are a choice morsel however prepared, a delicacy enjoyed throughout the world. Their only drawback is that they are relatively bony. The Chinese remedy this by employing an ingenious boning method, and with a little practice one becomes expert at it. Then the wings are stuffed with, for example, scallions and ham before they are fried. In this recipe I combine Eastern ginger, scallions, coriander, soy sauce, and sesame oil with some very Western cream cheese for a smooth, zesty stuffing. And instead of deep-frying the wings, I cook them in a hot oven. The result is an irresistible and truly appetizing morsel, a wonderful change of pace from the usual finger food served at parties.

The wings may be stuffed hours in advance; just keep them, tightly wrapped, in the refrigerator.

| | |
|---|---|
| 2½ pounds (about 16) large chicken wings | 1 tablespoon rice wine |
| | 3 tablespoons light soy sauce |
| CREAM CHEESE STUFFING | |
| 6 ounces cream cheese | 2 tablespoons fresh coriander |
| 2 tablespoons chopped fresh ginger | 1 tablespoon light soy sauce |
| 3 tablespoons chopped scallions | 2 teaspoons sesame oil |

To bone the chicken wings, cut to the bone above the joint joining the wing to the wing drummet. Grab the joint with a paper towel and twist; the bone of the drummet should come out. Push the meat up, exposing most of the bone. With your finger make a small pocket where the bone was lodged. Repeat the procedure for the joint between the wing and wing tip. Bone all the wings. Marinate the wings in rice wine and soy sauce for 1 hour in the refrigerator.

Preheat the oven to 500 degrees.

In a small bowl mix together the cream cheese stuffing ingredients. Stuff about 1 teaspoon in each wing using a small spoon or your fingers. Line the stuffed wings on a baking sheet skin side up. Reduce the oven

*Makes 32 servings*   temperature to 400 degrees and bake the wings for about 20 minutes, until golden brown. Serve immediately.

*Wine Suggestion:* a light, spicy California Zinfandel; or Chianti, young and served slightly chilled.

# Chicken-Asparagus-Sesame Salad

Cold chicken salad in a sesame-flavored dressing is a familiar dish in many parts of Asia and a popular favorite in America as well. Asparagus, however, is of European provenance and is still a relative rarity in Asia. This noble vegetable has been introduced into Chinese cuisine by the great chefs in Hong Kong and is becoming very popular there. Chinese cooks typically stir-fry asparagus, but I think it is delicious simply blanched and served with a sparkling dressing. Here, I use a variation of French vinaigrette spiced with an Eastern touch of sesame paste.

This easy-to-make dish is delightful in springtime and on warm days, and is perfect for picnics.

*8 ounces asparagus, diagonally sliced into 2-inch sections*

*1 pound boneless chicken breasts, cut into 3-inch by ¼-inch strips*

DRESSING
*1 egg yolk*
*1 teaspoon Dijon mustard*
*Salt and freshly ground black pepper*
*2 teaspoons finely chopped garlic*

*2 teaspoons sesame paste*
*¼ cup peanut oil*
*¼ cup olive oil*

*3 tablespoons shredded sun-dried tomatoes*
*1 cup basil leaves, loosely packed*

*3 tablespoons finely chopped scallions*
*2 pickled sweet red peppers, cut into strips*

Bring a medium-sized pot of water to a boil; blanch the asparagus and remove with a slotted spoon. Turn off the heat and add the chicken. Cover and steep for 4 minutes. Drain the chicken and set aside.

To make the dressing: In a small bowl, beat the egg yolk with the mustard, salt, and pepper. Add the garlic and sesame paste, and mix well. Add the oils in a slow steady stream, beating continuously until the oil is fully incorporated.

Toss the chicken and asparagus with the sun-dried tomatoes and the dressing. Add the basil leaves and scallions, and toss again. Top with the peppers and serve.

*Serves 4 to 6*

*Wine Suggestion:* a dry (under 1 percent residual sugar) California Chenin Blanc or a comparable Vouvray.

# Asian-Flavored Duck Salad

I have long enjoyed duck braised, roasted, or steamed in the Chinese manner, but I discovered duck salad only a few years ago in France. It is an admirable way to enjoy this rich fowl and is, besides, a savory way in which to use any duck leftovers. In this recipe I combine cooked duck meat with a traditional and distinctive Eastern dressing and, in a Western or at least non-Asian mode, Belgian endives and mangos. These touches work well together, balancing the robust taste of the duck. Roast the duck yourself or buy it already cooked from a specialty butcher or Chinese delicatessen. You will find this an unusually delectable salad.

*2 cups cooked duck meat, from ½ roast
   duck*

DRESSING
*1 tablespoon finely chopped garlic*
*2 tablespoons finely chopped scallions*
   *Salt and freshly ground black pepper*
   *to taste*
*2 teaspoons sesame oil*

*1 tablespoon dark soy sauce*
*3 tablespoons chopped fresh chives*

*2 Belgian endives, cored and leaves
   separated*
*2 mangos, peeled and sliced*

Shred the duck meat and set it aside.

Mix the dressing ingredients together and moisten the duck meat with

*Serves 4*

it. Make beds of Belgian endives on individual plates. Cover with duck salad and garnish with mango slices. Serve at once.

*Wine Suggestion:* a full-bodied California Gewürztraminer with a touch of sweetness; or a dry Sauternes on the order of Château "Y," Château "R," or Château "G."

# Fresh Tuna Salad

For me, Japanese cuisine is epitomized by fresh fish and the tastes and fragrances of the sea. The influence of Japanese styles and techniques on Western cooking has been profound and, I believe, enormously beneficial. This is particularly true in the matter of the presentation of food—the esthetics are as important as the freshness and the taste. I love Japanese simplicity versus the often baroque approach of the Chinese. In this recipe I adopt some Eastern styles and flavors (tuna fillets, rice wine, soy sauce) and marry them to Western treats (avocado and tomatoes) and present them in an almost Japanese fashion.

This intriguing and easy salad provides a fresh, light, and beautiful opener to any meal.

| | |
|---|---|
| ½ pound fresh tuna fillet, thinly sliced against the grain | 2 tablespoons Chinese white rice vinegar |
| 1 tablespoon light soy sauce | 1 tablespoon fresh chopped coriander |
| 1 tablespoon Chinese rice wine | ½ cup Tomato Concassé (see page 70) |
| ½ sweet red onion, peeled and very thinly sliced | 1 tablespoon sesame oil |
| | 1 large ripe avocado, peeled and sliced |

In a small bowl, mix the tuna with the soy sauce and rice wine and marinate for 20 minutes. Toss the red onion with the vinegar and coriander and marinate for 10 minutes. Combine the tomato concassé and sesame oil.

*Serves 4 as an appetizer*

On individual plates, arrange a composed salad of tuna, red onions, tomato, and avocado.

# Cold Tomato Cubes Tossed in Tarragon and Sesame Oil

This is a simple but delicious recipe that is particularly appropriate when tomatoes are in season. It combines Western fresh herbs with the pungent toasty and nutty flavor of Eastern sesame oil. It is very easy to put together but best if the dressing is put on just before serving.

1½ pounds fresh tomatoes
2 teaspoons fresh tarragon leaves

2 tablespoons finely chopped fresh
chives

DRESSING
1 tablespoon lemon juice
2 teaspoons Dijon mustard
1 teaspoon sugar

Salt and freshly ground black
pepper to taste
1 tablespoon sesame oil

Blanch the tomatoes in hot water for 10 seconds. Peel and juice them and discard the seeds. Cut the tomato flesh into large—1½-inch—cubes. Set them to drain in a large colander.

Mix all the dressing ingredients together in a small bowl.

When you are ready to serve, toss the tomato cubes well with the tarragon and chives, and blend in the dressing. Serve at once.

*Serves 4*

*Wine Suggestion:* a great dish for straightforward Italian whites such as Frascati or Fruili.

# Tomato Salad with Ginger-Scallion Vinaigrette

Ginger and scallions are a classic Eastern combination to which I have added a traditional Western salad dressing for a different sparkle and flavor. The results are delicious and refreshing.

*1 pound red or yellow cherry tomatoes*

VINAIGRETTE

*1 tablespoon finely chopped shallots*
*2 tablespoons finely chopped*
  *scallions*
*1 teaspoon very finely chopped*
  *ginger*

*2 tablespoons lemon juice*
*1 teaspoon Dijon mustard*
  *Salt and freshly ground black pepper*
  *to taste*
*¼ cup olive oil*

Cut the tomatoes in half. Place the shallots and scallions in a linen towel and squeeze the liquid from them. Combine them with the rest of the vinaigrette ingredients. Mix well, pour over the tomatoes, and serve at once.

*Serves 2 to 4*

*Wine Suggestion:* try a dry Chenin Blanc from California or a refreshing Spanish white from Rueda.

# SOUPS

*Soup for lunch! Mmmm, it's delicious.*      American Ad

*Of soup and love, the first is best.*      Old Proverb

Venite ad me omnes qui stomacho laboratis et ego restaurabo—*(Come to me, all those whose stomachs cry out, and I will restore you.)*
    Sign hanging over M. Boulanger's eighteenth-century Paris soup shop and, thus, the first restaurant

Soups are enjoyed by the peoples of both East and West. Within the different cuisines, however, soups have different functions and status. In Eastern cuisines, soups are either rarely prepared, as in India, or are seen as something to drink *(suimono)*, as in Japan. Among the Chinese, soup is not a prelude or first course but an integral part of the meal. Set in a large bowl in the center of the table and surrounded by all of the other dishes, the soup is consumed as the meal progresses. It serves as a refresher between the partaking of different dishes and as a beverage throughout the meal. Water is never served during the meal, and tea is brought out only before and after a Chinese meal. Eastern soups are delicious, I hasten to add; the point is simply that they are assigned a different place in Eastern cuisines.

In Western cuisines, soups may serve as appetizers, as first courses, or as complete meals in themselves. They are not side dishes or supporting actors, as it were. Why this central role was accorded soups in the West is unclear. It may have something to do with the relative abundance in Europe that allowed the concoction of so many hearty soups. Certainly, until the 1920s in America, soup and salad lunches and dinners were common, and most kitchens had stockpots simmering on the stove.

In the recipes included here I have taken popular soups from the various cuisines and introduced new spices and seasonings, enhancing the familiar flavors and adding a new dimension. See, for example, Cream of Ginger, Lemongrass, Corn Soup with Chili Bean Paste (page 105), and Goat Cheese Wonton Soup (page 98), with its saffron, chives, coriander, and scallions.

I have also included some cold soups, which are almost unknown in the East though in China a cold sweet soup may be served at a banquet. I have included a variation of that theme also—in the dessert section. In the West, where soups stand on their own, as it were, cold soups have a respectable place.

Remember, East or West, good soup requires a good stock.

# Cold Zucchini-Ginger Soup

I was inspired to make this dish by a soup I enjoyed at a great restaurant, the Gaddi, in the Peninsula Hotel in Hong Kong. Knowing my interest in blending East and West, Priscilla Chen of the Peninsula suggested this soup to me, and I saw at once that it was a true East-West dish. When I returned to California I immediately re-created the soup, adding some touches of my own.

It is an easy soup to prepare and is a refreshing way to begin any meal. It goes particularly well in a menu that features a roast such as Roast Pork with Chinese Spices (page 174).

2 pounds small zucchini, trimmed
  and julienned
1 tablespoon coarse salt
2 tablespoons butter
¾ cup finely chopped scallions
1½ tablespoons minced fresh ginger
1 tablespoon sugar

4 cups Basic Chicken Stock, page 67
1 cup heavy cream
Salt and freshly ground white
  pepper to taste
Purple chive flowers or minced
  scallions for garnish (optional)

In a stainless steel colander, mix the zucchini with the salt. Allow to sit for 30 to 45 minutes. Rinse off the salt. Wrap the zucchini in a towel and squeeze out as much liquid as you can. Set aside.

Heat the butter in a large sauté pan. Sauté the scallions and ginger gently without browning for about 5 minutes. Add the reserved zucchini and sugar. Mix well. Meanwhile, in a large pot, heat the chicken stock until it is boiling. Sauté the zucchini mixture for a few more minutes. Add the hot stock and remove from the heat.

While the mixture is still hot, ladle in small batches into a blender and process until completely smooth. Place the blended soup in a stainless steel bowl and allow to cool. To speed up cooling, place the bowl in another one filled with ice cubes and cold water.

When the soup is almost cold, slowly stir in the cream. Season to taste. Keep in the refrigerator until ready to serve.

*Serves 4 to 6*    Garnish with the chive flowers or minced scallions if desired.

*Teddy's Crystal Prawns with Fresh Basil, Peppers and Garlic*

*Goat Cheese Wonton Soup*

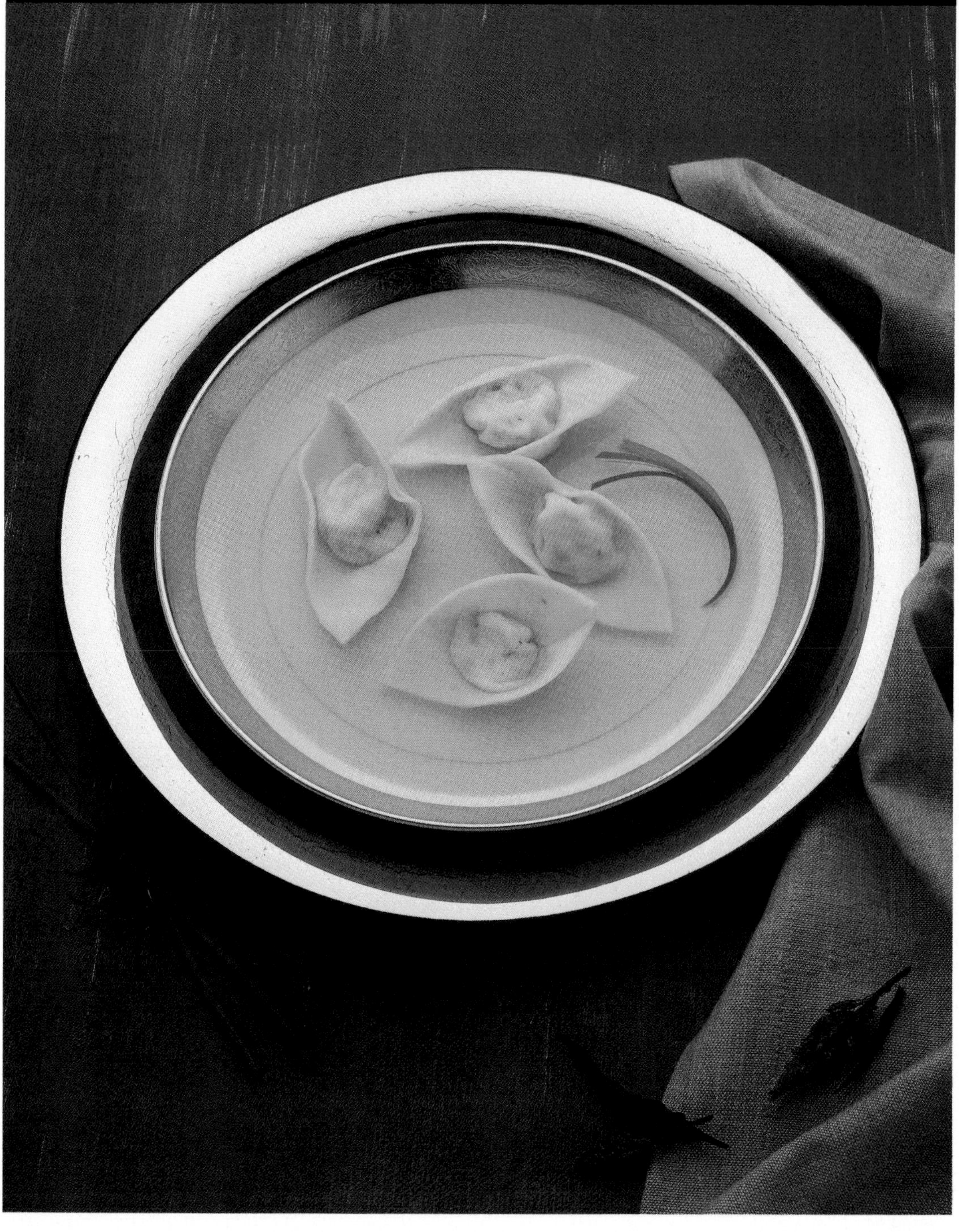

Broiled T-Bone Steak with Oyster Sauce and Bok Choy

Chinese Ratatouille

*Pasta in Black Bean Sauce with Triple Tomatoes*

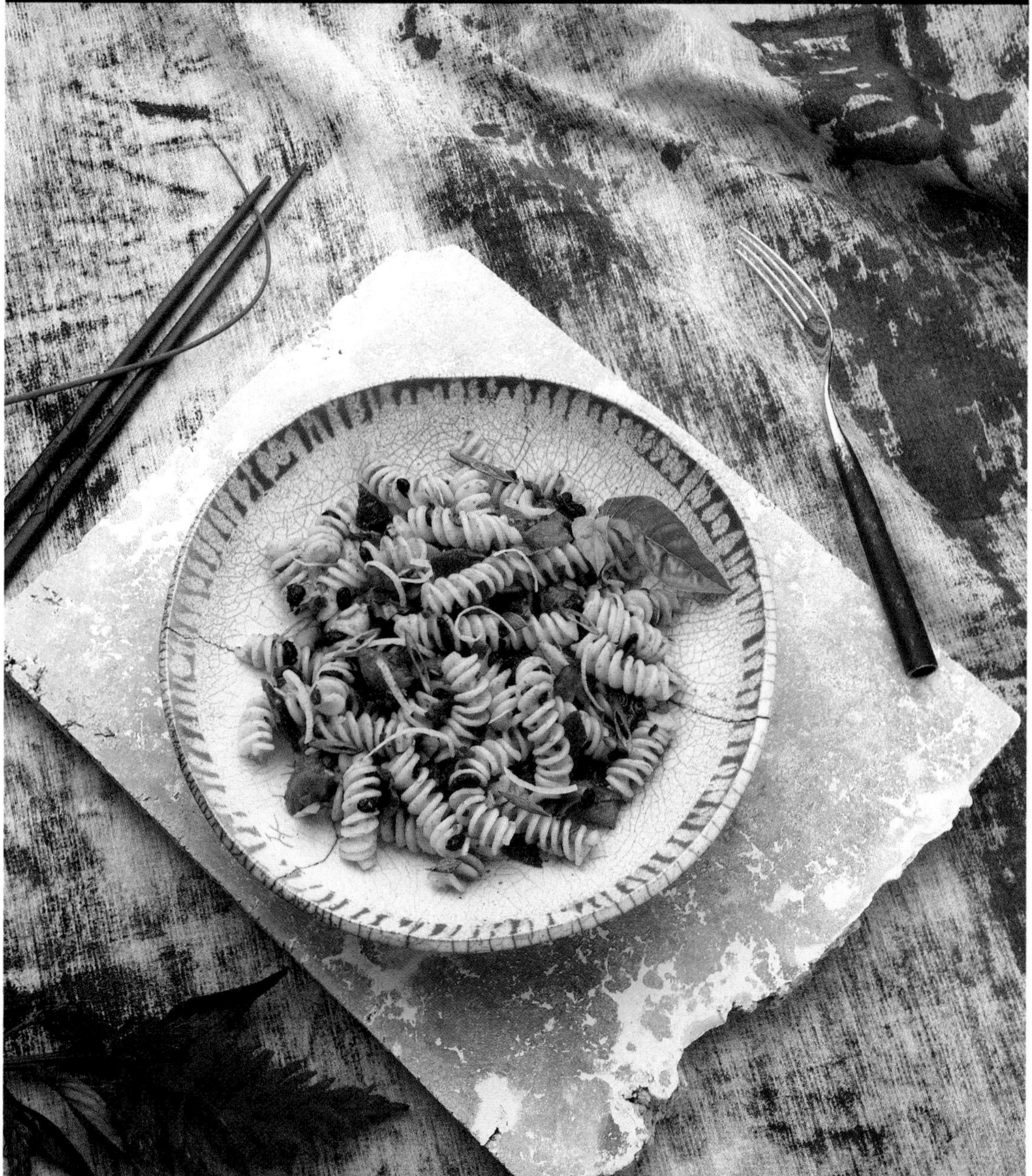

Baked Apples with Lemongrass; Warm Peach Compote with Basil

# Asian Pear Watercress Soup

This is a version of a simple Chinese soup that my mother made for me when I was a child. Her recipe was strictly Chinese, full of simple flavors. I have added two decidedly Western touches—butter and crème fraîche—for richer and even more satisfying results. The purée technique is Western; the Eastern palate prefers different textures simultaneously, but I believe the technique is appropriate in this case.

*1½ pounds (4 or 5) Chinese pear*
  *apples, peeled and cored*
*4 cups watercress leaves, loosely*
  *packed*
*4 cups Basic Chicken Stock, page 67*

*2 tablespoons butter*
*2 tablespoons Crème Fraîche, page 43*
*2 teaspoons sugar*
  *Salt and freshly ground white*
  *pepper to taste*

Cut the pear apples into quarters and set them aside. Wash the watercress leaves and blot them dry with paper towels.

Bring the chicken stock to a simmer in a medium-sized pot. Add the pear apple quarters and watercress leaves. Let the mixture cook for about 5 minutes over medium heat. Remove from the heat and let cool for a few minutes.

When it is cool enough to handle, puree the mixture in a blender until it is smooth. You may have to do this in several batches.

Return the pureed soup to the pot. Add the butter, crème fraîche, sugar, salt, and pepper. Bring the soup back to a simmer and let it cook 5 minutes more. It can be served warm or cold.

*Serves 4 to 6*

*Note:* Asian pears are sometimes known as sand pears because their skins have a sandlike surface; they may also be labeled Oriental apple pears or pear apples. When perfectly ripe, they have the heady bouquet of the best pears and the crisp crunch of apples. If they are unobtainable, use fresh local or in-season pears.

*Wine Suggestion:* here is an opportunity for an old, rather dry Sauternes from a vintage like 1977 or 1972.

# Goat Cheese Wonton Soup

All dumplings or wontons are equal, but some are more equal than others. I believe that the Chinese method of serving the dumplings in a rich but light broth brings out the best in the dumplings, especially when, as in this case, a delicate saffron flavor is present. Instead of the traditional Chinese stuffing of ground pork, I rely here upon the wonderful earthy flavor and texture of California goat cheese, a Western specialty whose strength and tang blend well with the chives, coriander, and scallions to form the stuffing. This recipe illustrates the strengths of both Eastern and Western cooking. It is a perfect cold weather dish and is a light meal in itself.

SAFFRON WONTON PASTA

| | |
|---|---|
| *¼ teaspoon saffron threads* | *1 egg white* |
| *2 teaspoons water* | *¼ teaspoon salt* |
| *1 cup flour* | *1 tablespoon peanut oil* |
| *1 medium-sized egg* | |

STUFFING

| | |
|---|---|
| *4 ounces California goat cheese* | *½ tablespoon finely chopped coriander* |
| *4 ounces fresh ricotta cheese* | *Salt and freshly ground black pepper* |
| *2 tablespoons finely chopped fresh* | *to taste* |
| *chives* | |
| *3 tablespoons finely chopped scallions,* | |
| *white parts only* | |

| | |
|---|---|
| *2 quarts Basic Chicken Stock, page 67* | *2 teaspoons salt* |
| *Salt to taste* | *Chopped scallion tops for garnish* |
| *2 quarts water* | *(optional)* |

Soak the saffron threads in 2 teaspoons of hot water for about 10 minutes. Meanwhile, combine the rest of the pasta ingredients in a bowl or food processor. Add the saffron-water mixture. Do not overprocess the pasta dough. Stop the machine before it forms the dough into a ball. Knead the pasta dough into a smooth ball by hand and then cover it with foil or plastic wrap. Let it rest for about 30 minutes.

To make the stuffing: In a small mixing bowl, combine the cheeses and seasonings together with a wooden spoon, mixing well.

Roll out the pasta as thinly as possible using a pasta machine. Dust it with flour from time to time to keep it from sticking. Cut the pasta into 3-inch squares. You should have about 25 squares.

Stuff each square with about 2 teaspoons of the stuffing mixture. Pull up the sides and pinch them together to seal. The moisture from the stuffing will be enough to seal the wontons, but be careful not to break the squares. Lay the stuffed wontons on a floured baking sheet.

Bring the chicken stock to a simmer and add the salt. In another pot, bring the 2 quarts of water to a boil and add the 2 teaspoons of salt.

Poach the wontons for about 30 seconds in the pot of water. When they float to the top, gently remove them with a slotted spoon or strainer and place them in the simmering stock. Cook for 2 or 3 minutes. You may have to do the wontons in several batches.

Pour the soup into a soup tureen or ladle into individual bowls. Garnish with the chopped scallions if desired. Serve at once.

*Serves 4 to 6*

*Wine Suggestion:* a light, fragrant California Sauvignon, or Fumé Blanc.

# Cold Tomato Soup with Lemongrass

Relatively speaking, tomatoes were introduced by the West into the venerable Chinese cuisine but yesterday, about one hundred years ago. They have nevertheless become universally popular. East does meet West. Here, I combine old-fashioned Western tomato soup with an Eastern standard, lemongrass. Its distinct but subtle flavor contrasts nicely with the smooth richness of the tomatoes and without the addition of any acidic elements as would follow the use of lemon juice. This is an excellent warm weather dish. It makes a perfect first course but may even serve as a light supper by itself.

It may be made ahead of time and refrigerated since it retains its unique flavor very well.

| | |
|---|---|
| 2 tablespoons butter | Salt and freshly ground white pepper |
| 1 tablespoon olive oil | to taste |
| ½ cup finely chopped scallions | 2 tablespoons heavy cream |
| ¼ cup very finely chopped fresh | 2 tablespoons finely chopped fresh |
| lemongrass | chives for garnish |
| 2 cups Basic Chicken Stock, page 67 | 1 tablespoon finely chopped fresh |
| 3 cups Tomato Concassé, page 70 | coriander for garnish |
| 2 tablespoons sugar | |

Melt the butter and olive oil in a medium-sized pan. Add the scallions and lemongrass. Cook over low heat for about 5 minutes.

Add the chicken stock and tomato concassé. Stir to mix well. Season the mixture with the sugar, salt, and pepper. Cook over low heat about 5 minutes more. Allow it to cool. Puree the mixture in a blender. You may have to do this in several batches.

Let the soup cool. Cover with plastic wrap and refrigerate. When you are ready to serve the soup, stir in the cream and garnish with the chives and coriander.

*Serves 4*

*Wine Suggestion:* a ``tamed'' Sauvignon, or Fumé Blanc, from California or a simple dry white Graves.

# Light Oyster Soup

My favorite soups in the Chinese and Japanese modes are the light, clear ones, each with its own subtle flavors. They are best made in the most straightforward manner, using simple fresh ingredients simply prepared. I have applied that rule to this oyster soup. The cuisines of China and Japan are celebrated for their seafoods, and fresh oysters are the essence of the sea. This soup, then, is decidedly Eastern in inspiration, and yet its taste is familiar to the Western palate. I use the ginger, as in Asia, to balance the natural richness of the oysters and to add a nice zest to the soup. Simple and quickly made, it serves as an elegant beginning for any meal.

2 cups Fish Stock, page 68
1 dozen oysters, shucked, and their
   liquor
1 cup Tomato Concassé, page 70
1 teaspoon finely chopped fresh ginger

1 tablespoon light soy sauce
1 tablespoon Chinese rice wine
2 tablespoons fresh coriander leaves for
   garnish

*Serves 4*

Bring the fish stock to a simmer in a medium-sized pot. Add the oysters, tomato concassé, ginger, soy sauce, and wine. Cook for about 5 minutes over low heat. Just before serving, garnish with the fresh coriander leaves.

*Wine Suggestion:* a light, young Champagne or a bright California sparkling wine.

# Oxtail Soup

In America, the story goes, we rarely make oxtail soup because when we are finished we don't know what to do with the rest of the ox. This is no doubt a commentary on our abundance. In Asia there has never been any such problem, and oxtail soup occupies an honored place in the cuisine of many Asian countries. Oxtail soup often appeared on my Chinese family table not only because of its economy but also because we loved to chew on the bones, whose hollows are filled with rich flavorful meat. Oxtails have a deep beef flavor, and I learned in my household to appreciate their delightful texture. After consuming the soup, we dipped our oxtails in a mixture of ginger, soy sauce, and scallions.

In this recipe I follow the traditional Chinese way of making the soup, but I substitute certain Western seasonings that I believe enhance the flavor of this venerable dish: mustard, capers, and garlic. The rice wine adds an appetizing aromatic flavor to the soup. It makes a wonderful hearty cold-weather treat—very satisfying and comforting.

*4 pounds oxtails*
*4 cups Basic Chicken Stock, page 67*
*1 cup rice wine*
*2 tablespoons light soy sauce*
*1 cup chopped scallions*

*5 tablespoons drained capers*
*2 teaspoons chopped garlic*
*3 tablespoons Dijon mustard*
*1 tablespoon sesame oil*

Blanch the oxtails in a pot of boiling water for 10 minutes.

In another pot combine the oxtails, chicken stock, rice wine, and soy sauce. Simmer slowly for 1½ hours, or until the oxtails are tender.

Remove the oxtails to a serving platter and keep warm. Mix together the scallions, capers, garlic, mustard, and sesame oil, and pour over the oxtails. Serve the liquid separately in bowls along with the oxtails.

*Serves 4 to 6*

*Wine Suggestion:* a fine California Chardonnay or a good-quality white Burgundy, 4 to 6 years old.

# Cream of Asparagus Soup with Coriander

Asparagus in season cannot be improved upon as a vegetable treat. When it is made into a soup, it must be allowed to display its virtues of taste, texture, and color. I therefore prepare it simply. In this recipe the crème fraîche provides a small touch of richness to the soup. The coriander, which is widely used as a soup seasoning in Thailand and southern China, adds an earthy flavor that goes especially well with the exquisite taste of the fresh vegetable. This is a soup to grace any table.

*1 pound asparagus, cut into 2-inch
  pieces
4 cups Basic Chicken Stock, page 67
  Salt and white pepper to taste
2 tablespoons finely chopped scallions*

*2 tablespoons butter
3 tablespoons Crème Fraîche, page 43
2 tablespoons finely chopped fresh
  coriander*

In a medium-sized pot, cook the asparagus in the chicken stock for 2 or 3 minutes. Allow the mixture to cool, then puree in a blender. Add the salt and pepper. Return the mixture to the pot and, over very low heat, stir in the scallions, butter, crème fraîche, and coriander. Cook for 1 minute, then serve.

*Serves 4*

*Wine Suggestion:* a medium-dry sherry, Amontillado, or California Golden.

# Scallop-Corn-Ginger Soup

Eastern ginger refreshes this combination of East-West favorites. The resulting soup deliciously reflects the complex flavors, tastes, and textures of the cuisines of both hemispheres. In Asia, chicken would be used rather than fish stock and the ingredients would not be puréed. However, I judge the soup to be much better with these two changes. It is easy to prepare, and it should be reheated slowly. This soup makes a splendid beginning course.

| | |
|---|---|
| *4 cups Fish Stock, page 68* | *1 tablespoon sugar* |
| *1 pound sea scallops* | *Salt and pepper to taste* |
| *2 cups fresh corn cut from the cob* | *½ cup heavy cream* |
| *2 tablespoons rice wine* | *1 tablespoon butter* |
| *1 tablespoon finely chopped fresh* | *3 tablespoons finely chopped fresh* |
| *ginger* | *chives for garnish* |
| *3 tablespoons chopped scallions* | |

In a medium-sized pot, bring the fish stock to a simmer, then add the scallops and corn. Simmer for 2 or 3 minutes. Add the rice wine, ginger, scallions, sugar, salt, and pepper, and simmer 1 minute more. Cool briefly, then purée the mixture in a blender. Return the soup to the pot and bring to a simmer. Adjust the seasoning and add the cream and butter, stirring to mix well.

Ladle into individual soup bowls or into a tureen and garnish with the chives.

*Serves 6 to 8*

*Wine Suggestion:* a fresh Moselle from a vintage like 1983 or a California Riesling with some sweetness.

# Cream of Ginger, Lemongrass, Corn Soup with Chili Bean Paste

Corn is not unknown in Asia today, but it is really a Western food. In this recipe I take a great favorite of my own—creamed corn soup—and heighten its pleasures by the addition of some of my favorite Eastern spices: lemongrass, ginger, and chili bean paste, which are used by Asian cooks who like spicy flavors. Here it is used to give a hot edge to a spicy citron-flavored corn soup. For those who enjoy a spicy soup, this is a winner in appearance, taste, and flavor. It is substantial but not too heavy as a first course. Allow each person to add chili bean paste to taste. If fresh corn is not available, fresh zucchini makes a very satisfactory substitute.

2 tablespoons butter
1 tablespoon finely chopped fresh ginger
2 tablespoons very finely chopped fresh lemongrass
2 tablespoons finely chopped shallots
½ cup finely chopped yellow onions
2 cups fresh corn cut from the cob

4 cups Basic Chicken Stock, page 67
Salt and freshly ground white pepper to taste
2 teaspoons sugar
½ cup half-and-half
2 teaspoons chili bean paste, or less according to taste, for garnish
Fresh coriander leaves for garnish

Heat the butter in a medium-sized pot. Add the ginger, lemongrass, shallots, and onions. Cook over low heat for about 2 minutes. Add the corn and cook 1 minute or so more. Add the chicken stock and bring the mixture to a simmer. Continue cooking over low heat for about 5 minutes. Add the salt and pepper, then the sugar and half-and-half. Take the pot off the heat and allow to cool to room temperature. Liquefy the soup in several batches in a blender. Puree each batch for at least 2 or 3 minutes. Return the soup to the pot and bring to a simmer.

To serve the soup in a large tureen, add the chili bean paste in the center and stir to make a swirling pattern. To serve in individual bowls, add ¼ teaspoon of chili bean paste or less to each bowl and swirl or mix in. Garnish with fresh coriander leaves.

*Serves 4 to 6*

*Wine Suggestion:* a white Zinfandel or a spicy French rosé from Provence.

# FISH AND SHELLFISH

Grilled Crab and Lobster
Steamed Scallops
Steamed Fish with
    Tomatoes and Basil
Crispy Whole Fish with
    Tomatoes
Ginger Fish Stew
Ginger-Steeped Fish Fillets
Teddy's Crystal Prawns
    with Fresh Basil,
    Peppers, and Garlic
Salmon Fillets with Ginger,
    Basil, Tomatoes, and Salt
    Sauce

Whole Fish in Papillote
    with Eastern Seasonings
Spicy Ragout of Ginger
    Prawns
Mussels with Lemongrass
    Butter Sauce
Stir-Fried Abalone with
    Broccoli
Seaweed Pasta with Squid
    and Scallops
Eastern-Flavored Crab
    Pancakes
Steamed Salmon in
    Chinese Cabbage

Steamed Fish with
    Scallions and Young
    Garlic Shoots
Shrimp with Mustard and
    Coriander
Jade Prawns with Italian
    Parsley, Coriander, and
    Basil
Stir-Fried Shrimp with
    Carrots and Asparagus
Shellfish in Black Bean
    and Butter Sauce
Bay Scallops with
    Mushrooms

**FISH**     Fish and shellfish are universally esteemed.

In China and Japan fish and shellfish are staples in the diet. Japan has for millennia depended upon the fruits of the sea, and the cuisine is characterized by the flavor, freshness, and aroma of all manner of seafood. China, with its many rivers and lakes and its long coastline, has similarly made fish central to its cuisine. Europeans need no lessons from Eastern chefs concerning the rich potential of seafoods. Americans, however, have been slow to fully exploit them.

And yet, Americans are today eating more and more fish. This may be because beef and other meats have gotten relatively more expensive, but it is probably due more to our increasing awareness that the American diet is weighted toward the consumption of too much fat, especially saturated animal fats. Among the dietary goals recommended by nutritionists is a decreased consumption of red meat and an increase in the consumption of fish. This suggestion, if followed, can only result in improved health and gustatorial delight: No food is as wholesome or delicious as well-prepared fresh fish and shellfish.

Another reason for the increased consumption of fish in America is the growing influence of Eastern cuisine here. Japanese and Chinese chefs have led the way in introducing fish dishes to the American diner. I know many Americans who today prefer to order fish when dining out because it tastes so delicious. Of course, many of these converts when children were familiar only with fried fillets or fish sticks which, while able to sustain a growing body, are devoid of culinary grace. It is authoritatively maintained that Americans learned to cook fish properly only in the 1920s, as a direct result of the efforts of a government agent. She taught and popularized the startling (to Americans) notion of not overcooking the tender flesh of the fish.

Many Americans were familiar only with canned or frozen fish, although it is true that Pacific Northwest, New England, Cajun, and Creole cooking are all emphatically seafood-based. Yet, the key element in the enjoyment of fish is freshness. No cook, no matter how talented, can overcome the deficiencies of stale fish. Only the freshest fish tastes as it should. In many places in the East, if the fish is not actually swimming, it is ignored for culinary purposes. In Hong Kong restaurants, large aerated fish tanks are set up in the dining and kitchen areas, and the fish marked for dishes on the menus swim about until they are selected for preparation. This is a very expensive custom but one that is deemed well worth the cost. It certainly ensures freshness. In the markets of Hong Kong, fish are filleted alive, "with their hearts still beating," as the saying goes there. Americans appear more and more to be insisting on truly fresh fish—"fresh frozen fish" is not fresh—and the insistence pays off in a deeper appreciation of the excellent qualities of the food.

It is true that fresh seafood is expensive; at least once in a while, however, take the plunge and experience the food as it is supposed to be.

SHELLFISH    Shrimp, prawns, crab, lobster, scallops, abalone, and other seafoods are popular in both the East and West. I have prepared these recipes to emphasize their delicious but delicate flavors, employing cooking techniques that best preserve and enhance those flavors.

Lobster is expensive and ordinarily reserved for very special occasions. Crab in season, however, is reasonable, and tasty varieties may be found in different parts of the country. I am most familiar with the West Coast Dungeness crab, with its meaty claws and substantial body meat, but the Atlantic, Gulf blue, and buster crabs, Florida stone crabs, and Alaska king crabs are all tasty treats.

Always get the freshest possible shellfish, preferably live specimens: The meat of dead crustaceans begins to lose its delicate, sweet flavor immediately. Many Chinese will not eat precooked crabs or lobsters because the flavor and taste are so reduced. Avoid overcooking shellfish. Technique is always important but nowhere more so than in the preparation of seafood, which is so delicate both in flavor and texture. Steaming, steeping, and properly done deep-frying are among the methods employed.

# Grilled Crab and Lobster

Lobster and crab have wonderfully delicate flavors that are preserved by grilling. Ginger-Scallion Mayonnaise (page 72) is excellent with this seafood grill. The delicate sweet flesh of the crab and lobster actually steams in the shells, preserving its moisture and natural flavors.

*2 live Dungeness crabs, about 1½ to 2
  pounds each, or 6 live blue crabs, or 4
  fresh stone crabs*

*2 live Maine lobsters or Pacific spiny
  lobsters, about 1 to 1¼ pounds each
  Olive oil for brushing*

Refrigerate the crabs and lobsters for 1 hour, to partially anesthetize them.

Split the crabs and lobsters in half lengthwise with a cleaver or heavy knife. Remove the fingery feathery lungs and discard, pull off the mouth and eyes, and remove the intestines. Leave intact the liver of the crab, which is yellow, and of the lobster, which is greenish-yellow.

Brush both sides of the shellfish lightly with olive oil. Set aside.

Make a charcoal fire. When the coals are ash white, grill the crab and lobster, turning frequently. The shellfish are done when their shells become bright red and, when cracked open, the flesh inside is a translucent white. Serve immediately.

*Serves 4 to 6*

*Wine Suggestion:* a drier-styled California Cabernet Blanc or a young Alsatian Tokay or a Muscat d'Alsace.

# Steamed Scallops

The gentle moist vapor of the steaming process retains and enhances the delicate flavors of the fresh scallop.

If Chinese rice wine is unobtainable and you don't care for sherry, try a dry white wine or substitute orange juice. The taste will be different, but the Eastern aspect will still come through.

*1½ pounds scallops, left whole if small*
*   or quartered if large*
*1 teaspoon Chinese Seasoned Salt,*
*   page 42*
*1 tablespoon shredded orange zest*

*1 tablespoon rice wine*
*4 tablespoons cold butter, cut into*
*   small pieces*
*1 cup finely chopped scallions, white*
*   part only*

In a medium-sized bowl, mix the scallops with the Chinese seasoned salt, orange zest, and rice wine. Marinate for 15 minutes. Place the marinated scallops on a plate or shallow bowl in a steamer or wok. Steam gently for 8 to 10 minutes. Drain the juices from the steaming plate and reduce in a saucepan. Whisk in the butter, a few pieces at a time, and add the scallions. Spoon a little sauce on each serving of the scallops.

*Serves 4 to 6*

*Wine Suggestion:* a fine-quality white Burgundy from Puligny or Chassagne, or a high-quality California Chardonnay.

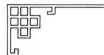

# Steamed Fish with Tomatoes and Basil

The key element of freshness is the taste of the fish—only the freshest fish tastes as it should. In this recipe I blend the Chinese technique of steaming with East-West flavors. Basil and tomatoes have affinities with both East and West, while the splash of butter and the fennel are typically Western.

*One 2½- to 3-pound red snapper, rockfish, sea bass, or any whole firm white-fleshed fish, cleaned*
*1 teaspoon coarse salt*
*½ cup fresh basil leaves*
*Leaves and stalks of 1 head fennel, roughly chopped*

*1 cup Tomato Concassé, page 70*
*1 tablespoon finely chopped shallots*
*4 tablespoons cold butter, cut into small pieces*

Prepare the snapper by cutting slashes 1 inch deep and 2 inches long crosswise from behind the gills to the end of the body. Repeat on the other side. Sprinkle the outside of the fish with salt and stuff the slashes with the basil leaves. Spoon the tomato concassé over the fish. Lay the fennel stalks and leaves on a plate as a bed for the fish. Place the fish on the bed of fennel.

Steam over slowly simmering water on a rack in a tightly covered wok or pot for 10 to 12 minutes, or until the flesh flakes easily.

Turn off the heat, drain off all the liquid accumulated on the plate, and pour into a wide skillet. Discard the fennel. Return the fish to the steamer to keep warm. Add the shallots to the steaming liquid and boil rapidly to reduce to about 1 tablespoon. Remove from the heat. Whisk in the cold butter a few pieces at a time and serve alongside the fish.

*Serves 4*

*Note:*  This is an excellent summertime dish. To serve cold, omit the butter sauce and add a splash of fresh lemon juice.

*Wine Suggestion:*  a dry white Graves or a fine Pinot Grigio from Italy.

# Crispy Whole Fish with Tomatoes

In China, deep-fried fish is often served with a sweet-and-sour or hot-and-spicy sauce. I was reminded of such a dish on a visit to Mexico when I was served a delicious Pacific rockfish, deep-fried and accompanied with fresh salsa. In this recipe I offer a variation on that theme of East-West techniques and flavors. For those who love their fish deep-fried, this is an especially delightful recipe. The cool, refreshing contrast of the sauce is a wonderful complement to the crisp, juicy fish.

FRESH TOMATO SAUCE
- 2 cups Tomato Concassé, page 70
- 1 tablespoon finely chopped fresh coriander
- 1 tablespoon olive oil
- 1/2 cup coarsely chopped basil leaves
- Salt to taste

- One 3½- to 4-pound rockfish, sea bass, red snapper, or any firm-fleshed white fish, cleaned
- Salt to taste
- 1 teaspoon freshly ground white pepper
- 4 to 6 cups peanut oil
- 1 cup cornstarch
- 1 head curly endive, washed and dried, for garnish

Mix the tomato concassé, coriander, olive oil, basil, and salt in a bowl and set aside.

Dry the fish thoroughly with paper towels. Cut 2-inch-deep and 2-inch-long slashes crosswise in the sides of the fish at 2-inch intervals. Season the fish with the salt and pepper.

Heat the oil to 375 degrees in a large wok or Dutch oven. Dust the fish with the cornstarch, shaking off any excess. Lower the fish into the oil with a strainer or large slotted spoon and cook for 5 minutes. Remove the fish with the strainer and reheat the oil. Lower the fish into the oil and fry a second time until golden brown and crisp.

Place the endive leaves on a platter with the fish on top. Serve immediately accompanied with the fresh tomato sauce.

*Serves 4*

*Wine Suggestion:* a good-quality blush or rosé wine, Zinfandel, or Cabernet Sauvignon, with good acid and a touch of sweetness.

# Ginger Fish Stew

Fish stews are more common in Western than in Eastern cuisine, although fish soups are popular in both East and West. Gentle stewing is another delicious way to prepare fish. In this recipe I emphasize the brisk, clean flavor of ginger as a counterpoint to the seafood and vegetables and to the other spices and flavorings. This may not be a true bouillabaisse, the standard by which I personally measure such stews, but it is a hearty and refreshing East-West variation of that classic theme, a fish stew with a taste, charm, and integrity of its own.

This dish is simple and easy to make. It can easily be doubled for a crowd. Serve it with the Garlic-Hot Pepper-Sichuan Peppercorn Mayonnaise (page 74).

*2 pounds firm white fish fillets, such as*
*sea bass, rockfish, and monkfish*

MARINADE
*2 teaspoons salt*
*2 tablespoons finely chopped coriander*
*2 tablespoons finely chopped scallions*
*1 tablespoon fresh ginger juice*
*3 tablespoons olive oil*
*1 teaspoon Chinese sesame oil*
*Fresh ground black pepper to taste*
*2 quarts Fish Stock, page 68*

*2 thick slices fresh ginger*
*3 cups Tomato Concassé, page 70*
*8 ounces snow peas, ends trimmed*
*2 ounces fresh kumquats, coarsely*
*chopped*
*Garlic-Hot Pepper-Sichuan*
*Peppercorn Mayonnaise, page 75; the*
*full recipe*

Cut the fish fillets into 1-inch by 2-inch pieces.

In a medium-sized bowl, mix the marinade ingredients, add the fish, and marinate for 30 minutes.

Bring the fish stock to a simmer in a medium-sized pot. Add the ginger slices and simmer in the stock for 15 minutes. Remove the slices with a slotted spoon and discard.

Add the marinated fish pieces and simmer for 5 minutes. Add the tomato concassé, snow peas, and kumquats, and simmer 5 minutes more.

*Serves 4 to 6*   Serve with the garlic-hot pepper-Sichuan peppercorn mayonnaise.

*Wine Suggestion:* a white Rioja from Spain or a rustic Frascati from Italy.

# Ginger-Steeped Fish Fillets

Ginger is indispensable in Chinese and other Eastern cuisines, especially when it comes to seafood cookery. Its pungent, pleasing taste works very well with almost any type of seafood and is particularly congenial to the delicate but distinct flavor of fish. In this recipe the fish has been gently steeped and allowed to absorb the seasonings in the broth without over-cooking. Once the fish stock is ready, the procedures are quite simple. The result is an elegant dish, especially when finished off with the colorful butter-tomato sauce. It can serve as a simple but sumptuous dinner for two, perhaps with a salad or as the first course in a more elaborate dinner.

*2 cups Fish Stock, page 68*
*1 tablespoon salt*
*Freshly ground white pepper to taste*
*1 tablespoon ginger juice*
*1½ tablespoons very finely chopped fresh ginger*

*1 pound fish fillets, such as red snapper, sea bass, and rockfish*
*1 cup Tomato Concassé, page 70*
*4 tablespoons butter*
*2 tablespoons finely chopped scallions*
*2 tablespoons Chinese rice wine*

Bring the fish stock to a simmer in a medium-sized pot. Add the salt, pepper, ginger juice, and finely chopped ginger, and simmer for 2 minutes.

Take the stock off the heat. Add the fish fillets and cover. Let the fish fillets steep in the hot fish stock for 5 minutes, then remove the fish fillets to a plate with a slotted spoon and cover with foil to keep warm.

Over high heat, reduce the cooking liquid in half. Add the tomato concassé, butter, scallions, and rice wine, and simmer 5 minutes more.

*Serves 4*    Serve at once over the fish fillets.

*Wine Suggestion:* an Alsatian Tokay or Riesling, or a dry California or Washington Riesling.

# Teddy's Crystal Prawns with Fresh Basil, Peppers, and Garlic

I originated this recipe to honor a dear friend on his fortieth birthday. The Chinese technique of salting leaves the prawns with a drier, cleaner taste and crisper texture. The fresh basil, stir-fried as a vegetable rather than added as a seasoning, together with the peppers and garlic, gives the prawns an aromatic Chinese-Provençal character. Stir-frying seals in the tenderness and succulence of the prawns. This is a simple, delicious dish.

*1 pound fresh prawns*
*2 tablespoons coarse salt*
*1 tablespoon olive oil*
*1 tablespoon peanut oil*
*2 tablespoons Chinese rice wine*

*1 red Anaheim chili, seeded and*
   *chopped*
*1 tablespoon finely chopped garlic*
*1 cup fresh basil leaves*

Without removing the shell, cut the legs off the prawns. With a sharp knife split the shell along the back. Remove the vein while keeping the shell intact. In a medium-sized bowl, combine the salt and prawns. Allow the prawns to sit for 30 minutes. Rinse them thoroughly under cold water and dry with paper towels.

   Heat a wok or large pan until it is hot. Add the olive and peanut oils. Add the prawns and rice wine, and stir-fry for 1 minute. Add the chili and garlic, and stir-fry 1 minute more. Add the basil leaves and, when they wilt, stir thoroughly. Serve at once.

*Serves 2 to 4*

*Wine Suggestion:* a straightforward French Chardonnay from Rully or Mâcon, or a young Italian Chardonnay.

# Salmon Fillets with Ginger, Basil, Tomatoes, and Salt Sauce

If imitation is the sincerest form of flattery, then this is the most sincere and flattering recipe I have ever created! I experienced the original version at Jacques Maximin's Chantecler, in the Hotel Negresco in Nice. It was a cold, nasty day in January, and I had driven with some friends for five hours from Marseille through one of the worst snowstorms ever to hit the south of France. There was indeed an edge to my appetite, but under any circumstances the beautiful and delicious *saumon frais au gros sel* would have been unforgettable. It was simplicity itself: a barely poached piece of salmon with a simple garnish of basil, tomatoes, and sea salt. I have not transcended it here but merely adjusted the original to give it an agreeable and delectable Eastern flourish, employing a sauce that complements the salmon and allows its virtues to shine through. This is a memorable dish that is simple to make.

*2 cups Fish Stock, page 68*
*1 pound salmon fillet, skinned*
*1 cup Tomato Concassé, page 70*
*2 teaspoons sesame oil*
*1 teaspoon finely chopped fresh ginger*

*1 tablespoon finely chopped fresh coriander*
*Sprinkling of coarse sea salt for each serving*

Bring the fish stock to a simmer in a medium-sized pot. Add the salmon fillet, cover, and turn off the heat. Steep for 30 minutes.

In a small bowl, mix the tomato concassé, sesame oil, ginger, and coriander, and refrigerate while the fish steeps.

Carefully remove the fish from the cooking liquid with a slotted spoon. Cut the fillet into 4 equal-sized pieces. Place on individual serving plates. Spoon some sauce over each fillet and sprinkle with sea salt. Serve at once.

*Serves 4*

*Wine Suggestion:* a rich California Sauvignon, or Fumé Blanc, or a similar French Sancerre.

# Whole Fish in Papillote with Eastern Seasonings

Steamed whole fish is popular in both East and West. In Asia, the fish is seasoned most often with the traditional and always pleasing trio: garlic, ginger, and scallions. Until recently the French used only the ancient papillote method: oiled or buttered paper forming a closed sack around the fish to allow the steaming process to work. Today it is recognized that papillote d'aluminium is an acceptable modern compromise. It may not have the charm of buttered or parchment paper but aluminum does perform better as a sealed container and as a moisture retainer, and has the advantage of being always at hand. The fish is steamed in its own moisture to perfection, its meat tender and succulent and suffused with the varied flavors of the Eastern seasonings. This is an impressive dish to serve at a dinner party; to make smaller portions, simply follow the same methods using fillets and cutting the cooking time in half.

*One 2-pound firm white-fleshed*
*    fish, such as sea bass or rockfish*
*1½ tablespoons coarse sea salt*
*½ cup shredded scallions*
*2 tablespoons shredded ginger*
*2 tablespoons fresh chopped*
*    coriander*

*3 tablespoons cold butter*
*1 fresh hot red chili, seeds removed*
*    and shredded*
*2 tablespoons light soy sauce*

Preheat the oven to 400 degrees.

Cut a length of aluminum foil, 1 foot wide and 6 inches longer than the fish. Rub both sides of the fish with salt and place on the foil. Scatter the scallions, ginger, coriander, butter, and chili over the fish. Sprinkle with the soy sauce. Seal the foil, wrapping the ends tightly.

Bake in the oven for 30 minutes, or until a thin bamboo skewer easily pierces the thickest part of the fish. Place the fish, still wrapped in foil, on a platter. Unwrap at the table and serve each portion with some of the aromatics.

*Serves 2 to 4*

*Wine Suggestion:* try a young Sauvignon, or Fumé Blanc, with oaky varietal character or a similar dry white Graves.

# Spicy Ragout of Ginger Prawns

The root meaning of *ragout* is "to restore one's appetite." A ragout, then, may be defined as any mixture or stew combining meat or fish and vegetables in such a way as to form a delicious and appetizing dish. Each locale in France boasts its own famous or extolled ragout. The many small pieces of various foods are cooked in a way reminiscent of Chinese claypot dishes. There is room in the flexible and hospitable ragout tradition for originality and experimentation. This ginger-prawn recipe clearly is well rooted in that tradition. The pungent but nonaggressive ginger works cooperatively with the crisp, clean prawn taste and texture; both enjoy and benefit from the accompanying sweetness and texture of the carrots and parsnips, all of them together in a nicely seasoned stock. This is indeed a tasty restorative to the appetite.

*1½ pounds prawns, shelled and deveined*
*2 teaspoons coarse salt*
*2 teaspoons cornstarch*
*1 small egg white*
 *Salt*
*1 tablespoon butter*
*1 tablespoon peanut oil*
*2 tablespoons finely chopped shallots*
*2 tablespoons finely chopped scallions*
*2 teaspoons finely chopped fresh hot red chilies*

 *2 tablespoons finely chopped ginger*
*½ cup finely diced turnips*
*½ cup finely diced carrots*
*½ cup dry white wine*
*¼ cup rice wine*
 *1 cup Fish Stock, page 68*
*2 tablespoons heavy cream*
*½ cup Tomato Concassé, page 70*
 *Freshly ground white pepper to taste*
*3 tablespoons finely chopped fresh coriander*

In a small bowl, combine the prawns and the coarse salt and set aside for 30 minutes. Rinse thoroughly under cold water and dry on paper towels. Combine the cornstarch, egg white, 1 teaspoon of salt, and prawns in a medium-sized bowl and marinate, refrigerated, for 30 minutes.

In a wok or medium-sized skillet, heat the butter and peanut oil. Add the shallots, scallions, chilies, and ginger, and stir-fry for 2 minutes. Add the turnips and carrots, and stir-fry 2 minutes more. Add the white wine and the rice wine, and reduce until the cooking liquid is nearly gone. Add the fish stock and reduce by two-thirds. Add the prawns, cream, tomato concasse, salt, and pepper. Cook for 5 minutes, stirring constantly. Add the coriander, stir well, and serve at once.

*Serves 4*

*Wine Suggestion:* a rich, fine-quality California Chardonnay or a similar white Burgundy.

# Mussels with Lemongrass Butter Sauce

Mussels are a staple in Eastern cuisine and a familiar item in the West, although it is true that the French and Italians have made much more of them than we Americans—clams and oysters seem to be our first choices. This is unfortunate, for mussels are every bit as tasty as these other bivalves, are relatively inexpensive, and can be prepared in many ways. The standard Chinese method is to stir-fry them, a good way to avoid over-cooking (they can get rubbery very quickly). I prefer to steam them just until they open; this takes very little time. Once steamed open, the juices released by the mussels need to be strained to remove any residual sand. With a sprightly sauce, Eastern seasonings, and a touch of butter, this recipe provides a delicacy to rival the best of clams and oysters.

*2 pounds mussels*
*¼ cup Chinese rice wine*
*1 cup Fish Stock, page 68*
*1 tablespoon finely chopped shallots*
*1 tablespoon scallions*
*1 tablespoon finely chopped fresh lemongrass*

*1 teaspoon chopped ginger*
*⅛ teaspoon saffron threads*
*Salt and freshly ground white pepper to taste*
*2 tablespoons cold butter, cut into small pieces*

Scrub the mussels under cold running water and pull off the wirelike beards. Steam the mussels open in a large covered pot filled with rice wine and fish stock. Remove the mussels with a slotted spoon and shuck them, discarding the shells. Strain the liquid into a bowl through a fine-meshed sieve.

Pour the liquid into a medium-sized skillet and add the shallots, scallions, lemongrass, ginger, and saffron. Cook over medium heat for 2 minutes. Add the salt and pepper. Whisk in the cold butter a few pieces at a time. Add the mussels and heat them through. Serve the mussels and the sauce in shallow bowls.

*Serves 4 to 6*

*Wine Suggestion:* an Alsatian Gewürztraminer or a spicy white California Pinot Blanc or dry Gewürztraminer.

# Stir-Fried Abalone with Broccoli

Abalone is a well-known, if expensive item, both fresh and dried, in Chinese and Japanese cuisines. In America this treat is known mostly in California. Delicately textured, vaguely reminiscent of clams, and tender when not overcooked, abalone is truly unique, and stir-frying is one of the best methods for cooking it. If fresh abalone is too expensive or unavailable, substitute scallops in this recipe. The broccoli is a traditional accompaniment for abalone, and it is excellent with scallops as well, being colorful and with a complementary assertive flavor. The abalone is deliciously at ease with the unusual East-West blend of crème fraîche and oyster sauce.

*1 pound broccoli
6 ounces fresh abalone meat or
scallops
1 tablespoon peanut oil*

*1 tablespoon finely chopped garlic
½ cup Crème Fraîche, page 43
2 teaspoons oyster sauce*

Trim the florets from the broccoli. Peel the remaining stems and cut into thin slices crosswise. Blanch the broccoli in a medium-sized pot for 1 minute and plunge in cold water. Drain.

Have your fishmonger shuck the abalone. Trim the edges and cut the abalone into thin slices crosswise. Pound the abalone briefly with a meat tenderizer or the side of a cleaver until tender but not mashed.

*Serves 2 to 4
as a first
course*

Heat a wok or medium-sized skillet and add the oil. Add the garlic, broccoli, and abalone. Stir-fry for 30 seconds. Remove the abalone with a slotted spoon. Add the crème fraîche and oyster sauce, and cook for 2 minutes. Return the abalone and stir. Serve at once.

*Wine Suggestion:* an outstanding California Chardonnay, 5 to 7 years old, or a rich, dry Sauternes.

# Seaweed Pasta with Squid and Scallops

Rome wasn't built in a day, but this pasta dish can be—and with spectacular results. In other words, this recipe takes time but is well worth the effort. Here, I use a Western pasta combined with the exotic Eastern staple, dried seaweed. The result is a pasta brimming with the flavor of the sea and an unusually appealing taste that goes perfectly with squid and scallops. The East-West spices and seasonings complete the harmony of the dish. This recipe is sure to be a favorite with anyone who loves seafood and pasta.

PASTA
*2 sheets dried Nori seaweed, finely*
  *chopped*
*2 cups flour*
*2 medium-sized eggs*

*1 egg white*
*2 tablespoons olive oil*
*2 teaspoons salt*

*1½ pounds squid*
*9 tablespoons olive oil*
*3 tablespoons finely chopped shallots*
*2 teaspoons finely chopped ginger*
*2 tablespoons finely chopped garlic*
*8 ounces sea scallops, cut in half*
  *crosswise if large*

*2 tablespoons chopped sun-dried*
  *tomatoes*
*1 cup Tomato Concassé, page 70*
*5 (about ½ cup) scallion tops, finely*
  *chopped*
*Salt and pepper to taste*

Make the pasta by combining the seaweed, flour, eggs, egg white, 2 table-spoons of olive oil, and 2 teaspoons of salt by hand or in a food processor. If you are making it by hand, mix until the pasta forms a ball easily. If you are using a food processor, mix the dough without letting it form into a ball. Remove and knead briefly. Cover with plastic wrap and let the dough rest in the refrigerator for 1 hour. Roll out the pasta on the thinnest setting of the pasta machine and cut into wide noodles.

To clean the squid, separate the tentacles from the body, removing the entrails as you pull. Cut the tentacles just above the eyes and with your fingers remove the hard beak. Split the body lengthwise without cutting through. Remove the transparent quill and any remaining entrails. Peel the skin. Score the body in a cross-hatch pattern by cutting halfway through the flesh at a 45-degree angle.

Fill a large pot with water and bring it to a boil. Add the squid and blanch for 5 seconds. Remove with a slotted spoon, rinse under cold water and set aside to drain in a colander. Reduce the temperature to low, so the water can continue to simmer, and cover the pot.

Heat 2 tablespoons of olive oil in a large skillet; add the shallots, ginger, and garlic. Add the scallops and cook for 1 minute. Remove the scallops with a slotted spoon. Add 2 more tablespoons of olive oil and the squid. Stir-fry for 1 minute and remove the squid with a slotted spoon. Add 3 tablespoons of olive oil, the sun-dried tomatoes, and the tomato concassé. Cook over high heat for 2 minutes. Turn down the heat to simmer.

While the sauce is simmering, cook the pasta in the boiling salted water for 30 seconds to 1 minute, until tender but still firm. Drain the pasta and toss with the remaining 2 tablespoons of olive oil.

Add the squid, scallops, scallion tops, salt and pepper to the skillet and heat through. Transfer the pasta to a large serving dish and ladle the sauce *Serves 4 to 6*    on top. Serve at once.

*Wine Suggestion:* a simple Entre-Deux-Mers, Vin de Sables, or a Manzanilla sherry.

# Eastern-Flavored Crab Pancakes

Pancakes are enjoyed in the East and West but in different forms. The pancakes I enjoyed as a child were definitely American, with lots of maple syrup. Unlike Chinese pancakes, which are made with just flour and water, I found the Western version fluffier, with a softer texture and a more delicate taste that is open to a variety of combinations. Here, I combine the Westernized pancake with crab meat and Eastern seasonings to create a delectable dish that also stretches the expensive crab meat a long way. The pancakes can be served with other fish dishes, such as Mussels with Lemongrass Butter Sauce (page 119), or alone as an appetizer with a bit of butter and lemon juice.

*1 cup all-purpose unbleached flour*
*1 cup fresh crab meat*
*2 small eggs*
*1 tablespoon sesame oil*
*2 teaspoons salt*

*1 teaspoon finely chopped ginger*
*3 tablespoons finely chopped scallions*
*1 cup low-fat milk*
*2 tablespoons fresh lemon juice*
*Peanut oil for frying*

*Makes about 16 pancakes*

Mix all the ingredients except the peanut oil in a large bowl. In a large nonstick skillet, heat a little oil and, for each pancake, ladle ¼ cup of the batter. Cook over medium heat until lightly browned, then turn over. Brown the other side. Serve them immediately or keep the pancakes warm in the oven.

*Wine Suggestion:* a lightly herbaceous Sauvignon, or Fumé Blanc, from California or a light white Graves.

# Steamed Salmon in Chinese Cabbage

Fresh salmon has vast appeal to many cooks. Its meat has firmness, texture, color, and exquisite taste, delicate but with great character—salmon has a unique combination of strength and subtlety. Such a fish has nobility enough to stand up to a spicy sauce, as in Salmon Fillets with Ginger, Basil, Tomatoes, and Salt Sauce (page 116), and it has an integrity sufficient to dignify the simplest combination, as here with Chinese cabbage. The salmon is wrapped in the cabbage, which helps both to keep its meat moist and to allow the sweetness of the cabbage to breathe through it. The salmon is thus gently steamed by hot vapors.

*Four 4-ounce salmon fillets*
    *4 large Napa cabbage leaves,*
      *blanched*
    *1 teaspoon sea salt*
    *2 teaspoons finely chopped fresh*
      *coriander*

*2 egg yolks, beaten*
*4 tablespoons cold butter, cut into*
    *small pieces*
*Salt and freshly ground white*
    *pepper to taste*

Place each fillet on one end of a cabbage leaf. Sprinkle with sea salt and fresh coriander. Roll up each leaf, folding in the sides as you go.

    Steam on a plate over simmering water for 8 minutes. Pour off the juice into a small bowl with the beaten egg yolks. Whisk the mixture and pour into a small saucepan. Over very low heat, cook the sauce until it lightly coats a spoon. Add the butter, a few pieces at a time. Add salt and pepper. Serve the sauce on the side with the stuffed cabbage.

*Serves 4*

*Note:* If you prefer, omit the sauce and simply squeeze on fresh lemon juice, or reduce the juices from the steaming process and mount it with a touch of butter.

*Wine Suggestion:* a rich, full-bodied California Chardonnay or a similar wine from Burgundy.

# Steamed Fish with Scallions and Young Garlic Shoots

I first discovered young garlic shoots in the south of France and immediately fell in love with them. Although they have a gentler impact than the mature version, their assertive flavor is nevertheless evident. They seem to pair well with foods that have a subtle taste. The Chinese are also quite fond of young garlic shoots and tend to use them mainly in stir-fried dishes. Steaming, however, points out the virtues of both the fish and the garlic shoots without one overwhelming the other. This is a simple and easy-to-make treat when young garlic shoots are available; substitute chives if they are not.

*Salt and freshly ground white*
*pepper to taste*
*1-pound halibut fillet, quartered*
*¼ cup shredded garlic shoots*

*¼ cup shredded scallions*
*½ cup Fish Stock, page 68*
*1½ tablespoons cold butter, cut into*
*small pieces*

Salt and pepper the halibut pieces. Place them on a plate and cover with the garlic shoots and scallions. Steam over simmering water for 5 minutes. Pour off the cooking liquid into a small saucepan and return the halibut to the steamer to keep warm. Add the fish stock to the saucepan and reduce by half. Whisk in the butter pieces, a piece at a time. Arrange the fish on a serving platter topped with the vegetables. Pour the sauce over the fish and serve.

*Serves 4*

*Wine Suggestion:* a straightforward young Chardonnay from Mâcon, California, or Italy.

# Shrimp with Mustard and Coriander

The more delectable the food, the easier it is to prepare an epicure's delight. In this case, it is fresh, plump, colorful, firm, succulent shrimp. A bit of mustard and fresh coriander, a touch of rice wine, butter, peanut oil, and fish stock, and you have an easy-to-make dish that is delicious and unusual at the same time.

*2 teaspoons peanut oil*
*2 tablespoons butter*
*1½ pounds prawns, peeled and*
   *deveined*
   *Garlic*

*2 tablespoons rice wine*
*½ cup Fish Stock, page 68*
*2 tablespoons Dijon mustard*
*2 tablespoons finely chopped fresh*
   *coriander*

In a wok or large skillet, heat the peanut oil and butter. Add the prawns and garlic, and stir-fry for 1 minute. Add the rice wine, fish stock, mustard, and coriander. Cook for 2 minutes over high heat, or until the prawns are translucent. Serve at once.

*Serves 4*

*Wine Suggestion:* a Pinot Noir Blanc from California or a Muscat d'Alsace from France.

# Jade Prawns with Italian Parsley, Coriander, and Basil

The green herbs give this recipe its name, derived from a similar dish I first encountered in Hong Kong. The fresh coriander, basil, and Italian parsley create a verdant field upon which the prawns display their own sparkling colors. As you will see, all the seasonings and spices, both Eastern and Western, blend into a harmonious unity. The dish is a delight to the eye as well as to the palate. Cooking the prawns in their shells preserves their flavor and succulence.

*2 tablespoons olive oil*
*1½ pounds prawns, with shells on*
*2 tablespoons chopped fresh*
  *coriander*
*1 tablespoon chopped fresh Italian*
  *parsley*

*3 tablespoons chopped fresh basil*
*1 tablespoon chopped garlic*
*3 tablespoons chopped scallions*
*1 tablespoon bean sauce*
  *Salt and freshly ground black*
  *pepper to taste*

Heat the olive oil in a wok or large skillet. Add the prawns and all the remaining ingredients. Stir-fry over high heat for 8 minutes. Serve immediately.

*Serves 4*

*Wine Suggestion:* a crisp California Sauvignon, or Fumé Blanc, or Pouilly-Fumé from France.

# Stir-Fried Shrimp with Carrots and Asparagus

Colors, textures, tastes, and contrasts abound in this simple but refreshingly appetizing dish; East-West ingredients are combined in a way that seems natural and that preserves their individualities. This is a quick and easy-to-prepare dish; it can also be served at room temperature as a cold salad.

*½ cup Basic Chicken Stock, page 67*

GARNISH
*8 ounces bok choy, prepared as on
    page 42 and blanched*

*1 tablespoon Chinese black vinegar
1½ tablespoons olive oil*

*1 tablespoon peanut oil
½ tablespoon butter
1 pound medium shrimp, peeled and
    deveined
8 ounces young carrots, peeled and
    blanched*

*8 ounces asparagus, trimmed, cut
    into 3-inch segments, and blanched
2 teaspoons finely chopped ginger
1 tablespoon finely chopped shallots
2 tablespoons rice wine*

Reduce the chicken stock in a small pan over high heat until you have just 2 tablespoons left and set aside.

In a medium-sized bowl, toss the bok choy with the vinegar and olive oil, and arrange on a platter.

Heat the peanut oil and butter in a large wok or skillet. Add the shrimp, stir-fry for 1 minute, and remove with a slotted spoon. Add the vegetables, ginger, shallots, and rice wine, and stir-fry over high heat for 2 minutes. Add the reduced chicken stock and return the shrimp to the wok. Stir-fry for 2 minutes. Spoon the shrimp and vegetables on top of the bok choy and serve at once.

*Serves 2 to 4*

*Wine Suggestion:* a full, rich Sauvignon Blanc, maybe of "reserve" quality, or a fine white Graves.

# Shellfish in Black Bean and Butter Sauce

For those who love shellfish as I do, clams and mussels are the epitome of seafood, with the salty tang of the sea in them. Combined with black beans, they are an unbeatable tasty alliance. Black beans are used widely in China with all types of food, and to very good effect, especially as a flavorful balance to the briny flavor of shellfish. Here, in an unorthodox manner—for the Chinese, that is—I blend the black beans with tomatoes, basil, and butter, to impart a rich complementary taste to the whole. I think this dish goes very well on top of Noodle Cake Stuffed with Basil and Tomatoes (page 218).

*1 pound fresh mussels*
*1 pound cherrystone or littleneck*
*   clams*
*1 cup Basic Chicken Stock, page 67*
*1 tablespoon black beans, page 41,*
*   coarsely chopped*

*2 cups Tomato Concassé, page 70*
*4 tablespoons cold butter, cut into*
*   small pieces*
*½ cup basil leaves for garnish*

Scrub the mussels and clams and soak them in several changes of cold water to rid them of any sand.

Heat the chicken stock and black beans in a large pot. Add the mussels and clams. Cook over high heat for 2 or 3 minutes, or until they open. Remove them at once with a slotted spoon and set aside. Discard any unopened clams or mussels.

Reduce the liquid by half over high heat. Add the tomatoes and cook for 30 minutes. Whisk in the butter a piece at a time. Return the cooked clams and mussels to the pot and reheat for 1 minute. Arrange the shellfish in a deep platter and garnish with the basil leaves. Serve at once.

*Serves 4*

*Wine Suggestion:* a rich white Zinfandel or a full-bodied dry Sauternes from France.

# Bay Scallops with Mushrooms

Bay scallops are unknown in Asia but abundant in America. They are sweeter than sea scallops, with a taste and texture that make them delicacies. They are at once easy to prepare and delightful to play with; that is, they lend themselves to combinations of vegetables, spices, and seasonings—even kumquats, as in this recipe. Despite the butter and bay scallops there is a tilt to the East here. No apologies—this is a delightful dish in any culture.

The challenge is to transcend the combination of subtleties. Scallops are delicious but demulcent—smooth, soothing; the word evokes the texture of the scallops. As for mushrooms, even Chinese and Japanese varieties are, if not anonymous, certainly unaggressive. All of the ingredients have their tasteful charms, but care must be taken to preserve and enhance them. In this recipe I combine Eastern and Western seasonings and vegetables in such a way as to ensure mutual respect and compatible relations between and among all the foods. There are distinctive tastes, but none is overpowering. The result is a delicious seafood platter that delights the eye before it beguiles the palate.

5 tablespoons butter
4 ounces snow peas, ends trimmed
1 small red pepper, seeded and
  shredded
1 pound fresh bay scallops
4 kumquats, thinly sliced
1 teaspoon ginger juice
  Salt and freshly ground black
  pepper to taste

1 cup Fish Stock, page 68
4 ounces Chinese black mushrooms,
  prepared as on page 45
8 ounces fresh oyster mushrooms or
  regular brown mushrooms
One 4-ounce package Enokitake
  mushrooms for garnish

Heat 3 tablespoons of the butter in a large skillet and stir-fry the snow peas and red pepper for 1 minute. Add the scallops, kumquats, ginger juice, salt, and pepper. Cook the scallops until they are opaque and almost firm. Remove the mixture and keep warm.

Reduce the fish stock by three-fourths in a small pan. Set aside.

Wipe the skillet clean, return it to the stove, and reheat. Add 2 tablespoons of butter and the mushrooms. Cook for 2 minutes. Add the fish stock and cook 3 minutes more, or until the mushrooms are soft. Arrange the scallops and vegetables in the center of a platter, surround with the cooked mushrooms, and garnish with the Enokitake mushrooms fanned around the dish. Serve at once.

*Serves 4*

*Wine Suggestion:* a California Pinot Blanc or dry Chenin Blanc, or try a very light Chardonnay from Italy.

# POULTRY

Grilled Hoisin Chicken
Grilled Mustard Chicken
    Thighs
Braised Chicken Thighs
    with Spicy Tomato and
    Ginger Sauce
Ginger-Orange Roast
    Chicken
Boned Stuffed Turkey
    Rice and Herb Stuffing
Mushroom-Stuffed Chicken
Honey-Glazed Squabs
Spiced Fried Cornish Game
    Hens
Chicken in Two Courses:
    Chicken Breasts in Rice
    Wine and Sichuan
    Peppercorn-Butter Sauce/

Grilled Marinated Thighs
    with Eastern Persillade
Chicken with Two Chinese
    Mushrooms
Boned Stuffed Quail
Ragout of Squab with
    Chinese Vegetables
Casserole of Spicy Chicken
    Wings
Duck in Two Courses
Squab Stuffed with Corn
    Bread
Ginger-Chili Corn Bread
Orange Duck, Peking-Style
Braised Duck
Chicken "Ragout"

Chicken Breasts with Red
    Peppers and Bok Choy in
    Cream Sauce
Marinated Grilled Quail
Marinated Roast Squab
    with Rice Wine-Butter
    Sauce
Sesame-Flavored Marinated
    Chicken
Stir-Fried Chicken with
    Snow Peas and Water
    Chestnuts
Roast Barbecued Duck
Sautéed Duck Liver and
    Chinese Duck Sausage

Chicken, turkey, duck, and other fowl are rightfully important foods in the cuisines of both East and West. Turkey, the All-American bird, has been enjoyed in France ever since the French Revolution, when the exiled Brillat-Savarin discovered it in New England and encouraged its cultivation in France. When properly prepared, all are delicious, nutritious, and relatively inexpensive.

**CHICKEN**    First prize, however, must go to the lowly, ubiquitous chicken, so universally utilized and so often taken for granted; its virtues are assumed, and our familiarity breeds indifference. There is little romance attached to this bird, for its most apparent strengths lie in the prosaic realm of cheapness, digestibility, and low calories/cholesterol. We need to be reminded of the subtle but unique flavor and texture of well-prepared chicken. Having experienced the noble duck, the glorious turkey, and the exotic game birds, we return to the sweet bird of our youth and are never disappointed. I emphasize "well prepared" because of the methods of production—today's chickens are unfortunately much less inherently tasty than those of yesteryear, though fortunately there is a move back to free-range chicken.

In China, that peasant nation par excellence where for ages the people have lived in harmony and understanding with the rest of creation, chickens have religious significance. In my childhood, respect for this delicious and versatile food was instilled in me. One may say that I read, marked, learned, and inwardly digested its significance and have retained an abiding respect for this familiar but uncommonly rewarding food.

In America, "chicken every Sunday" used to mean dinner built around the delicate, delicious flavor of the old-fashioned, naturally fattened barnyard chicken. Those were the days in America when chicken was more popular than turkey and before beef displaced it (and pork) as the most American of main courses. Today's chickens are "designer bred," as the eminent authority James Beard wrote: "They come to the market uniform in size, uniform in color, and uniform in lack of real flavor. They require a good deal of seasoning to give them any character. . . ." How true! And yet we eat more chicken today than ever before—it is an inexpensive, low-calorie, high-protein food, but it needs some work to make it interesting. Given that most commercially produced chickens are relatively tasteless, they therefore need some imaginative seasonings and stuffings. And all chickens need to be carefully cooked if the meat is to be moist and tender throughout. Roast chicken requires particular care in this regard.

In the East, chicken is braised, steamed, or deep-fried; it is rarely roasted, and then only in a special salt-roasting technique that leaves the chicken moist, tender, and not at all salty. Roasting is a common Western technique that brings with it the inescapable problem of any dry heat method: Parts of the meat may be overcooked and dried out in the process. The ideal method of roasting chicken is to use a revolving spit, where the juices of the chicken continuously baste the meat, keeping it moist. How can we roast a chicken in the Western mode and yet create a thoroughly cooked and moist dish?

My friend, the great French chef Jacques Pépin, suggests what I believe is the perfect solution: Roast the chicken upside down, with the juices flowing down the breasts and keeping them moist. Then, toward the end of the roasting period, turn the chicken over to brown it evenly. This technique works beautifully. It is unorthodox, but it has never failed me; once tried, it is invariably preferred.

The Japanese-Chinese technique of simmering-steeping is also most appropriate for chicken breasts (as you will discover in Chicken in Two Courses, page 148). The meat is tender to begin with, and our aim is thus to preserve its gentle taste and smooth texture. We therefore apply heat directly only in the brief simmering stage and then allow the residual heat to steep-cook the breasts to perfection.

Grilling is an appropriate technique for chicken thighs because that darker, richer meat needs more thorough cooking. And, being more robust, the thighs are compatible with strong marinades.

**TURKEY**

As with chicken, turkey needs and deserves some care in preparation. Commercially bred turkeys tend to be less robust in taste than their wild cousins. To compound the problem, many home cooks tend to overcook turkeys, producing a blander flavor throughout and dried-out white meat as well. My solution is to mix techniques: steaming, to preserve moistness, tenderness, and flavor; and roasting, to create the typical and auspicious golden brown color of the turkey. To these techniques I add one other step, the boning process, which I find myself saying over and over is not nearly as difficult as it sounds. It imparts to the turkey ease of cooking and carving and an undeniable and impressive elegance. I heartily recommend the boning process; if you are intimidated by it, have your butcher do it for you. Ask for the bones; they can be used for Rich Turkey and Chicken Stock (page 69). Always insist upon a fresh, small turkey.

**DUCK AND GAME BIRDS**

Duck needs no introduction, East or West. From the Chinese classic, Peking duck, to the French duck à l'orange, and every dish in between, this wonderful fowl has provided some of the most palatable dishes in every cuisine. I have included duck recipes that manifest the best of East and West flavors and techniques.

Quail is the prince of poultry in Japanese cooking, and in China, were it not for the abundance of pheasants, quail would be the most commonly used game bird. European and American cooks as well have traditionally prepared quail. This splendid game bird is thus universally appreciated (though in America too often it is overcooked). Truly wild game birds are lean and muscular, lacking the fat of their domesticated commercial cousins, but most quail available today have been raised on the farm. The traditional technique for preparing smaller, and drier, game birds such as snipe and woodcock call for the "four B's": Rub on or insert butter, bacon, or other fat, and broil and baste the bird over bread. (The bread absorbs the drippings.)

Cornish game hens are fairly inexpensive, nutritious, and easy to prepare. Unfortunately, they are also fairly bland, perhaps because they are rarely available fresh and because they are not true game birds but a cross between the Plymouth Rock hen and the Cornish game cock, commercially available for about twenty-five years. However, they do have the added virtue of a fine texture and, once properly marinated and then deep-fried, as in Spiced Fried Cornish Game Hens (page 147), can be a delectable dish.

Squab dishes are increasingly popular in this country and with good reason. Fresh squabs have their own special taste and texture, not to be confused with chicken's subtle flavor and substance. (I am reminded of the child protesting his mother's assurances that some strange new dish tastes just like chicken: "Why not just give me chicken then?") Squab *is* different. In China, and especially around Canton, squab is a venerable and traditional food. I was fortunate in my childhood to have enjoyed squabs many times. Because they were relatively expensive, I had them only at special family banquets, but they were always memorable. Briefly cooked in a dark braising sauce, hung to dry, and then deep-fried just before serving, they were a delicious treat. I particularly relished the combination of crispy skin and moist tender meat.

# Grilled Hoisin Chicken

Hoisin sauce provides a wonderful way to rescue our modern chickens from blandness. Thinning the hoisin sauce with a bit of rice wine and olive oil ensures that the flavor of the meat is not overwhelmed. For another unusual touch, substitute Chinese plum sauce for the hoisin sauce. These breasts are delicious cold at a picnic or as part of a buffet. They may also be cut into strips for an unusual chicken salad, and they are excellent with Cold Tomato Cubes Tossed in Tarragon and Sesame Oil (page 92).

MARINADE
*1 teaspoon fresh or ½ teaspoon
    dried thyme leaves*
*3 tablespoons hoisin sauce*

*2 tablespoons rice wine*
*1 tablespoon olive oil*

*Four 4-ounce chicken breast halves,
    boned*

Mix the marinade ingredients together and rub each chicken breast on both sides. Cover with plastic wrap and marinate for 30 minutes at room temperature or for 1 hour in the refrigerator. If refrigerated, bring to room temperature before grilling.

When the grill is hot or when the charcoal turns ash white, quickly grill the chicken breasts on both sides, being careful not to overcook them.

*Serves 2 to 4*

*Wine Suggestion:* a refreshing Beaujolais-Villages, or a light Zinfandel or Gamay from California.

# Grilled Mustard Chicken Thighs

I prefer the rich flavor and firm texture of chicken thighs because they provide more opportunities to play with East-West sauces and marinades. Here, I have combined typically Eastern ginger and scallion flavors with universally loved garlic and with Dijon mustard. Kumquats add a sweet and sprightly citrus counterpoint to both the sauce and the chicken. Fresh herbs such as thyme or tarragon may also be incorporated into the marinade. Thighs can take it! A good olive oil may be substituted for the sesame oil. My only caveat: Keep control of the ginger—if you add too much, it will run over the other seasonings and upset the balance of the marinade. The grilled thighs are wonderful cold, and perfect for picnics.

*1½ pounds (about 6) chicken thighs, boned and with skin on*
*1 teaspoon coarse salt*

*Freshly ground black pepper to taste*

MARINADE
*1 tablespoon finely chopped garlic*
*1 teaspoon fresh finely chopped ginger*
*¼ cup finely chopped scallions*

*2 tablespoons prepared Dijon mustard*
*2 tablespoons sesame oil*
*⅓ cup fresh thinly sliced kumquats*

Sprinkle the chicken thighs with the salt and freshly ground pepper. Mix the remaining ingredients together into a paste. With a spatula, smear each side of the thighs evenly with the marinade. Marinate in the refrigerator for at least 2 hours, covered with plastic wrap.

Take the thighs out of the refrigerator 30 minutes before you are ready to grill them. Grill over white hot coals with the skin side down. Turn when the skin becomes crispy. The thighs are cooked when they are slightly firm to the touch or pierce easily in the thickest part with a wooden skewer. Remove the thighs from the grill and set aside for 5 minutes before slicing and serving.

*Serves 4*

*Wine Suggestion:* a young Chianti or a very light young California Cabernet Sauvignon.

# Braised Chicken Thighs with Spicy Tomato and Ginger Sauce

The robust taste of chicken thighs is well suited to this assertive sauce of spicy tomatoes and ginger. All three flavors come through independently, and yet they blend together, too, to form a savory dish. This dish reheats very well, and most people say it tastes even better the second day.

| | |
|---|---|
| *1 tablespoon peanut oil* | *2 tablespoons finely chopped garlic* |
| *1½ pounds (about 6) chicken thighs* | *1 tablespoon finely chopped fresh* |
| *Salt and freshly ground black* | *ginger* |
| *pepper to taste* | *1 small fresh hot chili, chopped* |
| *1 can (28 ounces) peeled tomatoes* | *2 teaspoons sugar* |
| *without juice, coarsely chopped in* | *½ cup fresh coriander, loosely packed* |
| *a food processor or food mill* | |

In a medium-sized frying pan, heat the peanut oil over moderate heat. Brown the thighs on both sides, beginning with the skin side. Salt and pepper them while browning the second side. Drain the thighs on paper towels and set aside.

Drain the fat from the frying pan except for 2 teaspoons. Add the tomatoes, garlic, ginger, chili, and sugar, and cook over moderately high heat for about 8 minutes. Reduce to a low simmer.

Return the thighs to the skillet, cover, and braise slowly for 20 minutes. Add the coriander at the very end of the cooking.

*Serves 2 to 4*

*Wine Suggestion:* a medium-bodied California Zinfandel or a light Côtes-du-Rhône such as St. Joseph.

# Ginger-Orange Roast Chicken

Roast chicken is perhaps the easiest and least expensive main-course dish one can prepare. It can also be one of the most delicious if properly done, cooked carefully so that it does not dry out. Here, I offer what I believe is the perfect solution: Roast the chicken upside down, with the juices flowing down the breasts and keeping them moist. Then, toward the end, turn the chicken over, breast side up, to brown it evenly. I fill the chicken with spices and herbs that may be used either in a stuffing or simply packed into the chicken to flavor it. If you use only the flavors (not a stuffing), they may be taken out when the chicken is done and simmered briefly in some reduced chicken stock for a quick delicious sauce. Strain the sauce before serving it. Any cold leftover chicken makes a perfect picnic entree or light lunch.

*Salt and freshly ground black*
*pepper to taste*

*One 3- to 3½-pound chicken*

STUFFING
*1 orange, cut into 10 wedges*
*10 garlic cloves, crushed, with skin*
*left intact*
*12 sprigs fresh or 2 teaspoons dried*
*thyme*

*5 thin slices unpeeled ginger root*
*½ cup fresh coriander, loosely*
*packed*

Lightly salt and pepper the interior of the chicken. Place the orange, garlic, thyme, ginger, and coriander together in a bowl and mix well. Close the neck flap of the chicken with toothpicks or a bamboo skewer. Pack the interior of the chicken with the stuffing. Close the body cavity with toothpicks or a bamboo skewer.

Preheat the oven to 450 degrees. Place the chicken on a rack inside a roasting pan, with the breast side down. Roast for 15 minutes. Turn down the heat to 350 degrees and continue to roast for 40 minutes. Return the heat to 450 degrees, turn the chicken over, and roast for 5 minutes, or until the breast side skin is nicely browned.

If you are making a quick sauce, take the stuffing out and simmer with about 1½ cups of chicken stock for 20 minutes. Strain, return to the pan, and reduce by half over high heat. Carve the chicken after letting it sit for 15 minutes.

*Serves 2 to 4*        Serve with the sauce on the side.

*Note:*        Remember, the spices and herbs may also be used to make a traditional stuffing for the chicken with a rice or bread basis. It may be stuffed into the chicken or baked separately as a side dish.

*Wine Suggestion:* a fine Spätlese from the Rhine or Moselle, 3 or 4 years old.

# Boned Stuffed Turkey

Turkey needs and deserves some care in preparation because the breast meat is often dry by the time the rest of the bird is cooked. I suggest a two-step technique: steaming, to preserve moistness, tenderness, and flavor; and roasting, to produce the golden brown color. To these techniques I add one other step, boning, which is not nearly as difficult as it sounds. It imparts to the turkey ease of cooking and carving and a touch of elegance. If you are intimidated by boning, have your butcher do it for you. Ask for the bones; they can be used for Rich Turkey and Chicken Stock (page 69). Much of the preparation for this dish can be done at least a day ahead, reducing the pressures on the cook and making for a more relaxed holiday.

*One 12- to 14-pound turkey*
    *3 tablespoons kosher salt*
    *1 teaspoon freshly ground black pepper*

STUFFING
    *Rice and Herb Stuffing, full recipe follows*

SAUCE
    *Rich Turkey and Chicken Stock (page 69), full recipe*

*3 tablespoons sesame oil*
*½ cup fresh lemon juice*

Boning turkey:

Cut along the side of the neck to expose the wishbone. With a small sharp knife or poultry shears, cut the wing joint free. Pull the skin and flesh away from the carcass, cutting against the bone to release the skin and meat when necessary. Cut the thigh joints to free the carcass. Keep the tail detached and detach the rest of the bone. Scrape the meat from the thighs and legs. The body is now ready for stuffing.

Reserve the bones for making turkey and chicken stock.

Using a trussing needle and string, close the opening from the tail to the neck, leaving an opening 4 or 5 inches long for the stuffing.

Rub the boned turkey inside and out with the salt, pepper, sesame oil, and about 2 tablespoons of lemon juice. Place the turkey in a stainless steel or glass bowl, add the remaining lemon juice, cover, and refrigerate overnight.

Remove the turkey from the marinade and pat dry. Fill the turkey with stuffing and sew up the cavity. Tie the body crosswise at 2-inch intervals using heavy string. Tie the legs together to help the turkey hold its shape.

Place the turkey on a heat-proof platter on a rack in a large roasting pan or turkey roaster, back side down. Add enough water to the pan to 1½ inches underneath the rack. Cover the roasting pan or roaster tightly and bring the water to a boil over high heat. Reduce the heat to moderate and steam the turkey for 1½ hours, or until the thigh juices run clean when pricked and the center of the stuffing registers 160 degrees. Replenish the water in the pan during steaming if necessary. Remove the turkey from the platter, reserving any juices that have collected on the platter. Discard the water in the pan.

Preheat the oven to 450 degrees. Place the turkey on a rack in the roasting pan and roast for 15 to 20 minutes, or until golden brown.

While the turkey is roasting, pour the turkey and chicken stock and the reserved turkey juices into a medium-sized saucepan, and boil over high heat until reduced to 3 cups, about 8 minutes. Skim it while it is reducing. Strain the sauce. Season with salt and pepper to taste.

*Serves 8 to 12*     Carve the boned turkey and serve the sauce on the side.

*Wine Suggestion:* Beaujolais Nouveau or a light, fresh California Zinfandel, served chilled.

# Rice and Herb Stuffing

This stuffing has a genuine Eastern tang to it but nevertheless blends smoothly with the traditional Western holiday turkey. The Chinese pork sausage and duck liver sausage may perhaps sound exotic, but most Americans love them once they've tried them. Much of the preparation can be done well in advance. The stuffing is also delicious when served with chicken.

3 cups glutinous rice
2 tablespoons peanut oil
1 cup finely chopped shallots
½ cup finely chopped scallions
½ cup Chinese rice wine
8 ounces Chinese pork sausage, cut into ¼-inch dice
8 ounces Chinese duck liver sausage, cut into ¼-inch dice (substitute another 8 ounces Chinese pork sausage if duck liver sausage is unavailable)
3 cups Rich Turkey and Chicken Stock, page 69

1 teaspoon salt
Freshly ground black pepper to taste
2 cups (about 1½ pounds) peeled and chopped fresh water chestnuts
1 small sweet red or green pepper, seeded and diced
1½ teaspoons fresh tarragon
1 teaspoon fresh or dried thyme
¼ cup chopped fresh Chinese or Western chives

Place the glutinous rice in a large bowl. Add water to cover and soak overnight. Drain well.

In a large skillet or wok, heat the peanut oil over medium-high heat. Stir-fry or sauté the shallots and scallions for about 30 seconds. Add the wine and cook until nearly all liquid has evaporated. Add the pork and liver sausages, stir, and cook for 1 minute. Add the rice, stock, salt, and pepper. Cook, uncovered, stirring occasionally to prevent sticking, until all the stock is absorbed, about 8 minutes. Add the water chestnuts, pepper, tarragon, thyme, and chives, and cook, stirring frequently, for 3 minutes. Remove from the heat and let the stuffing cool to room temperature.

*Makes about 8 cups*

Use 4 cups of the stuffing to fill the boned turkey or 2 cups for a large roasting chicken. Spoon the remainder into a buttered baking dish and, before serving, bake at 350 degrees for 45 minutes.

*Note:*

One-half of the stuffing in this recipe goes into the boned turkey, and the other half is baked separately.

# Mushroom-Stuffed Chicken

This recipe centers on two of my favorite foods: chicken and mushrooms. I recommend white cultivated mushrooms and fresh shiitakes, or substitute dried Chinese black mushrooms for the shiitake. I have chosen to grill this chicken, but it could as well be roasted in the manner described in Ginger-Orange Roast Chicken (page 140). Grilling imparts a special smoky flavor to the chicken, accented by the mushrooms. This works especially well if you use the popular dome-lidded covered grill. The basil leaves add a touch of anise tang that balances the rich mushrooms. This is a rather time-consuming dish to prepare and a bit expensive, but well worth it. The preparation can be spaced out over a morning for a relaxed afternoon grill. Any leftovers would make a pleasant repast the next day, providing the basis for an elegant picnic, with a good bottle of red wine and crusty bread.

STUFFING

| | |
|---|---|
| *1 pound mushrooms, washed and patted dry* | *½ cup dried bread crumbs* |
| *1 pound fresh shiitake mushrooms, or 1 cup dried Chinese black mushrooms, page 45* | *2 cups fresh basil leaves or parsley, loosely packed* |
| *4 tablespoons butter* | *2 tablespoons fresh marjoram leaves* |
| | *Salt and freshly ground black pepper to taste* |

*Two 3½-pound chickens*

To make the stuffing, coarsely chop the mushrooms. Melt the butter in a large skillet, add the mushrooms, and cook at medium-high heat for 5 minutes, until most of their liquid has evaporated. Add the bread crumbs, basil, marjoram, salt, and pepper. Reduce the heat and cook the mixture for about 2 minutes. Set aside and allow to cool thoroughly.

To loosen the chicken skin, start at the neck and place your fingers under the skin. Lift up gently with your fingers, creating a gap between skin and flesh. Carefully repeat this procedure, working toward the body cavity, until most of the skin is loosened. Stuff the chicken under the skin and use any remaining stuffing to fill the body cavities.

*Serves 6 to 8*

Cook over ash white coals for 45 minutes to 1 hour, turning frequently to avoid burning the skin.

*Wine Suggestion:* a good-quality California Cabernet Sauvignon, 5 to 10 years old, or a similarly aged Bordeaux, Petite Château.

# Honey-Glazed Squab

Squab dishes are increasingly popular in this country, and with good reason. Fresh squab have their own special taste and texture completely unlike chicken's subtle flavor and substance. In China, and especially around Canton, squab is a venerable and traditional food.

In this recipe the squab are roasted, a technique that many cooks believe is the best way to prepare them. Instead of constant basting, the trick here is to "paint" on a coat of a honey-soy sauce-rice wine mixture that is most definitely of Chinese provenance. The Chinese seasoned salt and dried thyme are robust touches, but squab bears such seasonings with grace. You will taste all of these flavors, modulated by the unique flavor of the squab and set off against the crispy skin and moist tender meat. This is a dish to be slowly and thoughtfully savored.

I like to serve this squab with Cornmeal-Scallion-Ginger Waffles (page 203) or on a wedge of Noodle Cake Stuffed with Basil and Tomatoes (page 218).

*Four 10- to 12-ounce squab*

MARINADE

| | |
|---|---|
| *1 tablespoon Chinese Seasoned Salt, page 42* | *1 tablespoon rice wine* |
| *1 tablespoon dried thyme* | *3 tablespoons honey* |
| *1 tablespoon dark soy sauce* | *Cornmeal-Scallion-Ginger Waffles, page 203* |

Using a sharp knife, cut through the backbone of the squab lengthwise. Cut off the backbone and tail. Crack the breast bone so that each squab lies flat.

Mix the Chinese seasoned salt with the thyme in a small bowl. In a separate bowl, mix the soy sauce, rice wine, and honey.

Rub the inside of each squab with the seasoned salt-thyme mixture. Place the squab skin side up on a platter or roasting pan. Using a pastry brush, paint the soy-honey mixture on the skin of each squab. Marinate the squab for at least 1 hour at room temperature.

Preheat the oven to 450 degrees. Place the marinated squab skin side up on a roasting pan in the upper half of the oven and brown them for about 15 minutes.

Lower the temperature to 350 degrees and roast for 15 to 20 minutes, until the squab are cooked but the breast meat is still slightly pink. Remove the squab from the oven and let them cool for about 10 minutes. Cut the squab in half lengthwise and serve each half on a cornmeal-scallion-ginger waffle.

*Serves 4*

*Wine Suggestion:* an off-dry Vouvray or a full, rich California Chenin Blanc.

# Spiced Fried Cornish Game Hens

Cornish game hens are fairly inexpensive and easy to prepare. This recipe is, in fact, a Chinese variant of the American favorite, fried chicken. The marinade of salt, pepper, Chinese seasoned salt, and thyme is potent, a dry marinade combination I particularly like. Used in this recipe, the robustness of the marinade imparts to the hens a needed flavor but one that, as you will see, is also compatible and unassuming with the mild-flavored flesh. Flour is lightly sprinkled over the birds instead of a batter; deep-fried just before serving, the game hens emerge greaseless and transformed into crisp, clean, tender, and flavorsome treats. This recipe can easily be doubled or tripled, and is perfect for a large party. I like to serve the hens with Garlic-Sesame Seed Mayonnaise (page 75), which adds just the right contrast to the taste and texture of the game hen morsels.

*Two 1¼- to 1½-pound Cornish game
    hens*

MARINADE
*1 teaspoon coarse salt*  
*1 teaspoon Chinese Seasoned Salt,
    page 42*

*1 teaspoon freshly ground black
    pepper*  
*2 teaspoons dried thyme*

*3 cups peanut oil*  
*½ cup flour*

*Garlic-Sesame Seed Mayonnaise,
    page 75, full recipe*

Quarter the Cornish game hens. Pat them dry with paper towels.

Mix the marinade ingredients together in a bowl. Rub the marinade evenly on the Cornish game hen pieces and marinate for about 2 hours.

Heat the oil in a deep-fat fryer or wok. Lightly dust the hen pieces with the flour, shaking off any excess flour. When the oil is hot, about 350 degrees, deep-fry the Cornish game hen pieces until they are golden brown, then drain the pieces on paper towels. Just before serving, reheat the oil to 375 degrees and deep-fry the pieces for about 30 seconds. Drain and serve with garlic-sesame seed mayonnaise.

*Serves 4 as a
first course or
as appetizers*

*Wine Suggestion:* a slightly tannic young California Cabernet Sauvignon or similar Dolcetto from Italy.

# Chicken in Two Courses

In these recipes, the two chicken parts that by their natures deserve different treatment, the breasts and the thighs, receive their due. For the breasts, I employ steeping, a typical Chinese-Japanese cooking technique, and grilling, a more universal technique for the thighs. Grilling is, of course, an ancient and popular Western process, while among Japanese cooking techniques it is, along with simmering, second only to the preparation of raw fish.

The simmering-steeping technique is most appropriate for chicken breasts because the meat is tender to begin with, and our aim is to preserve its gentle taste and smooth texture. Heat is applied directly only in the brief simmering state; the residual heat then steep-cooks the breasts to perfection. That perfection consists of tender, moist, flavorful meat enjoyed within a spicy context of Sichuan peppercorns moderated, of course, by the rice wine and by the mellow butter. The butter is a Western touch; Eastern cuisine depends on lard or oil, which despite their virtues do not compare to butter in taste.

The grilling technique works for the chicken thighs because that darker, richer meat needs more thorough cooking. And, being more robust, the thighs are compatible with the assertive marinade, an East-West variant of the persillade I encountered years ago in southern France. Originally composed of chopped parsley and minced garlic, in this recipe it includes fresh coriander and orange zest, both of which add piquancy and strength to the marinade. Its lusty flavor also adds to the smoky effects of the grilling process.

These two chicken dishes, besides being delicious, demonstrate the natural contrasts between breast and thigh. They are perfect separate courses for any elegant dinner party.

# Chicken Breasts in Rice Wine and Sichuan Peppercorn-Butter Sauce

Salt and freshly ground white pepper
to taste
4 small boneless chicken breasts, with
skin removed
1 tablespoon Sichuan peppercorns

¼ cup rice wine
2 cups Basic Chicken Stock, page 67
6 tablespoons cold butter, cut into
small pieces
2 tablespoons chopped scallions

Lightly salt and pepper the chicken breasts, then marinate them in the peppercorns and rice wine for about 20 minutes.

In a large skillet, bring the chicken stock to a simmer. Add the chicken breasts along with the rice wine and peppercorns. Simmer gently for 5 minutes, skimming the liquid frequently. Turn off the heat and cover the skillet tightly. Allow the breasts to steep in the stock for about 20 minutes.

Remove the chicken and reduce the steeping liquid by two-thirds. Off the heat, whisk in the butter, a few pieces at a time. Add the scallions toward the end. Cut each breast into thin slices and cover with the sauce.

*Serves 4*

*Wine Suggestion:* a red Bandol or a red Sancerre.

# Grilled Marinated Thighs with Eastern Persillade

4 chicken thighs and legs
¼ cup finely chopped Italian parsley
¼ cup finely chopped fresh coriander
2 tablespoons finely chopped garlic

Zest from 1 orange (about 1
tablespoon)
¼ cup olive oil

To bone thigh and leg of chicken: Hold the thigh skin side down. Make a slit the length of the thigh and drumstick. Scrape the meat away from the bone with a sharp knife or cleaver. Be sure to keep the flesh intact so that it comes off the bone in one piece.

Prepare a charcoal fire. In a bowl or food processor, mix the parsley, coriander, garlic, orange zest, and olive oil until it forms a paste. Spread each thigh and leg with the mixture and marinate at room temperature for 30 to 40 minutes. Over white hot coals, grill the chicken, skin side down.

*Serves 4*

*Wine Suggestion:* a light California Gamay or a fresh Zinfandel.

# Chicken with Two Chinese Mushrooms

At first sight this recipe may seem like a case of the bland leading the bland: Chicken is hardly an aggressive taste, and mushrooms are generally mild. However, not only do these Chinese mushrooms have a distinctive texture and a subtle smoky character of their own, they also add substance without bulk to the dish while they absorb and retain the various flavors of the chicken, sauce, and shallots. This is an ensemble taste experience in which the separate ingredients retain their individuality as they combine: The whole is not separable from the sum of its parts. The crème fraîche is classically French, a mode that I enjoy. This is an easy-to-prepare dish, impressive in its simplicity and grace.

*½ ounce cloud ears\**
*One 3½-pound chicken, boned and*
*  skinned, as prepared on page 142*
*  Salt and freshly ground black*
*  pepper to taste*
*  Flour for dusting*
*1 tablespoon butter*
*1 tablespoon peanut oil*
*2 tablespoons finely chopped*
*  shallots*

*2 ounces dried Chinese black*
*  mushrooms, as prepared on page*
*  45*
*4 ounces fresh mushrooms, cut into*
*  thin slices*
*1 cup Basic Chicken Stock, page 67*
*½ cup Crème Fraîche, page 43*

Soak the cloud ears in warm water for 20 minutes and rinse well.

Cut the chicken into bite-sized pieces. Dust them with salt, pepper, and flour. In a large skillet, heat the butter and peanut oil, and stir-fry the chicken until lightly browned. Remove the chicken pieces with a slotted spoon. Add the shallots and cook for 1 minute. Add all the mushrooms and cook for 5 minutes. Add the stock and crème fraîche and cook over high heat for 4 minutes. Return the chicken pieces to the skillet and toss, coating thoroughly with the sauce. Serve immediately.

*Serves 4*

*Wine Suggestion:* a mellow California Zinfandel, or a Chianti Riserva, 5 to 7 years old.

\* *Cloud ears are a small, dark, crinkly Chinese fungus sold dried.*

# Boned Stuffed Quail

In this recipe the quail's distinctive taste is preserved even as the East-West stuffing and sauce add moisture and zesty flavors to the dish. The spinach, for example, not only adds color and its own special taste but also helps to keep the quail moist. The sweet rice is particularly appropriate. Neutral in taste, it is an exceptionally efficient absorber of other flavors, including that of the quail. Moreover, it blunts the iron-tasting edge of the spinach. You need not bone the quail, but it is an elegant touch.

STUFFING

*1 pound spinach leaves, making 8*
  *ounces cleaned*
*1 tablespoon butter*
*½ cup sweet rice, as prepared on*
  *page 143*

*1 teaspoon Chinese Seasoned Salt,*
  *page 42*
*½ cup Basic Chicken Stock, page 67*
*2 tablespoons chopped scallions*
*1 teaspoon sugar*

*Four 4-ounce quail, boned, as prepared*
  *on page 142*
*1 tablespoon butter*

*1 teaspoon peanut oil*
*½ cup Basic Chicken Stock, page 67*

Wash and drain the spinach several times to remove the sand. To make the stuffing: In a skillet, melt the butter and add the spinach, rice, Chinese seasoned salt, chicken stock, scallions, and sugar. Cook over medium heat for about 10 minutes, then allow to cool. Stuff the quail with the mixture and seal the ends of each quail with toothpicks.

In the same skillet, heat the butter and peanut oil. Add the stuffed quail and brown on all sides. Add the chicken stock and cook over medium heat for 5 to 8 minutes. Remove the quail with a slotted spoon and reduce the remaining liquid by half. Pour the reduced sauce over the quail and serve.

*Serves 2 to 4*

*Wine Suggestion:* a well-aged, high-quality Napa Valley Cabernet Sauvignon, or a fine classified Bordeaux, 10-plus years old.

# *Ragout of Squab with Chinese Vegetables*

The traditional Western ragout implies a harmonious unity of diverse vegetables, raw and more or less cooked, with some stock, butter or oil, and seasonings, simmered gently in a tightly covered pot. The technique is also the essence of Chinese clay-pot cooking, while Japanese "one-pot" cooking is a different matter, more like a fondue. The goal of such a technique is to create a dish that at one and the same time offers both a unique total identity of taste, fragrance, and texture and allows one to discern the separate, individual tastes of each ingredient. For example, in China, squab and vegetables are stir-fried individually, then simmered together in stock and spices in the clay pot, from which they are served directly at the table.

In this recipe I have adopted some French nouvelle cuisine techniques and applied them to the venerable clay-pot method. Specifically, the ingredients are precooked but are not simmered nearly as long as Chinese custom demands. The result is a delicious ragout in the classical sense with a modern slant. The Chinese vegetables impart their flavors to the mixture but retain their identities; the cloud ear mushrooms both blend in and make their presence known; the water chestnuts give sweetness and texture to the ensemble without disguising themselves; the squab are changed and yet remain the same through it all. This is elegance and delectation, quickly and simply made.

*Salt and pepper to taste*
*Two 1- to 1¼-pound squab, quartered*
  *2 tablespoons peanut oil*
  *1 ounce cloud ears, prepared as on*
    *page 150*
  *4 ounces fresh water chestnuts*
  *8 ounces bok choy, with core*
    *removed and cut into 2-inch*
    *lengths*

*8 ounces snow peas, with ends*
  *trimmed*
*2 tablespoons rice wine*
*1 cup Basic Chicken Stock, page 67*
*1 tablespoon dark soy sauce*
*1 tablespoon finely chopped chives*
  *for garnish*

Salt and pepper the squab pieces. Heat the peanut oil in a large skillet or wok. Add the squab pieces and brown them. Remove the squab with a slotted spoon. Add the cloud ears and stir-fry them for 1 minute. Add the water chestnuts, bok choy, and snow peas, and stir-fry them for 1 minute. Remove them with a slotted spoon. Add the rice wine, chicken stock, and soy sauce to the skillet. Add the squab and simmer for 10 minutes. Return the vegetables to the skillet and cook just long enough to heat through. Garnish with chives and serve immediately.

*Serves 2*

*Wine Suggestion:* a Beaujolais from Moulin-à-Vent, Brouilly, or a fuller-bodied California Gamay.

# Casserole of Spicy Chicken Wings

Do not underestimate chicken wings. True, you must compromise with knife and fork principles to extract their tender, succulent meats, but this is, after all, a family casserole dish and even, if you wish, a picnic treat. So, use your fingers.

In this recipe I draw upon the Latino-Mexican influence using Ancho chilies and blending them with a few Chinese flavorings. The result is a highly spiced and delicious marinade that turns the plebeian chicken wings into a specialty of the house. This is a simple dish to prepare, and I guarantee its popularity.

MARINADE
| | |
|---|---|
| *2 dried Ancho chilies* | *1 tablespoon light soy sauce* |
| *⅓ cup rice wine* | *2 tablespoons ground bean sauce* |
| *2 tablespoons chopped garlic* | |

*2 pounds chicken wings*

Soak the chilies in the rice wine for 45 minutes. Cut off the stems. In a blender, puree the chilies, rice wine, and the rest of the marinade ingredients. Marinate the chicken wings for 1 hour in an oven-proof casserole or baking dish. Preheat the oven to 400 degrees. Bake the chicken wings, uncovered, for 20 minutes, or until nicely browned.

*Serves 4 to 6*
*as a first*
*course*

*Wine Suggestion:* a young red Rhône such as Châteauneuf-du-Pape, or a young California Petite Syrah or a similar Valpolicella.

# Duck in Two Courses

This recipe is directly inspired by a traditional French custom of serving two courses from one duck. The origin of the custom is easy to imagine. It is based on the same necessities that lead one to substitute steaming for roasting a turkey: The breast cooks more quickly than the thigh. A boned duck breast may be grilled in less than 10 minutes; the rest of the duck takes closer to 45 minutes to cook. It makes sense to cut the duck into pieces before cooking and then to prepare at least two dishes, using different techniques. Most cooks understand that it is best to work with the cut-up duck.

Here, I separate the breasts from the rest of the duck. The boned and skinned breasts are then seasoned and marinated. After quick sautéing, the breasts are finished off in my Chinese vinegar and butter sauce. Remember that the Chinese vinegar is slightly sweet and will not offend the richness of the duck breast. I prefer my duck a bit pink, so you should let your taste guide your timing, but be careful not to overcook.

The duck legs are marinated in a traditional Eastern mixture of soy sauce and rice wine, a flavoring that the robust character of the duck nicely absorbs during the roasting process. In effect, you and your guests will enjoy and complete the first duck course just in time to welcome the second course as it emerges piping hot from the oven.

*One 4- to 4½-pound duck*
  *2 teaspoons Chinese Seasoned Salt,
    page 42*

MARINADE
  *2 tablespoons light soy sauce*          *1 tablespoon dark soy sauce*
  *1 tablespoon rice wine*


  *1 cup Basic Chicken Stock, page 67*     *1 teaspoon Chinese dark vinegar*
  *1 teaspoon dark soy sauce*              *2 tablespoons butter*

To obtain breast meat, cut through the length of the breast, slicing to the bone. With a boning knife, cut the meat away from the bone. Repeat the procedure for the other breast.

Cut the thighs from the carcass.

Skin the breasts and cut the skin into 2-inch pieces crosswise. Dust the breast meat with the Chinese seasoned salt. Mix the marinade ingredients in a heat-proof casserole or baking dish and add the thighs, tossing to coat evenly. Marinate for 40 minutes.

Render the duck fat by cooking the skin pieces over low heat in a medium-sized skillet for 20 minutes, or until the skin is crisp. Remove the skin (cracklings) with a slotted spoon and reserve. Turn up the heat and sauté the breasts for 2 minutes on each side. Remove the breasts from the skillet and keep them warm. Drain off the fat and return the skillet to the heat. Add the chicken stock and reduce to one-fourth cup. Add the soy sauce, dark vinegar, and butter, and stir to combine thoroughly. Remove from the heat. Cut each breast crosswise into slices. Cover a serving plate with a little sauce and fan the sliced breasts around it. Sprinkle with skin cracklings.

Preheat the oven to 400 degrees. Bake the thigh pieces, uncovered, along with the marinade for 40 minutes.

*Serves 4*

*Wine Suggestion:* Course 1: a mellow, refined Merlot from Pomerol or St.-Emilion, 5 to 7 years old.

Course 2: a good-quality French Pinot Noir, commune grade, 5 to 7 years old.

# Squab Stuffed with Corn Bread

Corn is a quite recent Western contribution to the Chinese list of staple foods; in Japan it remains an exotic flavor. Born in the U.S.A. as I was, corn and corn bread are as natural to me as Chinese sweet rice. My mother often used corn, and I remember enjoying it in many ways, but I especially love corn bread. I appreciate its texture and color, and the way its delicate flavor lends itself to different combinations of seasonings.

In this recipe I use, as a stuffing for the squab, previously made Ginger-Chili Corn Bread (recipe follows) soaked in buttermilk and soy sauce. To help keep the squab moist during the long baking period, I employ a traditional Chinese technique: wrapping the squab in caul fat. This covering melts away as the squab bake, flavoring them and keeping them moist. The result is a lusty squab entree, a rich and lightly spiced dish.

*Two 12-ounce squab, boned and
prepared as on page 142
Salt and freshly ground black pepper
Ginger-Chili Corn Bread, one-half
recipe which follows*

*½ cup buttermilk
2 teaspoons light soy sauce
2 pieces caul fat 9 inches by 9 inches
2 cups Basic Chicken Stock, page 67*

Season the squab inside and out with salt and pepper. Cook the corn bread and allow it to cool. Crumble the corn bread in a bowl and add the buttermilk and soy sauce.

Preheat the oven to 500 degrees. Stuff the squab with the corn bread-buttermilk mixture. Wrap each squab completely in the caul fat. Place them in a baking dish and bake for 10 minutes. Lower the heat to 400 degrees and continue cooking for 30 minutes.

Remove the squab from the baking dish and drain off the fat. Add the chicken stock, set the baking dish on a burner, and reduce by half over high heat. Cover a serving dish with the sauce, place the squab on top, *Serves 2 to 4* and serve.

*Wine Suggestion:* a full-bodied California Pinot Noir or a fine Burgundy from Côte-de-Nuits.

# Ginger-Chili Corn Bread

1 cup fresh corn, cut from 1 or 2 ears of corn
2 tablespoons chopped fresh hot red chili
2 tablespoons chopped ginger
2 tablespoons finely chopped scallions
Salt to taste
1 teaspoon baking powder
2 tablespoons sugar
1 cup coarse yellow cornmeal
4 tablespoons butter, at room temperature, plus enough to butter pan
3 medium-sized eggs, beaten
1 cup buttermilk

Preheat the oven to 400 degrees.

Combine the corn, chili, ginger, and scallions in a small bowl. In a bowl large enough to hold all the ingredients, combine the salt, baking powder, sugar, and cornmeal. Add the butter, eggs, and buttermilk to the dry ingredients and mix well. Add the corn mixture and stir thoroughly.

Butter a 9-inch-square baking pan. Add the corn bread mixture and bake for 30 minutes, or until a wooden skewer placed in the center comes out clean.

*Serves 6 to 8*
Cut into squares and serve.

# Orange Duck, Peking-Style

I first had orange duck in a French restaurant in Chicago. To my taste, the sticky sweetness of the orange sauce was overpowering and cloying. Years later, in France, I tried the dish again and found it delicious, with a light, smooth, tangy sauce that went perfectly with the duck. It became clear to me then that the two have a natural affinity, as long as some care goes into the preparation. I believe that the Chinese method of cooking duck is unsurpassed. I especially rely upon some of the principles that guide the making of Peking duck. For example, in this recipe I baste the whole duck and let it dry for a few hours. The secret of crispy duck is to let it dry until its skin is like parchment.

Another Chinese influence in this recipe is Cantonese in origin: the roast duck is filled with a liquid marinade. Here, the marinade is replaced by the orange juice that permeates the meat and keeps it moist. The basting liquid imparts a rich glaze and deep color to the duck; it also hastens the process by which the skin dries. The orange juice, the natural juices from the duck, and the elements in the sauce blend to create a mildly sweet compound that is subtle yet powerful. It is the perfect sauce for this elegant dish.

Any leftover duck may be used for a salad, such as Asian-Flavored Duck Salad (page 90).

*One 4-pound duck*
   *Salt and pepper*

*1 cup orange juice*

BASTING LIQUID
   *1 quart water*
   *3 tablespoons dark soy sauce*

*2 tablespoons honey*

   *1 cup water*

SAUCE
   *2 tablespoons grated orange zest*
   *1 cup Basic Chicken Stock, page 67*
   *1 tablespoon rice wine*
   *Salt and pepper to taste*

   *½ teaspoon chopped ginger*
   *1 tablespoon Grand Marnier liqueur*
   *2 tablespoons cold butter, cut into*
      *small pieces*

   *1 orange, peeled and cut into 8*
   *wedges, for garnish*

Season the inside of the duck with salt and pepper. Pour the orange juice into the body cavity. Close the 2 ends of the duck with skewers and secure with string wrapped lengthwise around the skewer.

In a medium-sized pot, combine the basting liquid ingredients and bring to a boil. Turn off the heat and baste the duck several times with the hot liquid. Allow the duck to dry either in a cool drafty place for 5 hours or in front of a fan for 2 hours. When the duck is properly dried, the skin will feel like parchment paper.

Preheat the oven to 500 degrees. Place the duck on a rack inside a roasting pan. Pour in 1 cup of water. Roast the duck for 20 minutes, turn down the heat to 400 degrees, and cook for 40 minutes. Return the heat to 500 degrees and roast 10 minutes more.

Remove the duck from the oven and release the juice inside the duck into a saucepan. Add the orange zest, chicken stock, rice wine, salt, pepper, ginger, and liqueur. Bring the sauce to a boil and reduce by half. Whisk in the butter and remove from the heat. Carve the duck and arrange on a serving platter garnished with orange wedges. Serve the sauce sepa-

*Serves 4*   rately.

*Wine Suggestion:* a full-bodied white Vouvray, off-dry; or if red is desired, a light, fresh red, like Beaujolais.

# Braised Duck

Braising cooks foods in two steps: first by browning briefly in hot oil or other fat, then by slow simmering with a little water or stock in a tightly lidded pot. The technique is much employed in Eastern as well as in Western cuisine. It is an excellent way to infuse delightfully compatible flavors into duck or any other food. In this recipe, instead of deep-frying the duck, as is commonly done in the East, I brown it Western-style in the oven. The combination of East-West herbs and seasonings nicely infuses the duck during the simmering stage; the plum sauce is traditional in Eastern braised dishes.

This is a relatively easy-to-prepare but still unusual duck dish. It reheats very well, and I like to let the duck cool, then remove all the visible fat, and serve it the next day.

One 4-pound fresh duck, quartered
Salt and pepper to taste
3 cups Basic Chicken Stock, page 67
2 tablespoons chopped fresh lemongrass
1 teaspoon chopped ginger
2 tablespoons chopped sun-dried tomatoes

1 tablespoon dried thyme
2 tablespoons rice wine
2 tablespoons dark soy sauce
1 tablespoon light soy sauce
3 tablespoons plum sauce
2 large sprigs fresh rosemary

Season the duck with salt and pepper. Preheat the oven to 500 degrees. Place the duck on a rack in a roasting pan and roast for 30 minutes, until nicely browned. In a pot, combine the duck and the rest of the ingredients. Braise, then cover for 40 minutes. Remove from the heat, skim the fat from the braising liquid, and serve.

Serves 4

Wine Suggestion: a rich, well-aged Bordeaux and Tiganello or similar fine-quality Cabernet Sauvignon.

*Chicken Sun-Dried Tomato Spring Rolls*

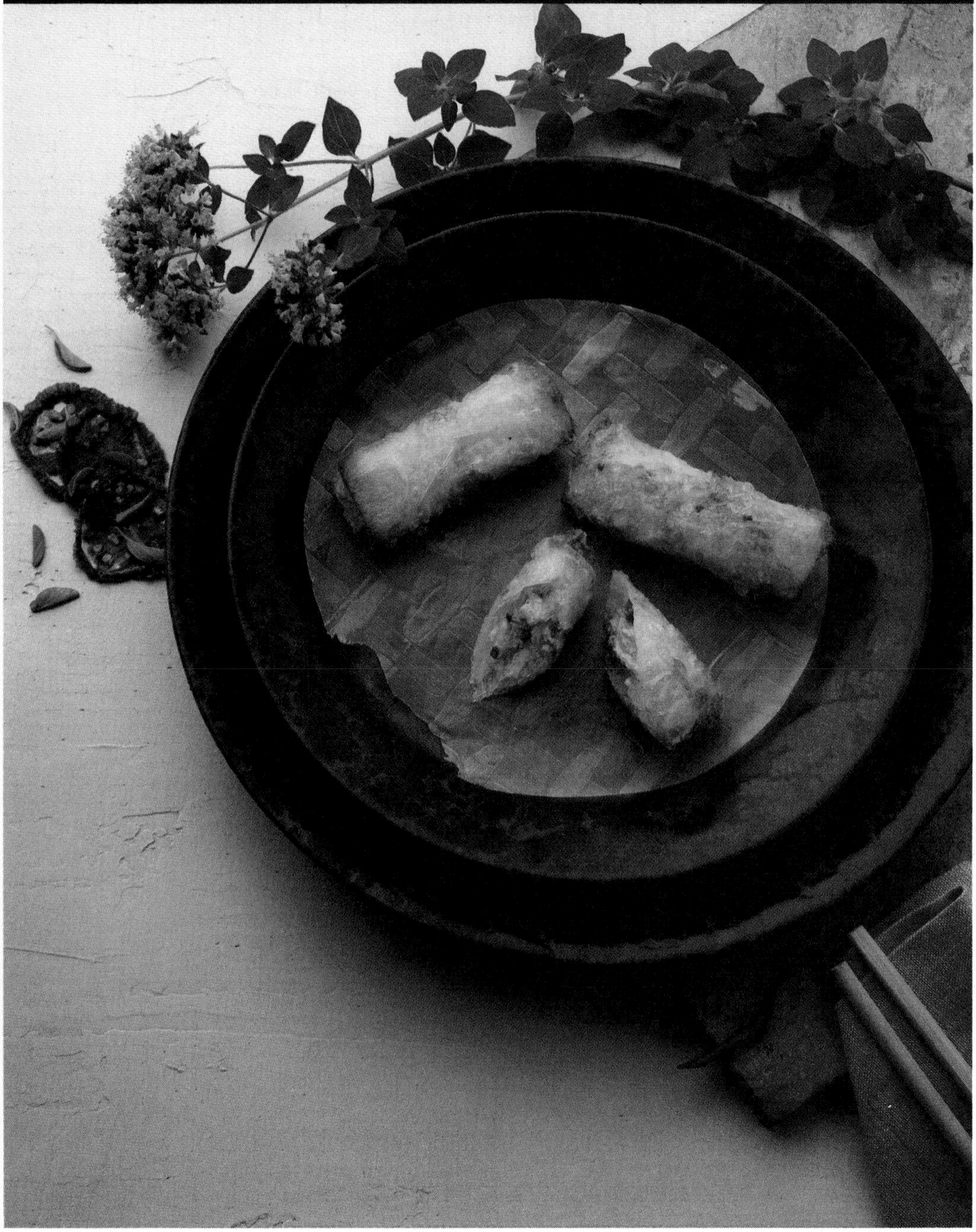

*Broiled Oysters with Three Sauces; Grilled Crab and Lobster*

*Barbecued Ribs with a Spicy Sauce; Vegetable Pasta*

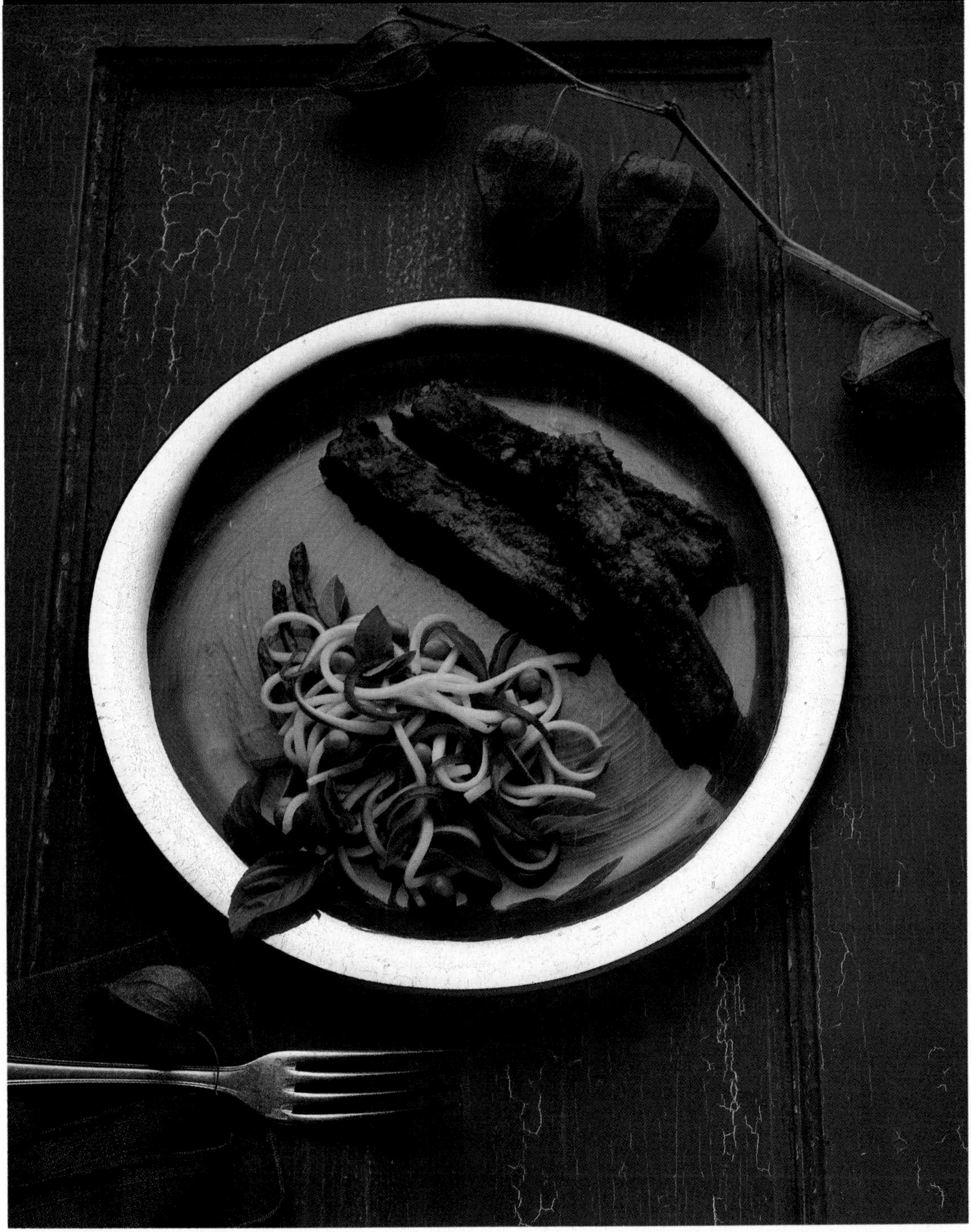

*Spiced Fried Cornish Game Hens; Garlic-Sesame Seed Mayonnaise; Fried Potato Chips*

Almond Madeleines; Orange-Ginger Custard with Raspberry Sauce

# Chicken "Ragout"

Yes, it is chicken stew, but with a Gallic-Chinese harmony. The chicken is steeped à la chinoise, assuring succulence and satin smoothness. In China the chicken would be served cold with a dipping sauce. Here, I add blanched vegetables and a sauce made from ingredients that are used in the traditional dipping relishes. With the crème fraîche added, the result is a delicious and colorful stew, rich in complementary tastes and textures.

*2 quarts Basic Chicken Stock, page 67*
*One 3½- to 4-pound chicken*
*8 ounces carrots, roll-cut*
*8 ounces asparagus, with stems removed and cut into 2-inch sections*
*10 whole scallions, cut into 2-inch sections*

*1 large (about 1 pound) sweet red pepper, seeded and cut into 1-inch strips*
*4 ounces snow peas, with ends trimmed*
*2 ounces black mushrooms, prepared as on page 45*
*2 tablespoons butter*
*¼ cup water*
*Salt and pepper to taste*

SAUCE
*2 tablespoons chopped fresh ginger*
*2 tablespoons finely chopped scallions*

*3 tablespoons finely chopped fresh coriander*
*tablespoons Crème Fraîche, page 43*

Simmer the chicken stock and add the chicken. Cook for 20 minutes, skimming frequently. Turn off the heat, cover, and let the chicken sit for 1 hour.

While the chicken is steeping, blanch the carrots and asparagus.

Remove the chicken from the pot and skim off any remaining fat from the cooking liquid. Reduce the liquid by half over high heat. Strip the meat from the bones and set aside.

In a large skillet, cook the vegetables with the butter, water, salt, and pepper for 3 minutes over high heat. While the vegetables cook, add the sauce ingredients to the reduced cooking stock. When the vegetables are done, add them along with the chicken meat to the sauce. Heat briefly and serve.

*Serves 4*

*Wine Suggestion:* a rich red from the Rhône, such as Hermitage or Côte Rôtie, approximately 5 years old, or a fine Oregon or Carneros Pinot Noir.

# Chicken Breasts with Red Peppers and Bok Choy in Cream Sauce

Chicken breasts are a favorite in America because of their white, delicately textured meat. In Asia they are not so highly prized because of their relatively bland taste. To me, the virtue of the chicken breast lies in its adaptability and congeniality. Precisely because it is bland, it can be paired with other ingredients. It readily absorbs sauces that change its taste but allow it to retain its chicken essence. In other words, it lends itself deliciously to gentle poaching. In this recipe I use bok choy, which is similar to Swiss chard but sweeter and leafier. This versatile vegetable combines well with the sweet red peppers, and both add their flavors to the complaisant chicken. The breasts are cut into strips, Eastern-style, but instead of being stir-fried they are poached and then simmered together with the vegetables until done, with the crème fraîche adding a classic Western touch.

*1 ½-pounds boneless chicken breasts*
   *Salt and pepper to taste*
*2 tablespoons chopped scallions*
*1 pound bok choy*
*1 cup Basic Chicken Stock, page 67*

*2 tablespoons butter*
*1 pound sweet red peppers, seeded and*
   *cut into 2-inch strips*
*2 tablespoons Crème Fraîche, page 43*

Cut the chicken breasts into strips 3 inches long and ¼ inch wide. In a medium-sized bowl, combine the chicken, salt, pepper, and chopped scallions.

Cut the bok choy stalks crosswise away from the stem. Separate the individual stalks and the central core. Divide the stalks lengthwise, using the point of a knife. Cut the stalks into 2-inch pieces. If using large bok choys, peel the skin from the core. Cut the core diagonally into thin slices.

Heat the chicken stock and butter in a medium-sized pan. Add the chicken and simmer for 3 minutes. Remove the chicken with a slotted spoon. Strain the stock into a bowl through a fine-meshed sieve. Return the stock to the pan, add the red peppers, and cook over moderate heat for 2 minutes. Add the bok choy and cook until the leaves wilt, about 1 minute. Remove the vegetables with a slotted spoon, add salt, pepper, and crème fraîche, and reduce the liquid by half. Return the chicken and vegetables to the sauce. Cook briefly until the chicken and vegetables are heated through. Serve immediately.

*Serves 4*

*Wine Suggestion:* Try your finer wines, such as "reserve" quality Cabernet Sauvignon from California, 5 to 10 years old, or classified Bordeaux, 7 to 10 years old.

# Marinated Grilled Quail

Besides being an appropriate way to cook many foods, the grilling technique involves very little food preparation. Delicious meals can be achieved with little labor, as in this recipe. The trick lies in the deceptively simple soy sauce, rice wine, and olive oil marinade. After only a short period of time, its distinctive and powerful flavors penetrate, enhance, and enliven the natural quail taste. Once grilled, the quail become delicious morsels to be eaten immediately or saved and served cold. They are also splendid picnic treats.

MARINADE
*2 tablespoons light soy sauce*      *1 tablespoon olive oil*
*1 tablespoon rice wine*

*Four 4-ounce quail*

*Serves 4 as a first course*

Combine the marinade ingredients, add the quail, and marinate for 1 hour at room temperature. Make a charcoal fire and, when the coals are ash white, grill the quail, turning once. The birds are done when just cooked but slightly pink inside.

*Wine Suggestion:* a very light, fresh red such as Chianti, young California Zinfandel, or a dry rosé from the Rhône, such as Tavel.

# Marinated Roast Squab with Rice Wine-Butter Sauce

Simplicity is a desirable characteristic in cooking as in other aspects of human endeavor. The problem often is, however, that there is sometimes more and sometimes less to a situation or process than meets the eye. To define simplicity, we rely not upon calculation but judgment. I always seek simplicity in my cooking, but my definition is based upon my own experience, my own judgment of what is simple. I regard this as a simple dish, both in its making and in its ingredients: squab marinated in a traditional Eastern mixture and simply roasted. Finished with a hint of butter and rice wine, the dish combines the best of both worlds.

*Two 12- to 14-ounce squab*

MARINADE
| | |
|---|---|
| *1 tablespoon light soy sauce* | *2 tablespoons rice wine* |
| *1 tablespoon dark soy sauce* | |
| *½ cup rice wine* | *2 tablespoons cold butter, cut into small pieces* |

Butterfly the squab by splitting them open and removing the backbone. Flatten them out with the palm of your hand. Make two small holes, one on either side of the breastbone, and tuck their legs through. This will help hold the shape of the birds while they roast.

Combine the marinade ingredients and marinate the squab in a heat-proof casserole or baking dish for 1 hour. Preheat the oven to 400 degrees. Roast the squab in the marinade for 30 minutes. Remove the squab from the dish and skim off any fat. Place the dish over a burner and deglaze with rice wine, scraping the bottom of the pan as you stir. Remove the dish from the heat and whisk in the butter. Spoon a few tablespoons of sauce on individual plates and place the squab on top.

*Serves 2*

*Note:*        This recipe can also be made with Cornish game hens.

*Wine Suggestion:* fine red wines such as Grand Cru Burgundy, 7 to 10 years old, or fairly mature Merlot from California, or Pomerol or St.-Emilion from Bordeaux.

# Sesame-Flavored Marinated Chicken

Fried chicken is appreciated in the East and West. Here, I use chicken thighs marinated in a robust sesame and garlic mixture. The nutty flavor of sesame dominates because of its strength and because the garlic loses some of its strong flavor when cooked. The dark thigh meat takes nicely to the sesame flavor and to the deep-frying method. A simple and tasty dish.

*1 pound chicken thighs, boned as
  prepared on page 149*

MARINADE
*1 teaspoon salt*                         *1 tablespoon sesame oil*
*1 tablespoon sesame paste*               *1 medium-sized egg, beaten*
*1 tablespoon chopped garlic*

*½ cup flour*                             *½ cup peanut oil*
*2 tablespoons roasted sesame seeds*

Cut the chicken into strips 3 inches by 1 inch. Combine the marinade ingredients in a medium-sized bowl and marinate the chicken for 1 hour. In a bowl, mix the flour and sesame seeds. Dredge the chicken strips in the flour mixture and shake off the excess. Heat the peanut oil in a wok or large skillet. Pan-fry the chicken until golden brown on both sides.

*Serves 2 to 4*

*Wine Suggestion:* light, refreshing red wines such as Gamay from California, lightly vinified Zinfandel, or young, fresh Beaujolais from France.

# Stir-Fried Chicken with Snow Peas and Water Chestnuts

I believe that this dish is not only easy to make but it also captures the essence of foods in ways that transcend both East and West. The stir-frying technique preserves all of the best qualities of the ingredients while changing them just enough to make them perfectly cooked. Here, the spices, olive and peanut oils, and thyme give the chicken thighs a delightful flavor; the snow peas and water chestnuts add colors, tastes, and textures that delight eye and palate. A simple, wonderfully balanced dish.

*1 pound chicken thighs, boned as*
*  prepared on page 149*
*  Salt*
*1 tablespoon Chinese Seasoned Salt,*
*  page 42*
*1 tablespoon dried thyme*
*1 tablespoon peanut oil*

*2 tablespoons olive oil*
*1 pound snow peas, with ends trimmed*
*8 ounces fresh water chestnuts, peeled*
*  and cut crosswise into ¼-inch slices*
*  Freshly ground black pepper to taste*
*3 tablespoons water*

Cut the chicken into strips 3 inches by ½ inch. In a medium-sized bowl, combine the chicken, 1 teaspoon of salt, Chinese seasoned salt, and thyme. Set aside for 20 minutes.

In a large skillet or wok, heat the peanut oil. Stir-fry the chicken strips for 3 minutes, or until they are golden brown. Remove the chicken with a slotted spoon. Add the olive oil, snow peas, water chestnuts, salt, and pepper. Stir-fry the vegetables for 2 minutes, add the water, and bring it to a boil. Return the chicken to the wok and heat through. Serve immediately.

*Serves 4*

*Wine Suggestion:* finer quality Beaujolais such as Fleurie or Chiroubles, a red Rioja from Spain, or a high-quality red generic blend from California.

# Roast Barbecued Duck

The French describe this duck, cooked in the Eastern mode, as "lacquered." It is an apt description because when finished the skin is hard, crispy, and shiny. This finish, however, is deliciously edible: The soy sauce-honey mixture has left its dark golden mark. At the same time, the hoisin sauce, thyme, and Chinese seasoned salt work their magic inside the duck. This is one of my favorite ways to serve and eat duck.

This dish can also be done on an outside grill.

One 3½- to 4-pound duck, butterflied
    as prepared on page 164
3 tablespoons hoisin sauce

1 tablespoon dried thyme
2 teaspoons Chinese Seasoned Salt,
    page 42

BASTING LIQUID
    2 quarts water
    3 tablespoons honey

3 tablespoons dark soy sauce

1 cup water

Season the interior of the duck with hoisin sauce, thyme, and Chinese seasoned salt.

In a medium-sized pot, combine the basting liquid ingredients and bring to a boil. Turn off the heat and baste the skin side of the duck several times with the hot liquid. Allow the duck to dry either in a cool, drafty place for 5 hours or in front of a fan for 2 hours. When the duck is properly dried, the skin will feel like parchment paper.

Preheat the oven to 400 degrees. Place the duck, skin side up, on a roasting rack inside a roasting pan. Pour 1 cup of water in the roasting pan. Roast the duck for 1 hour, until the skin is brown and crisp. Carve the duck and serve at once.

*Serves 4*

*Wine Suggestion:* an opportunity to be innovative. Try a rich, full-bodied Champagne, 4 to 7 years old, or a heavier, buttery Chardonnay from California, 3 to 5 years old.

# Sautéed Duck Liver and Chinese Duck Sausage

Duck livers are a favorite in both Chinese and French cuisines. Here, I put them together in a combination that will please any duck lover. Fresh duck livers are sautéed with a rice wine sauce and served with Onion-Ginger Confit (page 179) and Chinese duck liver sausages. The resulting dish is rich and luscious. Soaking the duck livers in milk overnight gives them a smooth texture and mild rice flavor. Steaming the duck sausages makes them plump and juicy. Serve this dish as an appetizer, as part of a larger menu, or as a main course.

*1 pound fresh duck livers*
*2 cups milk*
*4 ounces Chinese duck liver or pork sausages*
*Salt and freshly ground black pepper to taste*
*Flour for dusting*

*2 tablespoons peanut oil*
*1 tablespoon grated lemon zest*
*3 tablespoons rice wine*
*1 teaspoon sugar*
*½ cup Basic Chicken Stock, page 67*
*Onion-Ginger Confit, page 179*

Soak the duck livers in the milk overnight, covered, in the refrigerator. Drain and discard the milk. Trim the livers of the veins and fat, carefully keeping them as whole as possible. Gently blot them dry with paper towels.

Cut the duck sausages in half and put them on a heat-proof plate. Put about 2 inches of hot water and a trivet in the bottom of a steamer or wok. Place the sausages and plate on the trivet and gently steam for about 15 minutes.

Salt and pepper the duck livers and dust them lightly with flour. Heat the peanut oil in a wok or large skillet. Pan-fry the livers over high heat for about 1 minute on each side, until they are crispy and brown. Remove to a platter. Deglaze the wok or skillet with the lemon zest, rice wine, sugar, and chicken stock. Reduce the sauce by one-third and season with salt and pepper to taste. Pour this over the duck livers. Serve them with the sausages and onion-ginger confit. Serve at once.

*Serves 4*

*Wine Suggestion:* be adventuresome and match this dish with a youngish 5- to 7-year-old Sauternes.

# MEATS

Spicy Pork Chops
Roast Pork with Chinese
 Spices
Sautéed Apples
Roast Rack of Lamb with
 Asian-Style Marinade
Grilled Lamb Marinated
 with Rice Wine and
 Pomegranate
Barbecued Pork Cubes,
 Satay-Style
Onion-Ginger Confit

Barbecued Ribs with a
 Spicy Sauce
Braised Spicy Veal Shanks
Poached Anise Beef Fillet
 with Vegetables
Stuffed Veal Breast
Broiled T-Bone Steak with
 Oyster Sauce and Bok
 Choy
Country-Style Pork Stew
Lamb Chops with Leeks
Anise-Clove Pork Ragout

Crépinette of Pork and
 Chinese Sausage
Braised Oxtails in Plum
 Sauce
Braised Sweetbreads in
 Spicy Bean Sauce
Stuffed Leg of Lamb
Hoisin Pork Chops
Grilled Eastern-Flavored
 Lamburgers
My Mother's Braised East-
 West Oxtail Stew

*The line of customers moves slowly along the high marble counter, past the shelves and trays where the cuts of meat are aligned, each with its name and price on a tag stuck into it. The vivid red of the beef precedes the light pink of the veal, the dull red of the lamb, the dark red of the pork. Vast ribs blaze up, round tournedos whose thickness is lined by a ribbon of lard, slender and agile contre-filets, steaks armed with their invincible bone, massive rolled roasts all lean, chunks for boiling with layers of fat and of red meat, roasts waiting for the string that will force them to enfold themselves. Then the colors fade: veal escalopes, loin chops, pieces of shoulder and breast, cartilage: and then we enter the realm of legs and shoulders of lamb; farther on some white tripe glows, a liver glistens blackly . . . .* Italo Calvino, *Mr. Palomar*

*Heaven sent us good meat; the Devil sends cooks.* David Garrick

That there are differences in East and West approaches to food is no more apparent than the fact that in the East, for a variety of geographic, cultural, and religious reasons, meat of all sorts is defined as a secondary food; in China it is included among the foods whose function is "to help the fan, the rice, go down." In the West, for different geographic, cultural, and religious reasons, meats are seen as primary foods, central to any but the poorest diet. The American advertisement, "Meat makes the meal," could never have won acceptance among traditional Eastern consumers. This is slowly changing. All "modernized" countries seek to increase the availability of meat, seeing it as "progress" and as a response to consumer preference. The latter is probably correct. Even the Chinese would have integrated more meats into their noble cuisine had more been cheaply available.

This cultural difference, however, is no barrier to the blending of East-West cuisines. Meats lend themselves readily to the preparation of delicious dishes, sauces, and soups in any kitchen, regardless of cultural factors. All that is needed, as usual, is a little care and some imagination.

<u>PORK</u>

*Well roasted pig finds a fair sepulchre in the grateful stomach of the judicious epicure.*
                                              Charles Lamb, *A Dissertation upon Roast Pig*

Pork is a stable meat in both East and West, but it is the "red meat" of Chinese cuisine. It has been China's favorite meat for seventy centuries. All commercially raised pigs of today are descendants of the European wild pig, which the Chinese were probably the first to domesticate, over five thousand years ago. The Chinese, then, have been testing and tasting pork recipes for some time. The marvelous animal has entered into the very structure of Chinese culture. The Chinese ideograph for pork and for meat is the same, while the symbol for "home" is that of a roof with a pig under it.

In Chinese religious practices, especially among the southern Chinese, the offering of a whole pig is the highest act of devotional sacrifice to the divinities. In Cantonese religious custom this takes the form of a golden pig—one roasted whole with a malt sugar glaze that makes it scarlet gold, an "auspicious" color similar to the golden brown of the American Thanksgiving turkey.

Pork, moreover, is highly nutritious. It is an excellent source of the B vitamins; pork liver is rich in iron, and the meat includes significant amounts of other vitamins and minerals. For those concerned about cholesterol, I point out that pork meat is not marbled with fat, as most beef is, and the fat can easily be trimmed away. Finally, pork is economical and can be served at any lunch or dinner occasion, from snack to elegant banquet.

Please do not overcook pork. Whenever I serve Roast Pork with Chinese Spices (page 174), my guests, while delighted, quite often say it doesn't taste like pork. This is because they have experienced only dry, tough, and bland meat that is then covered with an inappropriate sauce designed to cloak the meat's deficiencies. And such, all too often, is the normal state of pork in America. Overcooking is the main cause of this situation, and that in turn derives largely from the fear of trichinosis. A word of reassurance is necessary. An internal temperature over 140 degrees will make the pork perfectly safe, assuming there were trichinae in the pig to begin with, a rare occurrence nowadays. I personally prefer a slightly pink roast pork, with an internal temperature of 150 degrees; most people like it cooked a bit more, say from 155 to 165 degrees. At those higher internal temperatures, the meat is no longer pink but closer to an off-white and still quite juicy. The essential point is that pork need not and should not be overcooked. There is no reason for it to be dry and tasteless.

I have noticed that pigs from China tend to be tastier, perhaps because of the way they are raised and the type of feed supplied to them. Judging the tenderness of pork, incidentally, and especially that of pork chops, is a highly problematical task. It is always best to use pork from a young pig, about six months old. Julia Child learned from the Department of Agriculture that the emotional state of the pig at the moment of slaughter is also important. An exhausted, frightened, or shocked pig's endocrinal system will render its flesh tough in reaction to stress. Such pork needs to be braised and not roasted. Perhaps we need laws to ensure that the little pigs who come to market are not traumatized along the way, but I may be cutting too close to the bone here.

## BEEF AND LAMB

*One sentiment does not exclude another: Mr. Palomar's mood as he stands in line at the butcher shop is at once of restrained joy and fear, desire and respect, egoistic concern and universal compassion, the mood that perhaps others express in prayer.*                    Italo Calvino, *Mr. Palomar*

Beef and lamb are familiar to both East and West. They are similar in that each has a strong and distinctive flavor, with lamb being rather more assertive.

Of beef, not much need be said. Its flavor, texture, variety, and robust readiness to combine with other foods are well known. Veal, however, needs a few words. Veal was a food alien to my Chinese culture and childhood. In this I was very much like most Americans. We eat about one hundred pounds of beef per capita each year and only two or three pounds of veal. Throughout Asia, however, the idea of butchering a calf unnecessarily is untenable; livestock is too valuable and scarcity too endemic a problem to consider such a step. The story is different in Europe. There, with the relative abundance of livestock, veal was a practical menu item, especially in the days when forage or feed was scarce: Better to slaughter the calf than to see it die of starvation. In Europe, at least, and certainly in France and Italy, veal became a standard and highly regarded delicacy.

Nevertheless, there are problems with veal which I, with my Chinese background, perhaps see too clearly. Veal is subtly flavored to a fault. I find it almost tasteless. If it is from too young an animal, the meat is as flaccid as a pudding; from too old an animal, it is beef without its heartiness. Veal must be cooked very carefully. It has little fat to begin with; overcooking dries it out and makes it tougher than it should be, while undercooking keeps the flavor locked up.

While a student in France, I ate veal shanks as an alternative to more expensive beef cuts. I soon learned that I much preferred the rich taste of the shanks to the bland tenderness of veal fillets. The secret lay in the sauce and in the technique—the shanks were braised. This technique, prized in both East and West, is perhaps the one best suited for veal; it is certainly the best way to prepare veal shanks. The large amount of connective tissue and the relatively tough leg muscles need long, slow, moist cooking.

Roast lamb, familiar in the West and a staple in Indian cuisine, plays no role in either Chinese or Japanese cooking. Roasting is not a standard technique in those two countries, and goats and sheep are more common than lamb. In China the meat is not highly prized because of what is regarded as its strong odor and taste. This latter belief is probably based on the practice of eating mutton, the meat of a mature sheep, rather than lamb, the meat of a young sheep. It is an interesting observation that in many Far Eastern languages goat and lamb are equated, suggesting perhaps the failure to exploit the animals' dietary potential. Young goat is tender, less greasily fat, and more delicately flavored than lamb. But young lamb itself is delicious when properly prepared, as the cuisines of Europe and America demonstrate in many recipes. I am very fond of roast lamb, and it is not a preference based on my mother's cuisine; it is, rather, a part of my American or Western heritage.

All of the recipes included in this section build on the strength and the ability of the meats to combine in so many ways with so many different spices and seasonings, resulting in new and delicious dishes.

# Spicy Pork Chops

This tasty but subtle dish brings a new flavor to pork chops, favorites in both East and West. This is a simple recipe and can be prepared well in advance of the actual cooking. With a cold vegetable or lettuce salad, it makes a pleasant meal on a warm summer day. Apple and Plum Sauce (page 73) is a welcome accompaniment to the chops.

Four 4-ounce loin-cut pork chops
1 tablespoon olive oil
2 teaspoons Chinese Seasoned Salt,
    page 42

½ teaspoon coarse salt
1½ tablespoons fresh or 2 teaspoons
    dried thyme

*Serves 2 to 4*

Dredge the pork chops in olive oil. Mix the Chinese seasoned salt, coarse salt, and thyme in a small bowl and sprinkle both sides of the chops with the spice mixture. Set aside for 1 hour. Make a charcoal fire and, when the coals are ash white, grill the chops. Turn them once and remove as soon as they are firm to the touch. Serve immediately.

*Wine Suggestion:* a fruity Rheingau from a vintage like 1983, Kabinett, or a California or Pacific Northwest Johannisberg Riesling, preferably young.

# Roast Pork with Chinese Spices

The fresh orange and lemon peels add to this dish what their name implies, zest. In the East, dried citrus peels are more often used and, because they are dried, their flavor tends to be stronger and sharper. I think the Western approach, fresh peels, works better here. Apple and Plum Sauce (page 73) is an excellent accompaniment to this dish. Leftover roast is delicious cold with Ginger-Scallion Mayonnaise (page 72).

MARINADE
1 tablespoon five-spice powder
2 teaspoons freshly ground black
  pepper

2 tablespoons coarse salt

One 3½- to 4-pound pork loin roast
  with bone in
¼ cup fresh sage leaves, loosely
  packed
2 tablespoons fresh marjoram leaves
6 garlic cloves, lightly crushed with
  skins on

2 tablespoons shredded fresh orange
  zest
1 tablespoon shredded fresh lemon
  zest
4 cups Basic Chicken Stock, page 67
  Fresh coriander sprigs for garnish

Mix the five-spice powder, black pepper, and salt in a small bowl. Rub the pork with the mixture and sprinkle with the herbs, garlic, orange zest, and lemon zest. Marinate for at least 2 hours in a cool place or overnight, covered, in the refrigerator.

Preheat the oven to 450 degrees. Roast the pork, fat side up, for 10 minutes. Reduce to 350 degrees and roast 20 minutes more. Remove from the oven and let the roast sit for 20 minutes. (This can be done hours in advance.)

Bone the roast and pour off and discard the fat from the roasting pan. Deglaze the pan with chicken stock over a burner, stirring to remove the flavorful bits from the bottom of the pan. Add the bones and gently simmer for 30 minutes. Skim the fat from the sauce and strain through a fine-meshed sieve. In a medium-sized saucepan, reduce the sauce by half and set aside.

One hour before serving, preheat the oven to 350 degrees and cook the roast for 20 to 25 minutes. Remove from the oven and allow to cool for

20 minutes before carving. Fan out the slices on a serving platter and moisten with the sauce. Garnish with fresh coriander sprigs and serve. Sautéed Apples (recipe follows) is an excellent accompaniment.

*Serves 6 to 8*

*Wine Suggestion:* a refreshing, spicy white from Alsace, such as Gewürztraminer or Riesling, or a comparable California drier-styled wine.

# Sautéed Apples

This is a traditional French recipe modified by the addition of Eastern seasonings. Cooked fruits are not common in the East; most fruits are eaten in dried form, and some are used in soups. Fresh fruits are an excellent accompaniment to heavier dishes such as roasts; they balance the heaviness of meats and are often as good as if not better than vegetables in that role. Apples and pears, for example, sometimes substitute for starches such as rice and potatoes.

Firm pears may be substituted for the apples. For a spicy variation, add one teaspoon of minced fresh ginger.

*2 pounds golden delicious apples, peeled, cored, and cut into ¼-inch slices*
*Juice from 1 fresh lemon*
*4 tablespoons butter*

*¼ cup finely chopped scallions*
*3 tablespoons finely chopped fresh coriander*
*Salt and freshly ground black pepper*

In a medium-sized bowl, toss the apple slices in lemon juice to keep them from turning brown. In a large skillet, melt the butter, add the apple slices, and sauté for 1 minute. Add the scallions and coriander. Sauté 1 minute more. Season with salt and pepper.

*Serves 4 to 6*

# Roast Rack of Lamb with Asian-Style Marinade

Here, as tender as it is, the lamb's distinctive taste is nevertheless robust enough to bear the East-West flavors of sesame oil, mustard, and soy sauce with grace and dignity.

Serve this lamb with roast potatoes and a green salad.

*Two 1½-pound racks of lamb, trimmed of excess fat*

*Peanut oil*

MARINADE

*2 teaspoons freshly ground black pepper*
*1½ tablespoons sesame oil*
*2 tablespoons roasted sesame seeds*
*1½ tablespoons sugar*
*2 tablespoons prepared Dijon mustard*

*1 tablespoon light soy sauce*
*2 tablespoons dark soy sauce*
*1 tablespoon finely chopped garlic*
*1 tablespoon coarse sea salt*

*1 tablespoon fresh or 3 tablespoons dry sage*
*½ cup Basic Chicken Stock, page 67*
*2 teaspoons sesame oil*

*2 teaspoons sesame paste or peanut butter*
*2 tablespoons butter*

Brown each rack of lamb in a nonstick pan with a little bit of peanut oil for 5 minutes, turning frequently. Allow the lamb to cool.

Mix the marinade ingredients in a small bowl and rub the mixture on the racks with a rubber spatula. Marinate for 1 hour.

Preheat the oven to 450 degrees. Place the lamb racks in a roasting pan. Moisten the fresh or dry sage leaves with some water and scatter them over the lamb racks. Reduce the heat to 400 degrees, cover the lamb racks with foil, and roast for 30 minutes. Remove the foil for the last 5 minutes if you want a more browned and crisp look.

Remove the lamb to a cutting board and allow the racks to rest for 20 minutes.

Skim off the fat from the roasting pan, add the chicken stock, and deglaze over a burner, scraping to remove the flavorful bits. Add the sesame oil, sesame paste, and butter to the sauce and mix thoroughly.

*Serves 4*

Carve the lamb racks, arrange them on a serving platter, and serve with the sauce.

*Wine Suggestion:* an opportunity to use well-made, generic reds from California, with generous blends of Cabernet Sauvignon. Try other hearty, simple red wines such as proprietary Bordeaux or Burgundies.

# Grilled Lamb Marinated with Rice Wine and Pomegranate

This lamb dish was inspired by Narsai David, a superb cook and highly regarded caterer. He is of Syrian extraction and, as might be expected, lamb figures prominently in his cuisine. Having sampled his lamb dishes many times, I was inspired to create a recipe that reflected his influence but displayed some of my own touches. It is a case of East Meets West in the Middle East. The Chinese rice wine and the ambrosial juice of the pomegranate bring all three areas together to celebrate and enhance the taste of lamb. Be sure to allow the marinade enough time to permeate the meat.

Boned leg of lamb is best for this dish; any leftovers are as delicious as the first serving. They also make great items for a picnic.

MARINADE

*¼ cup rice wine*
*1 tablespoon salt*
*1 tablespoon chopped garlic*
  *Freshly ground black pepper to taste*
*2 tablespoons olive oil*

*1 tablespoon sesame oil*
*¼ cup lemon juice*
*½ cup pomegranate juice*
*1 tablespoon fresh thyme*
*1 tablespoon finely chopped fresh coriander*

*One 2-pound leg of lamb, butterflied*

In a large glass or stainless steel bowl, combine the marinade ingredients. Marinate the lamb for 2 hours at room temperature. Make a charcoal fire and, when the coals are ash white, grill the lamb for 45 minutes, turning frequently. Allow it to rest on a carving board for 20 minutes, then cut into thin slices. Save any juices and serve them along with the meat.

*Serves 4*

*Wine Suggestion:* a petite Château red Bordeaux, 5 to 7 years old, would work well, or a moderately aged California Cabernet Sauvignon with soft tannins.

# Barbecued Pork Cubes, Satay-Style

On my frequent excursions to Asia, one taste treat I always seek is satay, a dish of Malaysian origin but popular throughout the East. Foods such as beef, lamb, chicken, or seafood are cut into thin slices, marinated, skewered, and then grilled. When done, it resembles a miniature shish kebab. The traditional marinade combines spices, lemongrass, peanuts, and coconut.

In this version I substitute a marinade of Western seasonings and Eastern flavors, and instead of thin slices of meat, I use cubes of pork. The result is a subtle but many-faceted treat, redolent of the two cultures.

You may serve this as an appetizer or as a first course.

MARINADE
*2 teaspoons light soy sauce*
*1 tablespoon dark soy sauce*
*2 tablespoons sesame paste or peanut
  butter*

*1 pound pork butt, cut into 1-inch
  cubes*

*1 tablespoon fresh marjoram
  Salt and freshly ground black pepper
  to taste*
*2 tablespoons rice wine*
*1 tablespoon fresh lemon juice*

Mix the marinade ingredients in a medium-sized bowl. Add the pork and toss thoroughly. Marinate for 1 hour or more in the refrigerator. Arrange the pork on bamboo skewers. Make a charcoal fire and, when the coals are hot, grill the pork 3 or 4 minutes on each side. Serve immediately. Onion-Ginger Confit (recipe follows) is an excellent accompaniment.

*Serves 4*

*Wine Suggestion:* accompany with a young chilled Beaujolais from France, Chianti from Italy, or Gamay from California.

## Onion-Ginger Confit

3 tablespoons butter
2 cups thinly sliced sweet red onions
½ cup thinly sliced shallots
2 tablespoons finely chopped ginger
1 cup Basic Chicken Stock, page 67

2 tablespoons sugar
Salt and freshly ground black pepper
to taste
1 cinnamon stick

*Makes about 2½ cups*

In a medium-sized skillet, heat the butter and sauté the onions and shallots until the onions are translucent. Add the rest of the ingredients and simmer for 5 minutes. Remove the cinnamon stick. Turn up the heat to medium and cook until all the liquid has evaporated. Serve warm or at room temperature.

# Barbecued Ribs with a Spicy Sauce

I grew up feasting on barbecued ribs prepared the Chinese way: marinated in a honey-hoisin sauce that gave the ribs a golden glaze as they hung roasting in a Chinese oven. The idea of grilling ribs is a Western and, no doubt, an American inspiration. I still like Chinese-style ribs, but grilled ribs are now my favorite. In this recipe I combine aspects of my East-West heritage, using both Chinese spices and Western seasonings that together form a lusty sauce worthy of the robust flavor of the ribs. Moreover, I employ two methods here—the preliminary low-heat roasting gets rid of unnecessary fat and shortens the grilling time, thus avoiding burnt barbecue sauce. This is a wonderful picnic or summertime grill treat, a unique East-West/All-American dish.

*3½ pounds pork ribs*

BARBECUE SAUCE

| | |
|---|---|
| *2 cups Tomato Concassé, page 70* | *2 tablespoons dark soy sauce* |
| *1 tablespoon peanut oil* | *2 tablespoons chili bean paste* |
| *½ cup chopped yellow onions* | *½ cup kumquats or tangerines* |
| *1 tablespoon chopped ginger* | *¼ cup sugar* |
| *2 tablespoons chopped garlic* | *2 tablespoons rice wine* |
| *3 tablespoons hoisin sauce* | *2 tablespoons light soy sauce* |
| *1 tablespoon sesame oil* | |

Preheat the oven to 250 degrees. Place the pork ribs in a baking dish and cook for 2 hours to render the fat and tenderize the meat. Remove the ribs from the dish and set aside.

Combine the barbecue sauce ingredients in a large saucepan and simmer gently for 45 minutes. Allow the sauce to cool, then puree in a blender.

Smear the ribs with the barbecue sauce. Make a charcoal fire and, when the coals are ash white, grill the ribs, basting with any remaining sauce. Cook the ribs for 5 to 10 minutes on each side, depending on thickness.

*Serves 4 to 6*   Serve immediately.

*Wine Suggestion:*   blush wines, such as white Zinfandel or white Cabernet, would go well, or try a good-quality rosé from Bandol or Tavel.

# Braised Spicy Veal Shanks

Here, I braise veal shanks in an East-West blend of spices and seasonings that enlivens the dish without overwhelming the flavor of the veal. The result has both subtlety and strength. This is a hearty cold-weather dish, served simply with rice and a salad. It reheats nicely.

*1½ tablespoons peanut oil*
*3 pounds veal shanks*
*2 tablespoons finely chopped yellow*
*  onions*
*1 tablespoon chopped garlic*
*1 tablespoon chopped ginger*
*4 cups Basic Chicken Stock, page 67*

*1 tablespoon light soy sauce*
*2 tablespoons curry powder*
*2 tablespoons rice wine*
*2 cups Tomato Concassé, page 70*
*  Salt and freshly ground black*
*  pepper to taste*

*Serves 4*

In a large skillet, heat the oil and brown the veal shanks. Remove the shanks with a slotted spoon and sauté the onions, garlic, and ginger for 2 minutes. Transfer the aromatics to a medium-sized casserole with the shanks and the rest of the ingredients. Stir and braise, covered, over low heat for 45 minutes, or until tender.

*Wine Suggestion:* a good-quality Beaujolais from Moulin-à-Vent or Brouilly, or a red Sancerre. From California, a good quality Zinfandel, 3 to 5 years old.

# Poached Anise Beef Fillet with Vegetables

Beef is eaten in the East and in the West, and lends itself to intercultural exchanges. Here, I draw upon two traditional recipes: the French Boeuf à la Ficelle and the Chinese anise-flavored beef soup. The heat of the simmering liquid seals the surface of the beef, keeping it succulent within. The slow steeping process, maintained until the beef is rare, allows the richly seasoned stock to permeate the meat, reinforcing its flavor. After the fillet has been cooked, you can reduce the stock over heat to concentrate it into a robust sauce or serve it in separate bowls as an additional soup course, with the vegetables added. This hearty dish goes especially well with Turnip-Parsnip-Ginger Purée (page 208)—a wonderful winter combination. Simple to make and quite out of the ordinary, it may be presented in an elegant fashion.

*3 pounds beef fillet*
*8 cups Basic Chicken Stock, page 67*
*6 whole star anise*
*3 tablespoons dark soy sauce*
*2 tablespoons Pernod or other anise-*
*flavored liqueur*
*Salt and pepper to taste*

*1 pound baby carrots, blanched*
*1 pound green beans, blanched*
*2 bunches scallions, trimmed and left*
*whole*
*Turnip-Parsnip-Ginger Purée, page*
*208, full recipe*

To secure the beef, tie string around the meat at 2-inch intervals. Tie 1 length of string all the way around the fillet lengthwise.

In a large pot, combine the chicken stock, star anise, soy sauce, Pernod, salt, and pepper. Simmer for 15 minutes. Add the beef fillet and simmer 10 minutes more. Turn off the heat, cover the pot, and let the meat steep for 1 hour.

Remove the meat with a slotted spoon and wrap it in foil to keep warm. Bring the cooking liquid to a simmer and add all the vegetables. Cook for 2 minutes, then remove with a slotted spoon. Strain the cooking liquid. Slice the fillet and arrange on a serving platter surrounded with the vegetables. Serve the cooking liquid in individual soup bowls enriched with the turnip-parsnip-ginger purée.

*Serves 6 to 8*

*Wine Suggestion:* fine, well-aged Cabernet Sauvignon or Merlot, or 7-to-10-year-old red Bordeaux.

# Stuffed Veal Breast

When displayed, breast of veal appears unpromising: a bony, irregularly shaped chunk. But it is a versatile meat and relatively cheap. Once stuffed, it is ready to be transformed into a delicious meal. Veal breast is usually sold in two pieces. Always ask for the ribbed half of the breast closest to the loin section; it is the more symmetrical piece and is easier to stuff. Here, both the stuffing and the Eastern spices permeate and brighten the delicate taste of the veal. The liquid resulting from the slow braising process makes a subtle blend of East-West flavoring that serves well as a sauce for the veal. The dish is excellent hot or cold and should be served with your favorite vegetables.

STUFFING

| | |
|---|---|
| *1 tablespoon olive oil* | *½ cup finely chopped blanched* |
| *1 pound ground pork* | *parsnips* |
| *1 tablespoon finely chopped shallots* | *2 tablespoons finely chopped sun-* |
| *½ cup chopped leeks* | *dried tomatoes* |
| *½ cup finely chopped blanched* | *Salt and freshly ground black* |
| *carrots* | *pepper to taste* |

| | |
|---|---|
| *One 3½- to 4-pound veal breast* | *2 teaspoons sesame oil* |
| *2 tablespoons olive oil* | *2 tablespoons finely chopped ginger* |
| *2 tablespoons light soy sauce* | *2 to 4 cups water* |

In a medium-sized skillet or wok, heat the olive oil and brown the meat. Add the remaining stuffing ingredients and cook for 5 minutes over low heat. Allow the stuffing to cool.

With a small sharp knife, cut an opening on the largest side of the breast. Expand the opening with your fingers, pushing up the top layer. Place the stuffing in the opening and pack it tightly. Seal the opening with string or wooden skewers.

In a large casserole, heat 2 tablespoons of olive oil and brown the stuffed veal breast. Add the soy sauce, sesame oil, ginger, and 2 cups of water. Bring the cooking liquid to a simmer, cover, and braise gently for 1 hour, or until tender. Add more water if necessary. Remove the meat with a slotted spoon, allow it to rest for 20 minutes, and remove the string. Cut the stuffed veal into slices crosswise between the bones. Briefly

*Serves 4 to 6*

reduce the cooking liquid, moisten the veal slices with the sauce, and serve.

*Wine Suggestion:* simple, straightforward Chiantis, young California Zinfandels, or fresh red table wines would accompany this dish well.

# Broiled T-Bone Steak with Oyster Sauce and Bok Choy

This was among my first encounters with East-West dishes, and it represents to me the naturalness of blending the two traditions. It was one of the most popular specialties at the restaurant where I served my apprenticeship; by popular, I mean with Americans. The Chinese eat beef, but there are no T-bone steaks in China. The oyster sauce seemed quite unexceptionable to the patrons, and the bok choy was relished. Clearly, the T-bone steak was reassuringly familiar and powerful enough to lead the customers past the cultural barriers; the point remains that people ate, enjoyed, and accepted the East-West blend. It is a simple but very satisfying dish, especially if you desire a substantial meal in a hurry.

*2 tablespoons sesame oil*
*Two 1-pound T-bone steaks*
*Salt and freshly ground black pepper to taste*

*2 pounds bok choy, prepared as on page 42*
*2 tablespoons oyster sauce*

Rub sesame oil on the steaks and season them with salt and pepper. Make a charcoal fire and, when the coals are ash white, grill the steaks. While the meat is cooking, briefly blanch the bok choy. Remove the bok choy and make a bed of it on a serving platter. Transfer the steak to a cutting board and cut into 1-inch slices crosswise. Arrange the meat on top of the bok choy, cover with a ribbon of oyster sauce, and serve.

*Serves 2 to 4*

*Wine Suggestion:* avoiding the temptation of a good-quality cold beer, this dish could show off some fine wines from Bordeaux, from vintages like 1974 and 1977.

# Country-Style Pork Stew

This is among my favorite foods, East or West. It is simple in conception, easy to put together, hearty, flavorful, and pleasing to look at. It is, in fact, a peasant dish but one sanctified by time and countless appreciative palates. The recipe builds upon the Western idea of a stew, to which I add classic Eastern spices and flavorings. The rock sugar imparts a glow to the dish while the pork bears the sprightly sauce with aplomb. The dish reheats very well and is perfect on winter evenings.

2 pounds country-style spareribs, cut into 1-inch cubes
1 tablespoon peanut oil
½ cup finely chopped leeks
8 ounces carrots, roll-cut
1 tablespoon sesame paste
2 tablespoons hoisin sauce
1 tablespoon chopped fresh or dried thyme

Salt and freshly ground black pepper to taste
2 teaspoons rock sugar
½ cup rice wine
2 cups Basic Chicken Stock, page 67
1 pound white potatoes, cut into large pieces

Blanch the ribs in boiling water for 2 minutes. Remove with a slotted spoon and drain on paper towels. In a wok or large skillet, heat the peanut oil and brown the meat. Add the leeks and cook for 2 minutes. Transfer the ribs and leeks to a clay pot or Dutch oven and add the rest of the ingredients except the potatoes. Cover and simmer gently for 25 minutes. Add the potatoes and cook 15 minutes more. Turn off the heat and skim the fat from the surface. Serve immediately.

*Serves 4 to 6*

*Wine Suggestion:* young, fruity red wines such as Beaujolais, California Gamay, or light Zinfandels.

# Lamb Chops with Leeks

Americans share with Chinese a certain coolness toward lamb; we eat but a few pounds of it per capita per year. This is unfortunate because lamb is delicious when well prepared and not overcooked. In this recipe I choose the choicest cut: loin lamb chops. The lamb retains its vigorous taste but the leeks have great character, and together with the garlic, rice wine, and seasoned salt, they nicely tame the meat. This is an easy but richly flavorful dish.

Three 12-ounce to 1-pound loin lamb
  chops
  1½ teaspoons Chinese Seasoned Salt,
    page 42
    1 tablespoon peanut oil
    1 tablespoon finely chopped leeks

1 tablespoon finely chopped garlic
2 tablespoons rice wine
1 cup shredded leeks
1 cup Basic Chicken Stock, page 67
1 tablespoon butter

Dust the chops with the Chinese seasoned salt. Heat a wok or medium-sized skillet and add the oil. Brown the lamb and remove with a slotted spoon. Add the chopped leeks and garlic, and stir-fry for 30 seconds. Add the rice wine, shredded leeks, and chicken stock. Cook over high heat until the leeks are tender. Turn down the heat. Return the lamb and cook for 5 minutes, turning frequently. Remove the lamb to a warm serving platter. Add the butter to the leeks and stir. Spoon the leek sauce over the lamb and serve.

*Serves 2 or 3*

*Wine Suggestion:* an opportunity for the finest red wines, outstanding California Cabernets from the mid-seventies, or fine Châteaux from Bordeaux, 10 years or older.

# Anise-Clove Pork Ragout

I enjoy pork in almost any mode—it is a favorite meat of mine. Pork is so tasty and succulent; it has such character and is yet so agreeable with other foods. It therefore provides me an opportunity to play, to experiment. Here, I take one of my favorite cuts of pork and slowly infuse into it a zesty blend of East-West spices and seasonings. I prepare the vegetables partly in my traditional Chinese way, cutting them into small pieces, and partly in the nouvelle cuisine manner—the pieces diced, not sliced. Everything then simmers together at the end. The result is an attractive and flavorful dish. It is easy to prepare and reheats well. I like to serve it with rice or pasta.

*3 pounds boneless country-style spareribs, cut into 2-inch cubes*
*1 tablespoon peanut oil*
*3 whole star anise*
*6 whole cloves*
*Salt and freshly ground black pepper to taste*
*3 tablespoons finely chopped shallots*
*1 cup Tomato Concassé, page 70*
*3 tablespoons hoisin sauce*
*3 tablespoons dark soy sauce*

*2 tablespoons light soy sauce*
*2 tablespoons plum sauce*
*1½ cups sauterne*
*2 cups Basic Chicken Stock, page 67*
*8 ounces carrots, blanched and finely diced*
*8 ounces parsnips, blanched and finely diced*
*8 ounces turnips, blanched and finely diced*

Blanch the ribs in boiling water for 2 minutes. Remove with a slotted spoon and drain on paper towels.

Heat a wok or large skillet, add the oil, and brown the ribs. Transfer the ribs to a large clay pot or Dutch oven. Add the remaining ingredients except the vegetables. Cover and simmer gently for 45 minutes, or until the meat is tender. Add the vegetables and simmer 5 minutes more. Skim off the fat from the surface and serve.

*Serves 4 to 6*

*Wine Suggestion:* simple, straightforward wines, such as Beaujolais, light Zinfandels, or Italian Chiantis.

# Crépinette of Pork and Chinese Sausage

This dish is an easy way to make your own homemade sausage. "Crepinettes" are named after the French technique of wrapping a savory meat and vegetable mixture in a caul or crépine, the fatty membrane that covers a pig's intestines. The caul fat is quite edible, with a mild rich flavor. Specialty butchers can supply you with caul; if none is available, you can wrap the stuffing in thin strips of fatback or bacon, tucking the ends under to form a sack. Here, I mix pork and Chinese sausage meat, along with a rich blend of Western herbs, resulting in a most palatable filling.

Once made, the crépinettes will keep in the refrigerator for hours before cooking; be assured that leftovers, if any, are delicious. The basil leaves give the crépinette a colorful look and subtle taste; if you wish, you may substitute fresh coriander or parsley.

*1 pound ground pork*
*1 cup (about 8 ounces) finely diced*
  *Chinese pork sausage*
*1 tablespoon chopped fresh thyme*
*1 tablespoon chopped fresh marjoram*

*½ teaspoon ground cumin*
  *Salt and freshly ground black pepper*
  *to taste*
*8 ounces caul fat*
*Basil leaves*

In a medium-sized bowl, mix the ground pork, pork sausage, herbs, cumin, salt, and pepper.

Cut the caul fat into 15 5-inch squares. Lay out a square of caul fat and place several tablespoons of pork onto 1 end. Place a basil leaf on top of the pork and fold the sides in to form a package. Repeat until you have used all the pork.

In a large nonstick skillet, brown the crépinettes over low heat, turning them frequently. Cook for 10 minutes, or until they are done. Serve immediately.

*Serves 6 to 8
as a first
course*

*Wine Suggestion:* well-made California Chardonnays, 3 to 5 years old, or a fine white Burgundy such as Puligny-Montrachet, 5 to 7 years old.

# Braised Oxtails in Plum Sauce

Oxtails, as with beef in general, transcend East and West cuisines. Understandably, because of their relative scarcity, oxtails are more appreciated in Eastern diets: In ancient China it was often forbidden to slaughter oxen because of their value as work animals. And in the West, ironically, because of the relative abundance of beef, oxtails are ignored or slighted. Such neglect is undeserved. Properly prepared, as in this recipe, in the slow-cooking, moist heat, braising method, oxtails are a succulent and flavorful treat. This is especially true when the oxtails are simmered in such an Eastern-inspired sauce as this, with flavors of lemon, plum, rice wine, and chicken stock. The slightly preserved fruity flavor offers a delicate contrast to the robust taste of the oxtails. With the potatoes and olives, we are back in the West. This hearty and economical meal is ideal for cold weather, and it reheats nicely.

If you are unable to get lemon sauce, substitute more plum sauce.

*3 pounds oxtails*
*4 cups Basic Chicken Stock, page 67*
*3 tablespoons plum sauce*
*3 tablespoons lemon sauce*

*1 cup rice wine*
*1 pound white potatoes, peeled and*
*cut into large pieces*
*½ cup Nice olives*

Blanch the oxtails for 10 minutes in boiling water. Remove with a slotted spoon and drain in a colander.

In a large clay pot or Dutch oven, combine the oxtails, chicken stock, plum sauce, lemon sauce, and rice wine. Simmer, covered, for 1½ hours, or until the oxtails are tender. Skim the fat from the surface. Add the potatoes and cook 15 minutes more. Add the olives, heat them through, and then serve.

*Serves 4 to 6*

*Wine Suggestion:* simple, refreshing red wines such as Beaujolais (nouveau if possible), Gamay, and Chianti, served slightly chilled.

# Braised Sweetbreads in Spicy Bean Sauce

Sweetbreads are not uncommon in Chinese cuisine, but I did not know of them as a child and didn't taste them until I went to Europe. I found them tasty and loved their rich texture. They are worth seeking out, even though they require a bit of work. Sweetbreads are enjoyable, as in this recipe, within the context of a flavorful Eastern sauce that preserves their taste and texture. Their ability to pair with other flavorings makes the time and work well worth the effort. This dish reheats well and may be prepared a day in advance.

*2 pounds sweetbreads*
*1 tablespoon peanut oil*
*1 tablespoon ground bean sauce*
*1 tablespoon chili bean paste*
*3 tablespoons tomato paste*

*Salt and pepper to taste*
*2 cups Basic Chicken Stock, page 67*
*1 tablespoon sugar*
*8 ounces carrots, finely diced*
*8 ounces turnips, finely diced*

The night before you plan to cook the sweetbreads, rinse them and soak them in cold water for 2 hours. Place them in a pot of cold water. Bring the water slowly to a simmer and cook the sweetbreads for 2 minutes. Remove with a slotted spoon and drain on paper towels. Peel the skin. Line a baking sheet with a single layer of paper towels, place the sweetbreads on the towels, and cover the sweetbreads with another layer of towels and a baking sheet. Weigh it down with several pounds. Leave overnight in the refrigerator.

Cut the sweetbreads into 2-inch pieces. Heat the peanut oil in a medium-sized pot and brown the sweetbreads. Add all the ingredients except the vegetables. Bring the sweetbreads to a simmer, cover, and gently braise for 30 minutes. Add the vegetables and cook 15 minutes more.

*Serves 4 to 6*    Serve immediately.

*Wine Suggestion:* a young Beaujolais-style wine or a straightforward California Gamay.

# Stuffed Leg of Lamb

Lamb has a strong and assertive taste. I believe it is improved when it must work with or even against a distinctive and equally assertive stuffing or sauce. In this roast leg of lamb I employ a mixture of Eastern and Western spices and condiments as a stuffing. The lamb is certainly affected by these seasonings, but its essential taste remains clearly present and, I believe, appetizingly enhanced. Any leftovers will be equally as tasty. You can also use this stuffing for a breast of lamb, applying the same technique as in Stuffed Veal Breast (page 183).

STUFFING

4 ounces black mushrooms, prepared
    as on page 45
1 tablespoon olive oil
3 tablespoons chopped sun-dried
    tomatoes

2 teaspoons chopped ginger
2 teaspoons chopped scallions
2 tablespoons chopped fresh
    coriander

One 3½- to 4-pound boned leg of lamb
2 teaspoons Chinese Seasoned Salt,
    page 42

Coarsely chop the mushrooms. In a medium-sized skillet, heat the oil and cook the mushrooms, tomatoes, ginger, scallions, and coriander for 2 minutes. Allow the stuffing to cool.

Preheat the oven to 400 degrees.

Spread the stuffing over the inside of the lamb. Carefully roll it up, secure with string, and place in a baking dish. Dust the lamb with the Chinese seasoned salt. Roast for 20 minutes. Reduce the heat to 350 degrees and cook the meat 1 hour more. Let the meat rest for 20 minutes before carving.

*Serves 4 to 6*

*Wine Suggestion:* a well-aged classified Bordeaux, 7-plus years, or a fine California Cabernet from the Napa Valley.

# Hoisin Pork Chops

There are times when nothing tastes quite as good as a meal that is satisfying, easy and, most important, quickly prepared. This is a no-fuss but quality dish that you can put together in little time but with great satisfaction. A few classic Eastern seasonings, a quick dip in the marinade, onto the grill with them, and you are home free. For those who are not as partial to pork chops as I am, lamb chops or small steaks may be substituted.

2 tablespoons hoisin sauce
2 pounds pork chops
1 teaspoon Chinese Seasoned Salt,
 page 42

½ teaspoon cayenne pepper
½ teaspoon cumin
 1 teaspoon salt

Spread the hoisin sauce on the pork chops and cover with the spices. Make a charcoal fire and, when the coals are ash white, grill the pork chops for 5 to 10 minutes on each side, depending on their thickness. Serve immediately.

*Serves 4*

*Wine Suggestion:* try a Pinot Noir Blanc, a richer white Cabernet, or an unusual Sancerre rosé.

# Grilled Eastern-Flavored Lamburgers

I first recognized the versatility of lamb during a brief stay in Morocco, where lamb is a diet staple. My Chinese heritage, which rather disdains lamb, did not prepare me for my encounter with it. In Morocco and in other places since then, I learned to appreciate its possibilities. Here, for example, I use ground lamb. This literally opens up the meat to other flavors—in this case, certain traditional Eastern seasonings—that enhance and balance and mute its own distinctive but somewhat assertive taste. The grilling technique is appropriate, for it allows most of the not very savory lamb fat to melt off, leaving the lamb itself tasting better. This dish is a fine alternative to grilled beef and adds a variety to any barbecue.

*1 pound ground lamb*
*1 tablespoon chopped garlic*
*1 tablespoon chopped ginger*
*2 teaspoons sesame oil*

*1 tablespoon Chinese Seasoned Salt,*
  *page 42*
*3 tablespoons chopped scallions*

In a medium-sized bowl, combine all the ingredients. Make four burgers. Make a charcoal fire and, when the coals are ash white, grill the burgers for 5 minutes on each side. Serve on buns with traditional hamburger condiments.

*Serves 4*

*Wine Suggestion:* a light California Pinot Noir, 3 to 5 years old, or a more straightforward southern red Burgundy such as Montagny, Rully, or Mercurey.

# My Mother's Braised East-West Oxtail Stew

The Chinese cuisine is famous for its receptivity and for the flexibility and adaptability of its techniques. This recipe demonstrates these virtues.

My mother—who to this day speaks only Chinese—often prepares braised oxtail stew, a dish that turns out to be a delicious combination of East and West. Although oxtail is a venerable Chinese food, the tomato-based stew is a Western concept adopted in China a scant one hundred years ago. The soy sauce used in the recipe is of course a staple in Asian cookery; the use of carrots, turnips, and potatoes is strictly Western in spirit. Combined as they are, using Chinese techniques, these different East-West ingredients result in a deliciously hearty dish that contains the best of both cultures.

This East-West oxtail stew is very easy to make, reheats well, and tastes even better when reheated. A perfect autumn or winter dish with plain rice. This recipe has the Asian balance of meat and vegetables: more vegetables than meat. If you like, you can add more oxtails *without* changing the recipe.

| | |
|---|---|
| 2 to 2¼ pounds oxtails | Zest from 1 lemon |
| 4 cups Tomato Concassé, page 70, or imported canned tomatoes, drained | 2 tablespoons light soy sauce<br>Salt and freshly ground black pepper to taste |
| 1 tablespoon olive oil | 1 pound carrots, peeled and cut into |
| 1 tablespoon peanut oil | 1-inch pieces |
| ½ cup yellow onions, peeled and coarsely chopped | 1 pound turnips, peeled and cut into 1-inch pieces |
| 2 tablespoons finely chopped garlic | 8 ounces potatoes, peeled and cut into |
| 3 tablespoons plum sauce | 1-inch pieces |
| 2 tablespoons hoisin sauce | ½ cup Nice olives |
| ½ cup rice wine or dry sherry | |

Blanch the oxtails for 10 minutes in boiling water, drain well in a colander, and pat dry with paper towels.

Put the tomatoes into the container of a food processor and blend for just a few seconds or put them through a food mill. Set aside.

Heat a heavy casserole pot over moderate heat, add the olive and peanut oils, and slowly brown the oxtails on all sides. Remove them with a slotted spoon and pour off the excess fat and oil, leaving just 1 tablespoon. Add the onions and garlic, and cook for a few minutes until they are translucent.

Add to the onions and garlic the oxtails, tomatoes, plum sauce, hoisin sauce, rice wine, lemon zest, soy sauce, salt, and pepper. Bring the mixture to a boil, lower the heat, cover, and simmer for 1½ hours, or until the oxtails are tender. Skim the fat from the surface from time to time.

Add the carrots, turnips, and potatoes and cook, covered, for 20 minutes more. Add the olives and heat them through. Skim off any surface fat and serve at once.

*Wine Suggestion:* an opportunity to use a fine French red Burgundy or a good quality California (Carneros) or Oregon Pinot Noir.

# VEGETABLES

Carrot-Ginger Purée
Stewed Parsnips
Potato Purée with Scallions
Stir-Fried Snow Peas with
    Carrots
Vegetable Pasta
Cornmeal-Scallion-Ginger
    Waffles
Scallion-Corn Soufflé
Grilled Corn and Scallions
    with Soy Butter

Chinese Ratatouille
Rice Wine Mushrooms
Turnip-Parsnip-Ginger
    Purée
Asparagus in Soy-Butter
    Sauce
Bok Choy-Sweet Rice
    Casserole
Stir-Fried Water Spinach
    with Garlic

Chinese Eggplant with
    Spinach-Ginger Stuffing
Braised East-West
    Mushrooms
Stir-Fried Summer
    Vegetables with Chinese
    Vinegar
Fried Potato Chips
    (Pommes Gaufrettes)

 Always buy the freshest vegetables in season, looking for firmness, freshness in appearance, and fragrance. And once you've got them home, rule number one on the cooking list should be: *Don't overcook them!* Give them the same attention and care as you would meat, fish, and fowl dishes. Vegetables are not merely accompaniments or complements to the main entree, they are also—or they can be—wonderfully tasty and highly nutritious foods in their own right. Those gourmets and gourmands are on the right path who maintain that the first indication of a quality restaurant is the freshness, taste, and succulence of its vegetable dishes.

Good cooks generally agree that the Chinese stir-frying method of cooking vegetables is the best way to prepare them. Stir-frying preserves the flavor, texture, colors, and nutrients of vegetables while rendering them even tastier and more palatable. The intense heat of the skillet or wok seals in the vegetables' juices and flavors, while the rapid tossing of the vegetables allows them to cook with little loss of nutrients (there being no water to dissolve them). It is a technique that deserves wide use, and I heartily recommend it.

Vegetables are almost never puréed in Chinese cookery because the process destroys the distinctive textures of the food. Among Westerners, however, and especially the French, puréed vegetables are common and popular. A pureed vegetable goes well with entrees that are coarsely textured and need to be set off by a subtle complemental dish. It is always appropriate to think in terms of complementary textures as well as flavors, tastes, and colors.

Stewed vegetables are more common than puréed dishes in Eastern cooking, and I include an East-West sample in my recipes, namely, stewed parsnips. Parsnips are among my favorite vegetables because of their earthy and distinct taste, although they are unknown in China. Carrots, however, are a great favorite, and it is the European carrot that is eaten. In the centuries after 1500 the indigenous root crops were replaced by the carrot because it is more nutritious, easier to produce and to prepare, and is less coarse and fibrous. I am happy to acknowledge this Western contribution to venerable Chinese cuisine!

<u>POTATOES</u>
<u>AND</u>
<u>TOMATOES</u>

Potatoes are not a common Eastern food, but we Westerners have had them as a staple in our diets for about two hundred years. I have enjoyed them since I can remember, especially pureed or mashed. My mother always mashed them with a fork so that bits of potatoes remained. Some people would say they were "lumpy," but to my mother (and to me) it was merely paying homage to the Chinese rule of contrasting and balancing textures. Commercial forms of pureed potatoes never satisfy my palate. They are starchy, without flavor, and have an "instant" taste, invoking memories of the potatoes I had at school that tasted like wallpaper paste. Good fresh Idahos are always preferable.

As for the tomato, it is neither of the East nor the West but rather of the New World. It was used in Europe only after the sixteenth century and introduced into China about one hundred years ago. In both East and West it transformed the cuisine while providing a new and valuable source of vitamins and minerals.

One important reminder: Most commercial varieties of tomatoes have been rendered thick-skinned and tasteless in an effort to make them transportable and longer-lasting from harvest to consumption. Buy tomatoes, then, only in your season or, better yet, grow your own. Commercially produced cherry tomatoes have not yet been subjected to the treatment accorded "beefsteak" tomatoes; they are available year-round and should be eaten plain. If you are lucky, they will be flavorful. Some cooks prefer Italian plum tomatoes, either fresh or canned imported, for a number of tomato sauce recipes.

It is worth experimenting with the various tomato types, as the Chinese cooks did when the first tomatoes made their appearance in China.

# Carrot-Ginger Purée

Purées make many people think of baby food: bland, soft, and mushy. But while all baby food is puréed, not all purées are meant for babies, as this easy-to-make and delicious recipe demonstrates. A puréed vegetable goes well with entrées that are coarsely textured and need to be set off by a subtle complemental dish. The Chinese almost never purée anything, but they especially refrain from applying the technique to vegetables, fearing that their distinctive textures will be lost. Among Westerners, especially the French, puréed vegetables are common, perhaps partly because it is considered bad form to include the same form of a vegetable twice in the same meal. Thus, a chef may serve carrots twice, but one will be boiled or sautéed and the other puréed.

To avoid the baby food syndrome, stop processing the carrots while they still have some of their coarse or grainy texture. Puréed carrots reheat nicely and may be prepared a day or two in advance.

*Salt*
*1 pound carrots, peeled and thinly*
*    sliced*
*3 thin slices ginger*
*4 tablespoons butter*

*⅓ cup sour cream*
*    Freshly ground white pepper to taste*
*2 tablespoons finely chopped*
*    coriander*

*Serves 4*

Add 1 teaspoon of salt to boiling water in a medium-sized pot and cook the carrots and ginger for 5 minutes, or until the carrots are tender. Drain the carrots and discard the ginger slices. In a food processor or food mill, partially purée the carrots, adding the butter and sour cream as you go. Add salt and pepper to taste and, just before serving, fold in the coriander.

# Stewed Parsnips

This dish has an added attraction in that it may be reheated with no real loss of flavor.

*1 pound parsnips, peeled and roll-cut*
*2 tablespoons butter*
*1 cup Basic Chicken Stock, page 67*
*½ cup Crème Fraîche, page 43*

*Salt and freshly ground white pepper*
*to taste*
*½ cup coriander leaves, loosely packed*

*Serves 2 to 4*

In a medium-sized skillet, simmer the parsnips, butter, chicken stock, crème fraîche, salt, and pepper for 10 minutes, or until the parsnips are tender. Turn up the heat to high, add the coriander leaves, and cook 5 minutes more. The liquid should be reduced by half. Serve at once.

# Potato Purée with Scallions

Here, I improve upon good, old-fashioned puréed potatoes by adding a touch of Eastern flavor—scallions. Puréed potatoes are rich, especially when lightened with cream and butter. The chopped scallions give a lightness and bite to the dish—these potatoes are anything but bland.

*2 pounds russet potatoes, peeled and*
*cut into 1-inch cubes*
*½ cup (1 stick) butter, at room*
*temperature*

*1 cup half-and-half*
*¼ cup finely chopped scallions*
*Salt and freshly ground black pepper*
*to taste*

*Serves 4 to 6*

In a large saucepan, cook the potatoes in boiling water for 15 to 20 minutes, or until tender. Drain and transfer the potatoes to a mixing bowl. Add the butter and ½ cup of the half-and-half. Using a whisk or large fork, whip the potatoes until smooth, gradually incorporating the remaining half-and-half. Blend in the scallions and season to taste.

# Stir-Fried Snow Peas with Carrots

Snow peas are increasingly popular in America, especially among younger chefs. They were once relatively expensive and hard to find, but they are becoming readily available and decreasing in price. Grown in one's own garden, they are even better.

Traditionally, snow peas are stir-fried with rice wine and soy sauce, but these flavorings, to my mind, tend to clash with the sweet delicateness of the snow peas. I prefer shallots, butter, salt, and pepper. Snow peas and carrots make a delicious and colorful vegetable accompaniment to any main dish. They may be served hot or at room temperature.

*2 medium-sized carrots, cut into
    julienne strips 2 inches by ¼ inch
1½ tablespoons butter
1½ tablespoons finely minced shallots*

*1 pound snow peas, with ends
    trimmed
Salt and freshly ground black
    pepper to taste*

In a medium-sized pot, blanch the carrots for 2 minutes in boiling water. Rinse under cold running water and drain well. Heat a wok or medium-sized skillet over low heat, add the butter and shallots, and stir-fry for 1 minute. Add the carrots and snow peas and stir-fry 30 seconds more. Add 1 or 2 tablespoons of water and stir-fry until the vegetables are tender. Season with salt and pepper, and serve at once.

*Serves 4*

# Vegetable Pasta

Here vegetables are cut into long, thin, spaghettilike strips and cooked using the Eastern technique of stir-frying. The flavorings are distinctively Western in concept. Olive oil has a lower burning temperature than most other cooking oils, so it is combined with peanut oil. This dish can be made ahead of time and served at room temperature with a splash of fresh lemon juice or a mild vinegar. For a nuttier flavor, add 2 teaspoons of sesame oil and increase the peanut oil.

*2 pounds small zucchini, cut into long
  julienne strips*
*1 tablespoon coarse salt*
*2 tablespoons olive oil*
*1 tablespoon peanut oil*
*2 teaspoons sesame oil*
*4 garlic cloves, peeled and thinly sliced*
*8 ounces thin asparagus, cut into
  2-inch sections*

*3 sweet red or yellow peppers, or a
  combination of the two, seeded,
  deribbed, and shredded lengthwise*
*1 cup fresh sweet peas (about 1 pound
  of pods), blanched*
*2 cups basil leaves*
*Salt and freshly ground black pepper
  to taste*

Sprinkle the zucchini with salt, place the strips in a colander, and let them sweat for 30 minutes. Wrap the zucchini in a kitchen towel and squeeze out the liquid. Set aside.

    In a wok or large skillet, heat the olive, peanut, and sesame oils. Add the garlic and stir-fry for 15 seconds. Add the asparagus, peppers, and peas. Stir-fry for 1 minute. Add the zucchini and stir-fry 2 minutes more. Toss in the basil leaves and, when they wilt, add the salt and pepper, and serve. If you like, you may serve freshly grated Parmesan cheese on the side for a mock pasta.

*Serves 4 to 6*

# Cornmeal-Scallion-Ginger Waffles

When well made and served with the appropriate accompaniments, waffles are a treat. Of northern European origin, they were already a common dish in America by 1800. Thomas Jefferson is supposed to have brought over the first waffle iron, but even earlier the Dutch settlers in New Amsterdam had introduced waffles to Colonial kitchens. Like pancakes, waffles lend themselves to many food combinations. Cornmeal waffles are a particularly delicate, tasteful, and rather more colorful version. They are mild, unassuming, and congenial breads, their mildness given a crispiness, a crunchiness, by the characteristic surface ridges that distinguish them. Here, I have given the waffles even more of a lift by adding a traditional Eastern seasoning of scallions and ginger. Roast squab or roast chicken served on a bed of such waffles, which soak up the juices running from the roasted bird, is an appetizing sight and a delicious meal.

The batter may be made hours in advance, but the waffles themselves must be made at the last moment.

*1 cup coarse yellow cornmeal*
*1 teaspoon salt*
*2 medium-sized egg whites*
*8 tablespoons (1 stick) butter, melted*
*2 teaspoons sesame oil*
*1 medium-sized egg yolk*

*½ cup flour*
*1 teaspoon baking powder*
*¾ cup milk*
*3 tablespoons finely chopped scallions*
*2 teaspoons finely chopped ginger*

In a small pan, bring the water to a boil, add the cornmeal and salt, and cook for 5 minutes. Allow it to cool.

Beat the egg whites until they are stiff, then set them aside.

In a food processor or a large bowl, combine the remaining ingredients. Be careful not to overmix.

Incorporate the cooked cornmeal and then gently fold in the egg whites.

Grease both sides of a hot waffle iron with melted butter or peanut oil. Pour the batter into the bottom half, close the top, and cook until browned. Repeat until all the batter is used. Keep the waffles warm in the oven until ready to serve.

*Makes 8 to 10 waffles*

# Scallion-Corn Soufflé

We tend to take our most common foods, such as corn, for granted. When my mother was a bit pressed for time she would transform kernels of corn into a delicious meal in a matter of minutes, using stir-fried corn, eggs, salt, pepper, and scallions. In my mother's hands, corn was always the basis for excellent dining, and I have never forgotten how adaptable that vegetable is.

My experience with soufflés in France—light, airy, delicious—led me to this corn soufflé. I use no flour in it, an idea prompted by a friend's allergy to flour. It is more fragile than a soufflé with flour; the starch in the corn suffices to hold the ingredients together. A fine East-West combination results when the soufflé is paired with Ginger-Tomato Sauce (page 76).

I use a tin-lined charlotte mold because it gets quite hot, hotter than a porcelain soufflé dish. This soufflé makes an elegant first course for any dinner.

*2 tablespoons butter*
*3 cups corn kernels, cut from 5 to 6 medium-sized ears*
*½ cup finely chopped scallions*
*½ cup heavy cream*
*Salt and freshly ground white pepper to taste*

*5 egg yolks*
*6 egg whites*
*Ginger-Tomato Sauce, page 76, full recipe*

In a large skillet, melt the butter and sauté the corn and scallions for 3 minutes. Add the cream and simmer 5 minutes more, uncovered. Season with salt and pepper.

Set aside ½ cup of the corn and purée the rest in a blender or food processor. Pour the puréed corn into a medium-sized bowl and mix in the egg yolks, stirring continuously. Add the reserved ½ cup of corn and set aside.

Butter a 2-quart tin charlotte mold and place it in the refrigerator.

Preheat the oven to 450 degrees. Beat the egg whites with a pinch of salt until they are firm with soft peaks.

Pour boiling water into a baking dish large enough to hold the mold and place the baking dish in the oven.

Mix one-fourth of the beaten egg whites into the corn mixture. Fold the rest in gently. Place the soufflé in the baking dish and turn down the temperature to 350 degrees. Cook for 40 minutes, or until a skewer placed in the center of the soufflé comes out clean.

*Serves 4 to 6*     Serve at once with the ginger-tomato sauce.

# Grilled Corn and Scallions with Soy Butter

Here is a true East-West marriage of flavors, textures, and colors. Corn is a relatively recent addition to the Chinese diet, as it is in fact to the Western cuisine—a New World vegetable that traveled both East and West. The scallions and soy sauce are typically Chinese, while the butter is a Western ingredient relatively unknown in China. The recipe involves an alternative technique to the usual boiled or steamed corn, namely grilling. I use dark soy sauce here because its deep rich flavor and color is better with the golden corn than the saltier light soy sauce. It also blends very well with the butter, combining to form a distinctive basting liquid. This dish is a wonderful accompaniment to grilled meat and seafood such as Grilled Mustard Chicken Thighs (page 138) and Grilled Crab and Lobster (page 109).

*6 tablespoons butter*      *4 ears sweet corn, shucked*
*2 tablespoons dark soy sauce*      *8 scallions, with tops trimmed*

In a small pan, combine the butter and soy sauce over low heat. Make a charcoal fire and, when the coals are ash white, grill the corn and scallions. Baste them with the soy butter and cook for 5 to 8 minutes, turning

*Serves 4*     frequently. Serve at once.

# Chinese Ratatouille

Simply defined, a ratatouille is a vegetable stew. But this is like saying a truffle is a fungus. It is true that the French *touiller* is a slang word meaning mix or stir, and that Cassell defines and translates the term as "coarse stew." However, the Provençal ratatouille and ragouts like it are much more than a mélange of vegetables tossed into a pot. Richard Olney writes of the "genial ratatouille, whose vegetables, intact but puree-tender, are cooked in a syrupy reduction of their own abundant juices. . . ." I propose a more Eastern variation of that description which better conveys my version of this dish.

I first prepared my Chinese vegetable ratatouille in 1982 on the occasion of Craig Claiborne's triple celebration: his sixty-second birthday, his twenty-fifth year with the *New York Times,* and the publication of his autobiography, *A Feast Made for Laughter.* I was one of the chefs and authors asked to honor him with a dish, and I offered this at his feast. It was held at the beginning of September, a time when fresh vegetables of many kinds are at their peak. I selected Eastern vegetables of distinctive tastes, colors, and textures, blending them into a spicy and well-seasoned stew. Instead of the traditional method of stewing the vegetables together, I cook them separately, then combine and stew them for a brief moment. It is, I believe, a delicious East-West variant of the Provençal classic.

It is well worth the effort to obtain the fresh Eastern vegetables, but if you cannot find them, by all means substitute fresh in-season domestic vegetables.

*8 ounces Chinese eggplant, roll-cut*
*8 ounces zucchini, roll-cut*
  *Salt*
*2 tablespoons butter*
*1 tablespoon olive oil*
*2 tablespoons finely chopped garlic*
*1 tablespoon finely chopped shallots*
*1 pound silk squash (Chinese okra),*
  *roll-cut*
*4 ounces baby carrots, peeled,*
  *blanched, and roll-cut*

*4 ounces fresh water chestnuts, peeled*
  *and sliced*
*1 cup Tomato Concassé, page 70*
*2 tablespoons finely chopped Chinese*
  *chives*
*2 tablespoons finely chopped chives*
*½ cup Thai (or Western) basil leaves*
  *Freshly ground black pepper to taste*
*¼ cup Basic Chicken Stock, page 67*

Place the eggplant and zucchini in a large colander and sprinkle with 2 teaspoons of salt. Let the vegetables sit for 30 minutes. Wrap them with a kitchen towel and squeeze out the moisture.

In a large skillet, heat the butter and olive oil. Add the garlic and shallots, and sauté for 1 minute. Add the eggplant, zucchini, silk squash, carrots, and water chestnuts. Cook for 2 minutes over medium heat. Add the tomato concassé, chives, basil, salt, pepper, and chicken stock. Simmer the ratatouille for 5 minutes, or until all the vegetables are cooked. Serve hot, at room temperature, or cold.

*Serves 6*

# Rice Wine Mushrooms

Here, a simple mushroom dish that is distinguished for its gentle power. The mushrooms retain their taste and charm, but are strengthened by the combined seasonings and flavorings. The dominant ingredient is the rice wine, rich and dry in a way reminiscent of sherry. The sauce is a perfect context for the mushrooms, and the result is a charming treat.

*1½ pounds fresh chanterelles or brown*
*    mushrooms*
*1 tablespoon olive oil*
*2 tablespoons finely chopped garlic*

*3 tablespoons rice wine*
*¼ cup fresh lemon juice*
*Salt and freshly ground black*
*    pepper to taste*

Remove any dirt from the mushrooms, using a towel. In a medium-sized skillet, heat the olive oil and sauté the garlic for 1 minute. Add the mushrooms, rice wine, lemon juice, salt, and pepper, and cook over high heat for 8 to 10 minutes, or until most of the liquid has evaporated. Serve immediately.

*Serves 4 to 6*

# Turnip-Parsnip-Ginger Purée

Turnips and parsnips are not high on the list of American favorites. In Europe they are treated with much more respect. Both vegetables, in different varieties, are found in the East and West, but I prefer the Western ones because I find them tastier than the Eastern versions. In this recipe you have the means to eat your turnips and have your parsnips too; both have their charm and virtues. Parsnips are as sweet as their carrot cousins, especially if they are thoroughly chilled before preparation. The cold sets off an enzyme reaction converting starch to sugar. Turnips have a robust flavor that must be tempered lest it overpower its blended neighbors. Here, I use the magic of ginger which both adds a zest to the dish and tames the turnip without neutralizing the sweet parsnips. Puréed foods are uncommon in Eastern cuisine, but it is a useful Western technique with wide applicability.

This dish goes well with poultry and meat, and is excellent in cold weather, when the vegetables are in abundance. Easily prepared, it holds its flavor and is eminently reheatable.

8 ounces turnips, blanched, peeled, and cut into large pieces
8 ounces parsnips, blanched, peeled, and cut into large pieces
2 tablespoons butter

2 teaspoons ginger
2 tablespoons scallions
Salt and freshly ground pepper to taste
¼ cup heavy cream

Purée the turnips and parsnips in a food mill or food processor. In a medium-sized skillet, heat the butter and sauté the ginger and scallions for 1 minute. Add the puréed vegetables, salt, pepper, and cream, and cook 5 minutes more over low heat. Serve at once.

*Serves 2 to 4*

# Asparagus in Soy-Butter Sauce

The Chinese diet, especially in the south, is remarkable for the variety of foods it includes. Blessed with a natural abundance, the southern Chinese are also open to new foods of foreign origin. One of the most recent adoptions is that delicious vegetable, asparagus, now grown commercially in Taiwan in large quantities. Moreover, asparagus has very quickly entered into the repertory of fine cooking in Hong Kong. Introduced there in the 1970s, it is now served regularly in homes and restaurants, where it is usually blanched or stir-fried. My favorite method, however, is to cook asparagus simply and very quickly in very little water. A sauce of Eastern soy and Western butter is prepared that preserves and enhances the essence of asparagus, and the sesame seeds add texture and flavor. This is an easy-to-make version of a wonderful vegetable.

*1 pound asparagus, with ends trimmed*
*1 cup water*
*1 teaspoon dark soy sauce*
*2 tablespoons butter*

*2 tablespoons heavy cream*
*1 teaspoon roasted sesame seeds for*
 *garnish*

Peel the skin from the bottom 2 inches of each asparagus stalk. In a medium-sized skillet, bring the water to a boil, add the asparagus, and reduce the heat to medium. Cook for 5 minutes. Remove the asparagus to a warm serving platter with a slotted spoon. Turn up the heat to high and reduce the cooking liquid to 2 tablespoons. Add the soy sauce, butter, and cream, stir, and remove from the heat. Pour over the asparagus and garnish with the sesame seeds. Serve at once.

*Serves 2 to 4*

# Bok Choy-Sweet Rice Casserole

When I lived in the south of France, my French "mother," Madame Taurines, often made a rice and spinach gratin dish that she called "tian." It was a delicious treat whose wonderful fragrance as it came out of the oven announced its pleasures and sharpened one's appetite. After my return to America, I often made adaptations of Madame Taurines' tian, using zucchini or artichoke in place of the spinach. In homage to her delicious recipe, to her southern French-Italian home cooking, I devised this Eastern version using sweet and sturdy bok choy and Chinese glutinous (or sweet) rice. The result captures the essentials of tian but with a delightful difference. This is an easy-to-make dish and is excellent either steaming hot or served at room temperature, which makes it a fine picnic treat.

1 cup glutinous rice
1 pound bok choy, as prepared on
   page 42
1 tablespoon olive oil
2 tablespoons chopped sun-dried
   tomatoes
3 tablespoons chopped garlic

Salt and freshly ground black pepper
   to taste
1 cup Basic Chicken Stock, page 67
6 medium-sized eggs, beaten
¼ cup finely chopped fresh coriander
3 tablespoons freshly grated Parmesan
   cheese

Cover the rice with water and soak it overnight.

Briefly blanch the bok choy and finely chop it. Drain the rice. In a wok or large skillet, heat the olive oil and add the sun-dried tomatoes, garlic, rice, salt, and pepper. Stir-fry for 1 minute. Add the chicken stock and cook until the liquid has evaporated. Let it cool.

Preheat the oven to 350 degrees. In a large bowl, combine the eggs, cooked rice, bok choy, and chopped coriander. Lightly oil a 12-inch gratin dish and pour in the egg-rice mixture. Sprinkle with Parmesan cheese and bake for 40 minutes, or until a skewer placed in the center comes out clean. Serve hot, at room temperature, or cold.

*Serves 6 to 8*

# Stir-Fried Water Spinach with Garlic

Water spinach is widely cultivated in tropical Asia, where it is prepared and served in many ways: soups, batter-fried, and stir-fried. It tastes like mild Western spinach, but its outstanding characteristic is the contrast between a crunchy stem and the soft wilt of its leaves. Be careful not to overcook the spinach. Once it wilts, it's cooked. If water spinach is unavailable, use fresh young spinach or watercress. Here, using the traditional stir-fry method, I quickly cook the delicate leaves and stems in a garlic-olive oil-basil mixture to create a very tasty vegetable treat.

*1 pound water spinach or watercress*
   *Salt to taste*
*1 tablespoon chopped garlic*

*1 tablespoon olive oil*
*2 tablespoons chopped fresh basil*

*Serves 2 to 4*

Remove the large tough stems from the water spinach and discard. Wash carefully to remove the sand. Drain well in a colander. In a wok or large skillet, stir-fry the salt and garlic in olive oil for 30 seconds. Add the water spinach and stir-fry for 1 minute. Add the basil, stir, and serve.

# Chinese Eggplant with Spinach-Ginger Stuffing

Asian eggplant, especially the long purple variety, is a traditional food in the East and among Mediterranean peoples. But eggplant is growing in popularity in the West. Eggplants are of many sizes, or lengths, and colors; I find the smaller varieties sweeter and more tender, but also more fragile, than the common American egg-shaped purple-black variety. Think of the eggplant as a sponge, capable of absorbing sauces and seasonings in a natural and congenial fashion. Here, combined with distinctive spinach and ginger flavors, in a sprightly many-seasons sauce, with eggs added for delicate taste and protein, the eggplant forms the substance of a delicious vegetarian meal. Western eggplant may, of course, be substituted.

2 pounds Chinese eggplant
Salt
1½ pounds (about 2 bunches) spinach
Olive oil for cooking the eggplant
1 tablespoon chopped fresh
lemongrass
2 teaspoons chopped ginger
1 tablespoon sesame oil

4 medium-sized eggs, beaten
1 teaspoon ground coriander
½ teaspoon ground cumin
3 tablespoons freshly grated
Parmesan cheese
Freshly ground black pepper to
taste

Cut the eggplant into thin slices lengthwise. If you are using large eggplants, cut off the tops, then cut them in half and into thin slices lengthwise. Place the eggplant in a colander and toss with 2 teaspoons of salt. Allow it to sit for 30 minutes, then wrap in a towel and squeeze out the liquid.

Wash and stem the spinach. Blanch it and wrap the leaves in a towel. Squeeze out the liquid and finely chop the spinach.

In a medium-sized bowl, combine the spinach and the rest of the ingredients, except the eggplant, seasoning to taste with salt and pepper. In a nonstick skillet, sauté the eggplant in olive oil over medium heat for 2 minutes on each side. Drain the slices on paper towels.

Preheat the oven to 400 degrees. Pour 2 inches of boiling water into a baking dish large enough to hold the mold and place the dish in the oven.

Line a 2-quart charlotte mold with the eggplant slices. Spoon in the spinach-egg mixture and cover the top with the remaining slices. Bake for 1 hour, or until a wooden skewer placed in the center comes out clean. Allow the mold to cool, cover with a plate, and invert it. The mold should slip out onto the plate. Discard any excess liquid. Cut into wedges and serve.

*Serves 8 to 10*

# Braised East-West Mushrooms

We tend to think of mushrooms as performing only in supporting roles. Properly prepared, however, mushrooms can take center stage. Here, I combine two types of mushrooms in an East-West seasoning that maintains their individuality and enhances their taste and texture. These are dried mushrooms that are soaked to restore them and then reheated with no loss of flavor.

*2 ounces dried cepe mushrooms*
*2 ounces black mushrooms, prepared as*
*  on page 45*
*2 tablespoons butter*
*2 tablespoons finely chopped shallots*

*2 teaspoons chopped ginger*
*1 pound fresh mushrooms, thinly sliced*
*2 tablespoons light soy sauce*
*2 tablespoons chopped fresh chives*
*1 cup half-and-half*

In a small bowl, soak the cepes in warm water for 30 minutes. Squeeze the excess water from the cepes by hand. Cut the black mushrooms into large slices. In a medium-sized skillet, heat the butter and add the shallots, ginger, and mushrooms. Sauté for 5 minutes. Add the soy sauce, chives, and half-and-half. Cook over moderate heat 10 minutes more, or until all the liquid has evaporated. Serve.

*Serves 4 to 6*

# Stir-Fried Summer Vegetables with Chinese Vinegar

Properly cooked young summer vegetables are one of the delights of warm weather. Here, they are seasoned with a touch of Chinese black vinegar, which is slightly sweet and mildly tart. It is very much like Italian balsamic vinegar, at once stimulating and reassuring.

*8 ounces red or yellow peppers*
*8 ounces small zucchini*
*8 ounces small carrots*
*1 tablespoon peanut oil*
*1 tablespoon olive oil*
*3 garlic cloves, peeled and crushed*
*½ cup Basic Chicken Stock, page 67*

*Salt and freshly ground black pepper to taste*
*2 tablespoons Chinese black rice vinegar*
*2 tablespoons finely chopped scallions for garnish*

Finely shred the pepper and set aside. Cut the zucchini in half.

In a medium-sized pot, blanch the carrots for 2 minutes in boiling salted water. Rinse under cold running water and drain well.

Heat a wok or medium-sized skillet over medium heat and add the peanut and olive oil. Add the garlic and stir-fry for 20 seconds, then add the peppers, zucchini, and carrots, and stir-fry for 1 minute. Add the chicken stock, salt, and pepper, and stir-fry until the vegetables are tender, 3 to 5 minutes. Season with the Chinese vinegar, garnish with the scallions, and serve at once.

*Serves 4*

# *Fried Potato Chips* (Pommes Gaufrettes)

These are classic fried potatoes, French-style. They are a fine accompaniment to meats but are delectable by themselves. In his classic *La Technique,* Jacques Pépin describes the appropriate method of preparing them. It is easy to do especially if you have a mandoline, a special device that assures even cutting. Simply slice the potatoes as thin and as even as possible. Another key to making these fried potatoes is to keep them in cold water for at least two hours and then dry them thoroughly before frying.

*1 pound potatoes, peeled*          *Salt to taste*
*4 cups peanut oil*

If you are using a mandoline, use the wrinkled or "teeth" blade: Hold each potato with the palm of your hand and cut straight down. Turn the potato 90 degrees and cut straight down in the other direction. Turn the potato 90 degrees for the next slice, and the result will be a crisscrossed slice. The slices should be about ⅛ inch thick.

Rinse the sliced potatoes gently in cold water to remove the starch. Cover them with cold water and leave in the refrigerator for at least 2 hours.

When you are ready to fry the potatoes, heat the oil to 375 degrees. Dry the potato slices gently and thoroughly. Deep-fry them until they are lightly brown and crisp. Salt to taste and serve at once.

*Serves 4*

# PASTA, NOODLES, AND RICE

Provençale Rice Noodles
Noodle Cake Stuffed with
  Basil and Tomatoes
Rice Noodles in Ginger-
  Tomato Sauce with Fresh
  Mushrooms

Chinese Greens-Stuffed
  Ravioli
Cannelloni Stuffed with
  Chinese Sausages
Rice Noodles Primavera

Pasta with Chinese
  Mushrooms and Morels
Duck Fried Rice
Pasta in Black Bean Sauce
  with Triple Tomatoes
Saffron Rice

Whatever its origins, it must be said that the Italians make the greatest pasta. Still, there is really no East or West when pasta lovers meet, though they come from opposite sides of the earth. The Chinese, after all, have almost as many varieties of pasta as the Italians. And they did invent rice noodles, which include among their virtues the property of not falling to pieces when things get hot. That is, in contrast to wheat-based noodles, they retain their shape when cooked in the sauce. This adds a welcome visual and textural pleasure to certain dishes.

The greatest virtue of fresh pasta is that, nutritious in itself, it provides a perfect base on which to build great dishes using meats, vegetables, sauces, and a wide variety of spices and seasonings. Only rice is comparable in this regard, and the recipes included here are a tribute to the sturdy virtues of these indispensable "fan" foods.

# Provençale Rice Noodles

Rice noodles are a staple in many Asian countries and figured prominently in our family's kitchen. Until recently they were rather a rare item in Western cooking. I began introducing them into my work when I discovered that a good friend was allergic to wheat-based foods. In this recipe I use thin rice noodles, a Thai and southern Chinese specialty. They have an interesting texture and a light, airy quality when cooked. Rice noodles share the same mildness as rice itself, which makes them quite adaptable to many different sauces and flavors.

Rich and varied Mediterranean flavors are used in tandem with an Eastern traditional spice, dried chilies. The mild noodles now shimmer with taste and zest. They are equally delectable served right from the skillet or at room temperature. They make a rewarding picnic or warm weather treat as well.

*8 ounces thin, dry rice noodles*
*3 tablespoons olive oil*
*3 dried hot red chilies, cut in half*
*2 tablespoons finely chopped garlic*
*1 teaspoon finely chopped fresh ginger*
*8 ounces zucchini, shredded*
*8 ounces sweet red peppers, seeded,*
  *deribbed, and shredded*

*2 tablespoons shredded sun-dried*
  *tomatoes*
  *Salt and freshly ground black pepper*
  *to taste*
*1 cup basil leaves*

Soak the rice noodles in warm water for about 30 minutes, then drain. Heat a wok or large skillet. Add the olive oil, dried chilies, garlic, and ginger, and stir-fry for 1 minute. Add the vegetables and sun-dried tomatoes, and stir-fry 2 minutes more. Add the rice noodles and stir-fry 5 minutes more. Season with salt and pepper, add the basil leaves, and mix thoroughly. Serve at once or as a cold noodle dish.

*Serves 4*

*Wine Suggestion:* an opportunity for fresh, straightforward white Zinfandel, or a simple rosé from Provence.

# Noodle Cake Stuffed with Basil and Tomatoes

This "cake" is in fact two layers of Chinese wheat-based egg noodles, familiar to Western cooking. In China the fresh thin noodles are slowly pan-fried into a golden crispness on one side, turned over, and then crisped on the other side. But the interior is left tender and soft, a delicious contrast of textures. Here, basil is used as a vegetable rather than a seasoning, and tomatoes provide a luxuriously tasteful filling for the cake. This noodle cake makes a pleasing bed for any shellfish dish, such as Shellfish in Black Bean and Butter Sauce (page 130), and a bed for Honey-Glazed Squab (page 145). It is a splendid alternative to potatoes and rice.

*1 pound Chinese thin fresh egg noodles*
*¼ cup olive oil*
*1 cup Asian or Western basil leaves*

*1 cup Tomato Concassé, page 70*
*Salt and freshly ground black pepper to taste*
*Water*

In a large pot, blanch the noodles for 1 minute. Drain and set aside. Heat a large nonstick skillet. Add 1 tablespoon of olive oil and half of the noodles. Pack the noodles tightly using a spatula. Add the basil, tomato concassé, salt, and pepper, and the other half of the noodles. Pack down the noodles. Reduce the heat to low, add a little more olive oil, and 1 or 2 tablespoons of water to moisten the noodles. Cook for 10 minutes, or until the noodles are crisp. Flip the noodle cake over, add a little more olive oil and water, and brown the other side. Remove from the skillet, cut into wedges, and serve.

*Serves 4*

*Wine Suggestion:* a rich, oily Chardonnay from the Côte de Beaune or a fine-quality California Chardonnay from Napa or Sonoma.

# Rice Noodles in Ginger-Tomato Sauce with Fresh Mushrooms

Chinese rice noodles include among their virtues the property of not falling to pieces when the heat is turned on. In this recipe the noodles are mingled in the sauce with two types of mushroom, the shiitake and the chanterelle. The result is a light, flavorful pasta enhanced by contrasting colors and textures. It offers a pleasing change from the more common Western pasta dishes.

8 ounces thin rice noodles
2 tablespoons butter
8 ounces fresh shiitake mushrooms,
  cleaned and with stems removed
8 ounces fresh chanterelles, cleaned
  Salt and freshly ground black pepper
  to taste

Ginger-Tomato Sauce, page 76, full
  recipe
¼ cup finely chopped scallions for
  garnish

In a large bowl, soak the rice noodles in warm water for 30 minutes. Drain and set aside. In a large skillet, heat the butter and add the mushrooms, salt, and pepper. Cook for 4 minutes over medium heat. Add the ginger-tomato sauce and rice noodles, and cook 5 minutes more. When the dish is done there should be almost no liquid left in the pan. If the sauce is too watery, reduce it over high heat. Garnish with the scallions and serve hot or at room temperature.

*Serves 4*

*Wine Suggestion:* an Alsatian Riesling or a dry California Riesling.

# Chinese Greens-Stuffed Ravioli

Bok choy has a wonderfully distinctive earthy taste that is slightly reminiscent of Swiss chard, except bok choy is sweeter. In this recipe, conceived by a good French-Italian friend of mine, bok choy flavored with pork is used as a stuffing for ravioli, which lends itself to East-West cuisine because it can be stuffed with almost anything that tastes good and makes sense. This dish is ideal. The simple flavor of the bok choy resounds throughout. You can serve this with Ginger-Tomato Sauce (page 76), or you can, as I do, serve it with just a little heavy cream, butter, and Parmesan cheese. This way you can taste the true delicious bok choy flavor. Salt and pepper bring out the natural flavors of the bok choy.

1 pound bok choy, prepared as on
    page 42
1 tablespoon olive oil
1 pound ground pork
    Salt and freshly ground black pepper
    to taste
2 tablespoons finely chopped fresh
    coriander
1 medium-sized egg, beaten
1 tablespoon water

Pasta, minus saffron as on page 98,
    two full recipes
Flour
Ginger-Tomato Sauce, page 76
    (optional)
Heavy cream, Parmesan cheese, and
    butter (optional)
2 tablespoons finely chopped fresh
    chives for garnish

Finely chop the bok choy. In a medium-sized skillet, heat the oil and brown the pork. Pour off the excess fat. Add the bok choy and cook for 2 minutes. Transfer to a bowl and allow to cool. Add the salt, pepper, and coriander, and mix well. Combine the egg and water, and set aside.

Run the pasta through a pasta machine on the next to thinnest setting. Cover a ravioli maker with a sheet of pasta and press down on the mold with the plastic plate to form indentations in the pasta. Fill the pockets half full. Brush the pasta with the egg-water mixture and cover with another sheet of pasta. Seal and cut the pasta by pressing down firmly with a rolling pin. The ravioli should fall through the holes in the mold. Dust with flour and place on a baking sheet. Repeat this process until all the pasta and filling are used.

*Makes about 8 dozen to serve 4 to 6*

Bring a large pot of water to a rolling boil. Add the ravioli and cook for 2 minutes. Remove them with a strainer or slotted spoon. Serve with ginger-tomato sauce or with heavy cream, Parmesan cheese, and butter. Garnish with the chopped chives.

*Wine Suggestion:* a light, somewhat oaky California Chardonnay or a white Burgundy from Mâcon.

# *Cannelloni Stuffed with Chinese Sausages*

Cannelloni, like ravioli and wonton, are made to be stuffed with delightful flavors and to be eaten with zestful appreciation of the wonderful combination of pasta, sauce, and filling. Perhaps because the Chinese have almost as many varieties of pasta as the Italians, I was a young man before I first ate cannelloni. It was in the south of France, and the dish was prepared by the French-Italian mother of a good friend of mine. I remember it well. She stuffed the pasta with a meat and spinach filling laced with Provençal herbs. I have eaten cannelloni many times since, but none has ever tasted better to me. It is at least partially because I despaired of ever surpassing that paragon of pasta that I undertook to create an Eastern approach to the dish. Glutinous (sweet) rice and Chinese sausage seasoned with ginger and scallions make a worthy filling for fresh cannelloni. A perfect dish for a large crowd or party, it may be made in advance (it even freezes well); reheated slowly, it retains its rich tastes and textures.

FILLING

1 tablespoon olive oil
1 pound ground pork
1 cup glutinous rice, prepared as on
   page 143
1 tablespoon finely chopped garlic
2 teaspoons finely chopped ginger
3 tablespoons finely chopped scallions

4 ounces Chinese sausage, finely diced
2 tablespoons rice wine
1 tablespoon light soy sauce
2 cups Basic Chicken Stock, page 67
   Salt and freshly ground black pepper
   to taste

Pasta, as on page 98, two full recipes
Olive oil
Ginger-Tomato Sauce, page 76, one
and a half recipes

Freshly grated Parmesan cheese

In a wok or large skillet, heat the olive oil and brown the pork. Pour off the fat and add the rest of the filling ingredients. Cook, stirring frequently, for 10 minutes over low heat, or until most of the liquid has evaporated. Transfer to a bowl and allow to cool.

Roll out the pasta to the second thinnest setting on a pasta machine. Cook the pasta sheets for 2 minutes in a large pot of boiling water. Drain and dry on linen towels. Cut the sheets into 4-inch squares.

Preheat the oven to 400 degrees.

Rub a large baking dish with olive oil. Spoon several tablespoons of filling along one edge of the pasta square and roll it up. Place in one corner of the baking dish. Repeat until all the filling is used. Cover the cannelloni with the ginger-tomato sauce and Parmesan cheese. Cover with foil and bake for 30 minutes. Uncover and bake 10 minutes more, or until browned. Serve at once.

*Serves 6 to 8*

*Wine Suggestion:* an earthy Pouilly-Fumé from the Loire or a similar California Sauvignon, or Fumé Blanc, possibly from the Santa Barbara area.

# Rice Noodles Primavera

Far be it from me to imply that pasta dishes are inescapably heavy and hard to digest. My use of Chinese rice noodles in this variation of a classic Western mélange of pasta and fresh vegetables signifies only that they are an excellent alternative to the standard wheat-based egg noodle pasta. Rice noodles cook up light and fluffy; they adapt themselves nicely to the colors and tastes of fresh vegetables; and their natural dry texture (even though they are soaked) makes them receptive to the bright flavors of Eastern spices. Use the freshest and best vegetables you can find in season. This dish is delicious served hot or at room temperature.

*8 ounces thin dried rice noodles*
*8 ounces broccoli*
*8 ounces carrots, peeled and roll-cut*
*8 ounces asparagus, diagonally sliced*
*  into 2-inch sections*
*2 tablespoons olive oil*
*2 tablespoons chopped garlic*
*3 tablespoons chopped scallions*

*1 tablespoon chopped ginger*
*  Salt and freshly ground black pepper*
*  to taste*
*¼ cup Basic Chicken Stock, page 67*
*8 ounces red or yellow sweet peppers,*
*  seeded, deribbed, and cut into strips*
*1 cup Tomato Concassé, page 70*
*½ cup freshly grated Parmesan cheese*

Soak the rice noodles for 30 minutes in a medium-sized bowl of warm water. Drain and set aside. Cut the broccoli florets from the stems. Peel and thinly slice the stems crosswise. Blanch the broccoli and carrots for 3 minutes, then rinse under cold water. Blanch the asparagus for 1 minute, then rinse under cold water.

In a wok or large skillet, heat the olive oil and add the garlic, scallions, and ginger. Stir-fry for 30 seconds. Add the rice noodles, salt, pepper, and chicken stock, and stir-fry 2 minutes more. Add all the vegetables and tomato concassé, and stir-fry 5 minutes more over high heat. Transfer to a serving platter, sprinkle with Parmesan cheese, and serve.

*Serves 4*

*Wine Suggestion:* blush wines, such as white Zinfandel or Cabernet Blanc, or try a straight-forward French rosé from Provence.

# Pasta with Chinese Mushrooms and Morels

This is a very simple but exquisitely subtle combination of tastes and textures. The mushrooms have delicate smoky and earthy flavors that permeate the sauce. The spices harmonize well with the light pasta. Mushrooms generally work very well with pasta, and these two varieties do so extraordinarily.

2 ounces black mushrooms, prepared as
　on page 45
6 ounces fresh or dried morels
4 tablespoons butter
1 tablespoon finely chopped garlic
3 tablespoons finely chopped shallots
　Salt and freshly ground black pepper
　to taste

1 tablespoon dark soy sauce
1 cup heavy cream
1 cup Tomato Concassé, page 70
　Pasta, as on page 98, full recipe
　minus the saffron
　Freshly grated Parmesan cheese
3 tablespoons finely chopped chives for
　garnish

Stem the Chinese mushrooms and cut them in half. If the morels are dried, soak them, squeeze out the moisture, and cut them in half.

In a large skillet, heat 2 tablespoons of butter and cook the garlic and shallots until the shallots are translucent. Add the mushrooms, salt, pepper, soy sauce, and heavy cream, and cook for 4 minutes. Add the tomato concassé and mix well. Remove from the heat.

Roll out the pasta to the thinnest setting of the pasta machine. Cut the pasta sheets into noodles 1½ inches wide by 5 inches long. Bring a large pot of water to a rolling boil and cook the pasta for 2 minutes. Remove with a strainer and toss with the remaining 2 tablespoons of butter. Transfer the pasta to warm individual plates, add some sauce on top, and sprinkle with Parmesan cheese and chives. Serve at once.

*Serves 4*

*Wine Suggestion:* young, simple red wines from Beaujolais or a light California Zinfandel or Gamay.

# Duck Fried Rice

Rice is usually associated with Asian cuisine, but it is in fact of almost universal significance as a foodstuff. (Incidentally, wheat, not rice, is the staple grain in much of China.) Rice is increasingly popular in America, probably because of the growing influence of Chinese and other Asian cuisines. There is no doubt that it is a nutritious and versatile substitute for pasta, potatoes, and bread. Here, we have a traditional Chinese dish that is also an American favorite: fried rice. The duck adds elegance and wonderful substance and taste, while the combination of East-West vegetables, spices, and seasonings elevates the dish above the ordinary in color, texture, and taste. Once the ingredients have been assembled, this dish is quickly prepared. Serve it hot or as a cold rice salad.

2 tablespoons peanut oil
2 tablespoons butter
3 cups cooked white rice
   Salt and freshly ground black pepper to taste
1 teaspoon Chinese Seasoned Salt, page 42
2 cups shredded cooked duck meat
4 ounces snow peas, with ends trimmed and shredded
4 ounces fresh water chestnuts, peeled and shredded

3 tablespoons finely chopped scallions
2 cups shredded iceberg or Romaine lettuce
1 tablespoon shredded fresh hot red chilies
1 sweet red pepper, seeded, deribbed, and shredded
2 medium-sized egg yolks
1 tablespoon sesame oil

In a wok or large skillet, heat the peanut oil and butter. Add the rice, salt, pepper, and Chinese seasoned salt, and stir-fry for 2 minutes over high heat. Add the duck, snow peas, water chestnuts, and scallions, and stir-fry 2 minutes more. Add the lettuce, chilies, and red pepper, and stir-fry 2 minutes more. Mix the egg yolks and sesame oil and add them to the wok. Stir, cook briefly, and serve.

*Serves 4 to 6*

*Wine Suggestion:* try a medium-bodied mellow Cabernet Sauvignon from California or a moderately aged red Bordeaux from an unclassified Château.

# Pasta in Black Bean Sauce with Triple Tomatoes

In this recipe I capitalize on the Italian *al dente* style of pasta, which is unknown in the formal cuisines of the East. The "bite" or substance of the pasta lends itself to a more demanding sauce, in this case one based on fragrant and flavorful Chinese black beans and chili. And the tomato brings its noticeably different texture, color, and concentration of flavor to the dish. The classical ruling triumverate of Eastern seasonings—ginger, scallions, and garlic—traditionally accompanies black beans and performs its usual noble work here.

1 pound dried fusilli pasta
3 tablespoons olive oil
2 tablespoons finely chopped fresh hot red chili, or 1 tablespoon coarsely chopped dried red chili
2 tablespoons finely chopped garlic
3 tablespoons finely chopped sun-dried tomatoes
6 tablespoons finely chopped scallions

3 tablespoons chopped basil
2 tablespoons finely chopped ginger
2 tablespoons coarsely chopped black beans
3 tablespoons tomato paste
½ cup Basic Chicken Stock, page 67
Salt and freshly ground black pepper to taste
1 cup Tomato Concassé, page 70

Bring a large pot of water to a rolling boil and cook the pasta until it is tender but firm. Drain and set aside.

In a wok or large skillet, heat the olive oil and add the chili, garlic, sun-dried tomatoes, 3 tablespoons of scallions, basil, ginger, and black beans. Stir-fry for 1 minute. Add the pasta and stir-fry 2 minutes more. Add the tomato paste, chicken stock, salt, and pepper. Stir-fry 1 minute more, then add the tomato concassé. Stir and serve garnished with the remaining 3 tablespoons of scallions.

*Serves 4 to 6*

*Wine Suggestion:* a fresh, fruity Beaujolais-Villages or a straightforward light California Zinfandel.

# Saffron Rice

Saffron, rarely used in Chinese cooking, is redolent of India and Indian cookery. With the beginning of the spice trade it quickly became popular in Western cooking, especially when used with fish and shellfish. I find it equally good with rice and apply it here in an easy-to-prepare dish that can accompany any entrée.

*2 tablespoons butter*
*2 tablespoons finely chopped shallots*
*1½ cups long-grain white rice or*
  *converted rice*
*2¼ cups Basic Chicken Stock, page 67*

*Salt and freshly ground white*
  *pepper to taste*
*¼ teaspoon saffron threads*
*3 tablespoons finely chopped fresh*
  *chives or scallions for garnish*

Heat a medium-sized pot and add the butter. When it is hot, lightly sauté the shallots, add the rice, and cook for about 1 minute. Then add the chicken stock, salt, and pepper, and saffron threads and bring the mixture to a boil. Turn the heat to very low, cover the pot, and cook gently for about 20 minutes.

When the rice is cooked, stir in the chives or scallions, and serve at once.

*Serves 2 to 4*

*Wine Suggestion:* use a fine, oak-aged California Chardonnay with 3 to 5 years bottle age or a similar white Burgundy such as Puligny-Montrachet or Chassagne-Montrachet.

# DESSERTS

| | | |
|---|---|---|
| Tangerine Sorbet | Orange-Ginger Custard | Fresh Water Chestnuts with |
| Cold Coconut Cream | Baked Apples with | Rum Butter Sauce |
| Litchi Sorbet with | Lemongrass | Ginger Crème Brûlée |
| Raspberry Sauce | Cold Melon-Coconut Soup | Almond Custard |
| Almond Madeleines | Warm Peach Compote with | Lemon Cream Tart |
| Blood Orange-Ginger | Basil | Mango Ice Cream with |
| Sorbet | | Candied Ginger |

*Dost thou think, because thou art virtuous, there shall be no more cakes and ale?*
William Shakespeare, *Twelfth Night*

Despite Kipling's ode, East does meet West, but it is true the twain rarely meet for dessert. Desserts in Western cuisine are the finale, often the grand finale, to the symphonic menu. In the East, in China and Japan, desserts play no such role; they are not a part of the formal structure of meals. The Japanese prefer the understatement of a slice of fresh fruit; the Chinese expect to have no appetite left by the end of the meal and therefore, except in the case of great banquets, the dessert course is alien to them. Such sweets and sweet snacks as were traditionally consumed had a naturally sweet vegetable or fruit base and were eaten separately or in the middle of a banquet, as refreshers between courses.

Fortunately for their cuisines, refined sugar was not generally introduced in the East until late in the nineteenth century. The Eastern diet is now under the assault of this unfortunate "food" which destroys the palate and fills one with empty calories. The Chinese snacks known as dim sum, some of which are sweet, are increasingly popular among Westerners, but in the Chinese cuisine, dim sum are not meant to be served as dessert. Rather, they are regarded as snacks with a range of flavors from salty savories and hot or spicy tidbits to sweet puddings and pastries served throughout the meal.

In any case, the dessert course is standard in our Western cuisine. What I have done in these recipes is combine into various dishes fruits, spices, flavorings, cream, custard, and sugar that capture the sweetness of both East and West.

# Tangerine Sorbet

I have transformed a classical French sorbet by adding to it an Eastern accent—star anise. It is a delightful finale to any meal, but it works especially well as an end to a highly seasoned meal. For a more Eastern taste, substitute one teaspoon of fresh ginger juice for the star anise. The sorbet will have a sharper flavor, but the ginger provides a wonderful cooling effect.

Nothing beats a fresh sorbet scooped directly from the ice-cream machine. If the sorbet is made ahead of time, be sure to stir it well before serving.

*1 cup water*
*½ cup sugar*
*3 whole star anise*

*1 vanilla bean*
*2 cups fresh tangerine or orange juice*
*Pinch of salt*

In a medium-sized pan, bring the water to a boil. Add the sugar, star anise, and vanilla bean. Reduce the heat and simmer the mixture for 5 minutes, or until the sugar has completely dissolved. Set the mixture aside to cool. Transfer to a bowl and refrigerate.

Strain the syrup and discard the vanilla and star anise. Combine the juice, syrup, and salt, and mix well. Pour into an ice-cream machine and make the sorbet following the manufacturer's directions.

If you don't have an ice-cream machine, don't despair! The mixture can be placed in ice trays in the freezer. It will require 2 or 3 mixings (every 30 minutes) to break up the formation of ice crystals. The result won't be a true smooth sorbet, but the final product is still delicious.

*Yields 3 cups*

# Cold Coconut Cream

In this dessert recipe I offer an Eastern variation (coconut is very popular in Asia) of a rich crème anglaise. It can be made hours ahead. Give it a good stir before serving, and serve it with fresh fruits or berries as I do, if you wish.

One 1½-pound fresh coconut*
  2 cups heavy cream*
  ½ cup milk*

6 tablespoons sugar
2 large egg yolks
  Sliced fresh fruit or berries
  (optional)

To prepare the coconut cream, tap all around the coconut shell with a hammer to loosen the shell from the meat. Poke holes in the dark-colored "eyes" using a screwdriver; drain and discard the liquid. Break the coconut open with a sharp blow. Remove the meat and peel the brown skin. Cut the coconut into small pieces and place in a small saucepan. Cover with 1 cup of cream and the milk, and simmer for 5 minutes. Allow it to cool, then process in a blender on high speed for 1 minute. Let it stand for 15 minutes, then strain. Using the back of a wooden spoon, squeeze all the liquid from the chopped coconut. Return the cream to the saucepan, add 3 tablespoons of sugar, and simmer for 5 minutes.

In a small bowl, beat together the egg yolks and 2 tablespoons of sugar. Take the saucepan off the heat and gradually add the coconut cream to the egg-sugar mixture in a slow steady stream, beating all the while. Pour the cream into a medium-sized saucepan and simmer slowly for 2 or 3 minutes. Whisk continuously to keep it from curdling. The cream should easily coat a wooden spoon. Allow the coconut cream to cool.

Beat the remaining 1 cup of cream and the remaining 1 tablespoon of sugar in a bowl until slightly stiff. Fold the mixture into the coconut cream. Refrigerate until ready to serve. Stir thoroughly before serving and garnish with fresh fruit slices, if desired.

*Serves 4 to 6*

*Wine Suggestion:* a Mission del Sol from California or a Muscat de Beaumes de Venise.

* Or substitute 3 14-ounce cans of coconut milk for the above ingredients

# Litchi Sorbet with Raspberry Sauce

The litchi (or lychee or leechee) is actually a fruit. It is native to Southeast Asia and is the most treasured fruit in China. It grows on trees in clumps like cherries; fresh, it has a strawberry look, but when peeled it reveals a translucent, whitish, grapelike pulp that is deliciously sweet. Once you taste the fresh variety you will see why centuries ago the venerable Shen Fu wrote: "One of the keenest pleasures of my whole life was tasting the fruit of the litchi in Canton."

It is appropriate to combine this jewel of the East with a splendid Western fruit, raspberries, to create an admittedly rich sorbet but one that allows the virtues of the fruits to manifest themselves beautifully: the treasured litchi reflected in a pool of raspberry sauce. I think this is a perfect East-West dessert.

| | |
|---|---|
| *2 pounds fresh litchi fruit, peeled and pitted* | *¾ cup sugar* |
| | *¼ cup fresh orange juice* |
| RASPBERRY SAUCE | |
| *2 cups fresh raspberries* | *¼ cup sugar* |

In a blender, purée the litchi fruit. Add the sugar and orange juice, and freeze according to the ice-cream manufacturer's instructions.

Puree the raspberries in a blender. Strain into a small bowl through the fine-mesh strainer. Mix in the sugar. Refrigerate until ready to use.

To serve, make a pool of raspberry sauce on a small plate and add the sorbet in the center.

*Serves 4*

# Almond Madeleines

Madeleines were famous long before Marcel Proust parlayed his appreciation of France's national cookie-tea pastry into his own immortality in *Remembrance of Things Past.* Therein he recalled his mother sending out for "one of those squat plump little cakes called 'petites madeleines,' which looked as though they had been molded in the fluted valve of a scallop shell." The popularity of madeleines is well founded. They are light, pretty, moist, golden-buttery, and deliciously not too sweet.

Here, I follow the classic French recipe, adding only a touch of roasted almonds borrowed from the traditional Chinese delight, almond cookies. These tea cakes are an excellent dessert by themselves; served with Litchi Sorbet with Raspberry Sauce (page 232), they are exquisite.

You will need madeleine or barquette molds for this recipe.

*½ cup (about 4 ounces) blanched
  almonds
2 medium-sized eggs
½ cup sugar*

*8 tablespoons (1 stick) butter, melted,
  plus additional for molds
1 cup sifted flour*

Preheat the oven to 375 degrees.

Place ¼ cup of almonds on a baking sheet and roast for 10 minutes, or until browned. Cool the almonds and finely chop them.

In a medium-sized bowl, beat the eggs and sugar together. Mix in the butter and the remaining ¼ cup of whole almonds. Slowly fold in the flour.

*Makes about
24*

Butter the molds and fill them two-thirds full. Bake for 20 minutes, or until lightly browned. Pop them out of the molds onto cake racks and let them cool.

*Wine Suggestion:* a good-quality Portuguese or California Tawny Port. Good for dipping the cookies.

# Blood Orange-Ginger Sorbet

In Chinese cuisine, oranges of many varieties are enjoyed for their sweetness and esteemed for their red and orange colors, scarlet gold being a revered religious color. My family always had oranges when they were available; we usually ate them as a refreshing dessert. We often exchanged oranges with other families during visits—the gift signifies a wish for health and good luck. We are spoiled nowadays with oranges readily available throughout the year, although, to my taste, they are not nearly as sweet as they used to be. I can remember when they were a prized Chinese New Year gift to children, bright gold sweetness in the gray depths of a Chicago winter.

One type of orange unknown to the Chinese, however, is the blood orange, so named because of its reddish pulp and red-streaked skin. It is popular in France, where I first sampled it. There are some rather tart varieties of blood oranges, and I know that the Chinese would love them: They prefer tart tastes and would find the color richly appropriate. Here, I take this French favorite and blend in a Chinese favorite, candied ginger, whose sharp pungency works well with the strength and sweet tartness of the blood orange. Try it this way first; if it is too "hot" for your taste, reduce the amount of candied ginger.

*4 cups blood orange juice*　　　　　　*2 tablespoons minced candied ginger*
*½ cup sugar*

Combine all the ingredients in a medium-sized bowl. Pour the mixture into an ice-cream machine and follow the manufacturer's instructions.

If you don't have an ice-cream machine, don't despair! The mixture can be placed in ice trays in the freezer. It will require 2 or 3 mixings (every 30 minutes) to break up the formation of ice crystals. The result won't be a true smooth sorbet, but the final product is still delicious.

*Yields 4 cups*

# Orange-Ginger Custard

This is a rather fancy dessert, colorful and esthetically appealing, remarkable for its richness, sweetness, and distinctive flavors. I was led to elaborate the dish after a memorable day in France. I rose at 4:00 A.M. and with a group of friends drove madly from Paris all the way to Crissier, Switzerland, where at 1:00 P.M. we sat down to lunch at the restaurant of M. Fredy Girardet. It was well worth the journey. The entire meal was a delight, but one dish in particular charmed me: Gratin d'Oranges—Madame France. Here, I have taken that concept and added my Chinese favorite, ginger, a spice that I find has a natural affinity with oranges. The raspberry sauce and custard makes this a luscious dessert worthy of a special occasion.

| | |
|---|---|
| 6 medium-sized eggs, beaten | 1 tablespoon fresh lemon juice |
| ½ cup plus 2 teaspoons sugar | 3 medium-sized oranges, peeled and |
| 1 cup heavy cream | sectioned |
| Pinch of salt | Raspberry Sauce, page 232, full |
| 1 tablespoon butter plus additional for | recipe |
| preparing dishes | 3 tablespoons shredded orange zest for |
| 1 tablespoon fresh chopped ginger | garnish |

In a medium-sized bowl, combine the eggs, sugar, heavy cream, salt, butter, ginger, and lemon juice. Butter an oval gratin dish or individual 5-ounce ramekins and pour in the mixture. Cover the top with orange sections. Wrap with foil and bake for 35 minutes, or until a wooden skewer placed in the center comes out clean.

To serve, ladle several tablespoons of raspberry sauce on a small plate. Add a serving of custard in the center and garnish with orange zest.

*Serves 6*

*Wine Suggestion:* an unusual late harvest Gewürztraminer, a richer muscat from Italy, or Vino Santo.

# Baked Apples with Lemongrass

Apples are universally enjoyed by all temperate-climate peoples. Baked apples, however, along with apple sauce and apples baked in pastry, are of Western origin; in the East, apples are eaten as a raw or preserved fruit and cooked in soups. Here, I take the traditional baked apple and spice it with lemongrass, thus adding a mild bite of lemon flavor to the old favorite. The crème fraîche is a smooth and enriching touch; some may prefer a small dollop of fresh, homemade vanilla ice cream.

In choosing apples, look for those that are firm to the touch and without bruises, soft spots, or scars.

*2 pounds Golden Delicious or McIntosh apples, peeled, cored, halved, and cut into ¼-inch slices*
*2 ounces Chinese rock sugar*

*2 tablespoons chopped fresh lemongrass*
*1 vanilla bean, quartered*
*Crème Fraîche, page 43, full recipe*

Preheat the oven to 400 degrees.

Cut 4 10-inch squares of foil. Place one-fourth of the apple slices in the center of each square. Add one-fourth of the rock sugar and lemongrass and a piece of vanilla bean to each square. Seal the foil squares. Place on a baking sheet and bake for 30 minutes.

Transfer the foil packages to individual plates. Bring them to the table and let each person open the package. Serve with a bowl of crème fraîche on the side.

*Serves 4*

*Wine Suggestion:* a late harvest Johannisberg Riesling from California or an Auslese from the Rhine, from a vintage like 1975 or 1976.

# Cold Melon-Coconut Soup

Despite the "soup" in the title, this is a dessert. Most Americans or Westerners do not realize that the coconuts they are used to seeing, those whose white interior pulp has dried and hardened, are mature samples. Asians much prefer the immature coconut with its still-soft, jellylike pulp that can be eaten with a spoon and whose "milk" is exceedingly sweet. Such coconuts make an excellent dessert or sweet snack base. Because in the West we get only mature coconuts, we must sweeten them artificially.

The inspiration for this recipe comes from a cold soup I enjoyed at the Sichuan Restaurant in Hong Kong; it included tapioca, a favorite Eastern thickener derived from the cassava plant. It is thus more like a thick soup. Here, I have omitted the tapioca and have substituted, in Western style, milk and half-and-half. The coconut-flavored milk and honeydew melon are congenial partners, each with a distinct flavor and yet combining synergistically into a refreshing overall taste. Adjust the amount of sugar according to your taste. Although this may be prepared several hours beforehand, I recommend against keeping it overnight. And give it a good stir before serving.

*10 to 12 ounces coconut meat (from a*
*    1½-pound fresh coconut, as*
*    prepared on page 231)*
*2 cups half-and-half*

*1 cup low-fat milk*
*5 tablespoons sugar*
*2 honeydew melons, cut in half and*
*    seeded*

To prepare the coconut milk, cut the coconut into small pieces and place in a medium-sized saucepan. Cover with the half-and-half and low-fat milk and simmer for 10 minutes. Allow to cool, then process in a blender on high speed for 1 minute. Let stand for 15 minutes, then strain. Using the back of a wooden spoon, squeeze all the liquid from the chopped coconut. Return the cream to the saucepan, add 3 tablespoons of sugar, and simmer for 10 minutes. Allow to cool.

Make ½ cup of melon balls and set aside for garnish. Scoop out the rest of the melon and purée it in a blender. Add the remaining 2 tablespoons of sugar and pour the purée into the bowl containing the coconut milk. Mix well, transfer to a soup tureen, and serve garnished with the melon balls.

*Serves 6*

237

# Warm Peach Compote with Basil

This is a peach we may all dare eat. The query concerns the basil: Basil with peaches? In Asia, anise, with its licorice lilt, is the most common flavoring in savory and sweet dishes, and it works very well. Following that line of reasoning, I thought of using sweet basil, the "royal herb" that lends its mild presence so congenially to so many other foods. If Chartreuse benefits from a touch of basil, I thought, why not try peaches and basil? I did, and they work deliciously, as you will see. This, incidentally, is a good way to prepare peaches that are not quite at their peak of ripeness; cooked slightly in this manner, they grow softer and sweeter.

*½ cup sugar*
*1 cup water*
*2 pounds peaches, peeled, pitted, and*
*  sliced*

*1 vanilla bean*
*4 tablespoons butter, cut into small*
*  pieces*
*½ cup basil leaves, loosely packed*

*Serves 4*

In a medium-sized skillet, combine the sugar and water and cook until the sugar dissolves. Add the peaches and vanilla, and simmer for 2 minutes. Remove the vanilla. Whisk in the butter, a few pieces at a time, and the basil leaves. Cook until the basil leaves wilt, then serve at once.

*Wine Suggestion:* a fine-quality Sauternes, preferably 10-plus years, would be a wonderful accompaniment.

# Fresh Water Chestnuts with Rum Butter Sauce

Fresh water chestnuts, raw as well as cooked, are a common delicacy in Asia and enjoyed both for their texture, at once crunchy and succulent, and their sweet nutty taste. Water chestnuts in sugar syrup or candied are popular items in the street market stalls. Here, cooked with a rum butter sauce, they make a delicious treat. This is a simple and exotic dessert, easy to make but nonetheless intriguing.

*8 ounces fresh water chestnuts, peeled*
*   and sliced*
*¼ cup fresh lemon juice*

*2 tablespoons sugar*
*¼ cup rum*
*2 tablespoons butter*

In a medium-sized skillet, cook the water chestnuts, lemon juice, and sugar for 5 minutes over low heat. Raise the heat to high, add the rum and butter, and flambé. When the flame has subsided, reduce the liquid to a thick syrup. Serve at once.

*Serves 4*

*Wine Suggestion:* a full-bodied cream sherry from Spain or California. Try Meloso Cream Sherry.

# Ginger Crème Brûlée

It is easy enough to burn the sugar; the trick is to snatch it out of harm's way and in so doing come up with a delicious treat. This archetypical Western dish, originating, so the story goes, centuries ago in King's College, Cambridge, has come a long way and remains a popular favorite. It is not, I need hardly note, a standard item in Chinese cuisine. I remember first being impressed with it many years ago at Chez Panisse in Berkeley; I have enjoyed it many times since, especially at San Francisco's Hayes Street Grill, where it is a standard and, for good reason, a very popular offering. The basically simple and subtle blend of eggs, cream, and sugar, with a caramelized crust, lends itself to inventiveness. Everyone seems to have his or her own preferred way of making it, and I am no exception. Here, I have added my own favorite spice, ginger; this Eastern touch adds a new dimension to the classic Western crème brûlée.

*1 tablespoon butter*
*2 teaspoons finely chopped fresh ginger*
*3 tablespoons sugar*

*2 cups heavy cream*
*4 medium-sized egg yolks*
*2 tablespoons brown sugar*

Preheat the oven to 450 degrees.

In a small skillet, melt the butter, add the ginger and 2 tablespoons of sugar, and cook over low heat for 2 minutes. In a small saucepan, scald the cream and remove it from the heat. Beat the egg yolks and the remaining 1 tablespoon of sugar together. Add the cream to the yolks in a slow steady stream, beating as you go. Add the ginger-sugar mixture to the cream-yolk mixture. Pour into an oval gratin dish.

Fill a large baking dish with 1 inch of hot water. Place the gratin dish in the baking dish and bake in the oven for 30 minutes, or until a wooden skewer placed in the center of the dish comes out clean.

*Serves 4 to 6*   Sprinkle with brown sugar, place under the broiler, and cook until caramelized, about 2 minutes. Allow it to cool, then serve.

*Wine Suggestion:* an opportunity for a rich, satisfying, classified Sauternes, 5-plus years old.

# Almond Custard

One of my most vivid memories of dessert, while growing up, was a sweet, warm almond soup which we always had at the close of Chinese banquets. I have been in love with almonds since, which even today are among my favorite treats. Here I have combined them with a custard that makes them a perfect coda for any dinner. This is delicious warm or cold and is very easy to make.

| | |
|---|---|
| *½ cup slivered blanched almonds* | *5 egg yolks* |
| *1 vanilla bean, split in half* | *1 cup milk* |
| *½ cup sugar* | *1 cup cream* |

Preheat the oven to 350 degrees. Brown the almond slivers on a baking tray for about 8 minutes or until they are golden brown. Allow them to cool and grind them in a blender or food processor.

Remove the seeds from the vanilla bean and combine them with the sugar. Beat the egg yolks and sugar-vanilla seeds together until they are pale yellow and the mixture falls like a thick ribbon from the beaters or whisk.

Combine the shell of the vanilla bean with the milk and cream in a medium-sized pan; scald the mixture. Remove the vanilla bean and slowly incorporate the hot milk/cream mixture into the sugar/egg mixture. Add the ground almonds. Pour the mixture into individual ramekins.

*Makes about 12 small or 8 medium-sized ramekins*

Pour hot water into a roasting or baking pan. Add the ramekins and bake for 30 minutes in the hot-water bath or until a skewer placed in the center of the custard comes out clean.

# Lemon Cream Tart

Citrus, in the form of fresh orange wedges, was a familiar dessert in my home. It was a satisfying and refreshing way to end a meal, and light and healthy as well. Later in France, I discovered the wonderful world of tarts —and, of course, I immediately loved the ones containing any type of citrus. Here, I offer a lemon cream tart, delicious, easy to make, and sweeter and richer than my simple Chinese fruit dessert, but nonetheless an appropriate ending to any meal.

PASTRY
| | |
|---|---|
| *1 cup flour* | *1 egg* |
| *¼ cup sugar* | *6 tablespoons cold butter* |
| *Pinch of salt* | |

LEMON CREAM
| | |
|---|---|
| *1 cup cream* | *Pinch of salt* |
| *2 eggs* | *½ cup lemon juice* |
| *1 egg yolk* | *Zest from 1 lemon* |
| *½ cup sugar* | |

Mix all the pastry ingredients together in a bowl. Roll the dough into a ball on a lightly floured board. Wrap it with plastic wrap and refrigerate for about 30 minutes.

Preheat the oven to 350 degrees. Mix the lemon cream ingredients together and set aside.

Roll out the pastry to about ⅛ inch thick and press into a 9-inch tart pan. Place a sheet of foil over the surface of the pastry and put about 2 cups of dried beans on the foil to weigh down the pastry. Bake the pastry for about 10 minutes.

Remove the beans and the foil from the tart pan. Lightly pierce the pastry surface with a fork. Return it to the oven and bake for 8 minutes more.

*Yields one 9-inch tart*

Add the lemon cream mixture and bake for about 40 minutes, until the filling is set and lightly browned. Allow the tart to cool thoroughly before serving.

*Wine Suggestion:* a late harvest Johannisberg Riesling from California would do nicely, as would a rich Auslese from the Rheingau.

# Mango Ice Cream with Candied Ginger

Mango is an exotic fruit, unique in many ways and with a wonderful flavor. Here, I have combined it with the zest of candied ginger for a lovely fruity ice-cream dessert.

*2 cups fresh mango purée*
*1½ cups low-fat milk*
*2 tablespoons finely minced candied
  ginger*

*3 egg yolks*
*¼ cup sugar*
*1 tablespoon lemon juice*

Sieve the mango purée, removing excess fibers.

Combine the milk and ginger in a medium-sized pot and scald the mixture.

Mix the yolks and sugar together until they form a thick ribbon. Gently incorporate the hot milk and ginger. Pour the mixture into a medium-sized saucepan and simmer slowly for 2 or 3 minutes. Whisk continuously to keep it from curdling. The mixture should easily coat a wooden spoon. Allow the mixture to cool.

Combine the egg mixture with the mango purée and lemon juice. Pour the mixture into an ice-cream machine and follow the manufacturer's instructions.

*Yields 4 cups*

*Wine Suggestion:* try a Muscato d'Asti from Italy or find an equally lively fresh Muscat from California or Australia.

# East-West Menus

*with Wine Suggestions by Darrell Corti*

## EAST-WEST THANKSGIVING MENU

• *Boned Stuffed Turkey with Rice and Herb Stuffing and Rich Turkey and Chicken Stock*
• *Potato Purée with Scallions*
• *Apple and Plum Sauce*
• *Stir-Fried Snow Peas with Carrots*
• *Tangerine Sorbet or Fresh Fruit*

The turkey, native to America, is unknown to Asians. But it is easily adaptable to Asian flavors such as those in this stuffing, which combines Eastern and Western flavors and textures, and relies upon rice instead of bread for its substance. Turkey meat has "character," and this combination of spices, meat, herbs, and vegetables with a rice texture makes for a delicious and robust partner. The stuffing is delicious by itself, and I recommend baking half of the stuffing separately; if there's any left over, it is wonderful the next day.

The blandness and heaviness of the potato is given a light but sharp bite with the flavor of minced scallions, transforming a mainstay dish into something both a bit new and quite delicious.

For another variation, this time away from cranberry sauce, I combine homemade applesauce with Chinese plum sauce, which is available commercially. Because this is a rather heavy meal, I recommend a simple but colorful vegetable dish, stir-fried for freshness and crispness—green snow peas and orange carrots—to balance and brighten the golden brown turkey. Finally, I think the most appropriate dessert would be a light fruity sorbet such as Tangerine Sorbet or simple fresh fruit.

*Wine Suggestion:* This East-West Thanksgiving menu allows for a lot of advance preparation and then rather unhassled service. The wine service follows in this mode.

The boned stuffed turkey with its rich sauce needs a medium-bodied, slightly tannic red wine with a good fragrance, something to refresh the palate. Since it is a holiday celebration, the festive touch of a glass or two of a Champagne or sparkling wine will set the mood. Other suggestions are: California Carneros-region Pinot Noir of 1 to 4 years of age; a light-style Zinfandel; a not-too-tannic Cabernet Sauvignon from a good vintage like 1981; a red Bordeaux from 1979–1980, from the Médoc or St.-Emilion; a Chianti Classico Riserva of 1979–1981.

Ices tend not to accompany wine well, and perhaps this dessert ought to be enjoyed and then wine drunk, in the Chinese fashion. A rich, smooth, and aromatic Malmsey Madeira, sweet Oloroso sherry, mature Tawny Port, or rich Australian Muscat would be appropriate here.

## SUMMER GRILL MENU

- *Grilled Crab and Lobster with Ginger-Scallion Mayonnaise*
- *Marinated Roast Squab with Rice Wine-Butter Sauce*
- *Cold Tomato Cubes Tossed in Tarragon and Sesame Oil*
- *Stir-Fried Summer Vegetables with Chinese Vinegar*

Grilling is much more popular in the West than in the East, which doesn't mean the two approaches can't work together. When this Western cooking technique is combined with Eastern herbs, spices, and condiments, familiar dishes acquire new and appetizing characteristics, as this summer grill menu demonstrates. The grilled crab and lobster are served with a ginger-scallion mayonnaise, an Eastern combination that enlivens as well as complements the rich, distinctive flavor of the seafood. Similarly, the squabs are marinated in soy sauce and Chinese rice wine marinade— Eastern flavors subtly influencing a Western technique. The grilled foods have a distinctive mildness and delicacy of flavor, transforming a simple barbecue into something special. The cold tomatoes in fresh tarragon provide the cool accompaniment to the grilled foods. Rather than olive oil, I use sesame oil, which imparts a distinctive "toasty" flavor to the tomatoes. The summer vegetables are stir-fried with Chinese vinegar, which wakes them up nicely.

*Wine Suggestion:* The Summer Grill menu screams for wines with direct, refreshing simple tastes that can be served cool or cold. The oily texture of mayonnaise and the richness of the shellfish need white wine of medium to full body with high acidity, such as some California Chardonnay and most French Mâcon or White Burgundy. Sauvignon Blanc, if not in the aggressive style, would be appropriate also. Examples are Sauvignon Blanc from Sonoma, the Central Coast, and Santa Barbara or Livermore. Sancerre or Pouilly-Fumé from France and several white wine types from northern Italy such as Chardonnay or Sauvignon from the Veneto or Friuli would work also. The drier styles of Germany's 1983–1985 Rieslings such as Kabinett or Spätlese would fit the bill.

The balance of the menu needs young red wine that is silky, easy to drink, rather low in tannin, and served cool or cold. Beaujolais and its vineyard area wines such as Julienas or Chiroubles would be good. Young Chianti and Dolcetto from Italy, young, fresh California Zinfandel, and Gamay or Pinot Noir would also work. Young red Rioja from Spain, Dão from Portugal, and the unique Lemberger from Washington's Yakima Valley would be serviceable. Fruity, not overly aggressive Cabernet Sauvignon styles or Merlots would also fit the bill.

Finally, one of the rich, very sweet and refreshingly high-acid late harvest Rieslings or Gewürztraminers from California, Washington State, Germany, or Australia would be a dessert all by itself.

## FLAVORS OF PROVENCE WITH A CHINESE TOUCH

• *Cold Tomato Soup with Lemongrass*
• *Roast Rack of Lamb with Asian-Style Marinade*
• *Chinese Ratatouille*
• *Almond Custard*

I have spent time in the south of France, visiting the parents and relatives of a good friend, and nowhere else have I felt so at home. I know the sights and smells of the area, and I love its cuisine; I have always felt those in Provence have carried taste, inventiveness, and a simple refinement in the preparation of food to the highest level. Whole cookbooks have been written about the Provençal cuisine without exhausting its richness and variety. In any event, for myself and for many other Americans, Provence represents the best of French cuisine. Its delicious freshness and pungent smells, together with the warmth of the people and the sounds and excitement of the markets, remind me of Hong Kong and the south of China.

This menu represents perhaps the most dramatic meeting of Eastern and Western culinary traditions. The truly distinctive foods and techniques of Provence are blended with typical Eastern foods and spices. The cold tomato soup is flavored with both Chinese basil, evocative of Provence, and lemongrass, a Southeast Asian herb growing in popularity in the United States that imparts a light, lemony but non-acid flavor to the soup.

The rack of lamb is typically Provençal, marinated in a true marriage of Western-Provençal herbs—thyme and marjoram—and Chinese spices.

Chinese ratatouille is almost a contradiction in terms since the Chinese do not generally stew but stir-fry their vegetables. However, in this ratatouille (which roughly translates as vegetable stew) Chinese vegetables such as silk squash and Chinese eggplant are stewed along with carrots and tomatoes, but briefly. Each of the vegetables is cooked separately and then stewed for about five minutes together. The whole is indeed a ratatouille in the traditional sense but with a savory Eastern flavor.

The almond custard forms an appropriate coda to the menu. The almond, common to both East and West, probably originated in the Middle East. From there it moved in both directions to China and Europe. In each culture the almond, ground into a light custard, is enjoyed as a sweet, delicate dessert following a spicy and stimulating menu.

*Wine Suggestion:* This menu, evoking the rich, earthy aromas of the late summer, needs wines that are hearty enough to stand up to tomatoes—light red wines or heavier rosés—followed by a fuller wine to go with the lamb.

The famous Provence rosés from France come first to mind: Côte-de-Provence Rosé, Tavel, Bandol, and the like. A drier style of California blush wine, white Zinfandel or Cabernet, or a drier Cabernet Sauvignon Rosé would also do well. This wine could also work as a single wine for this entire menu.

Red wines for the lamb course could include medium- to full-bodied California Zinfandel, Cabernet Sauvignon, or Merlot 3 to 4 years of age. The lighter Côtes-du-Rhône and Côtes-de-Provence or Bandol from France would accompany well. For large groups, some of the Cabernet-tinged jug red wines from California and Australia could also do double duty and be served throughout the meal.

The dessert wine should be tasty and aromatic without being ponderous. Light Italian or California muscats such as Moscato d'Asti, Moscato Ama-bile, or Muscat Canelli are appropriate. Sweeter Alsatian or Californian Gewürztraminer, usually called late harvest wines, would be good choices. Just make sure they are not excruciatingly sweet.

## DUCK LOVER'S MENU

• *Sautéed Duck Liver and Chinese Duck Sausage*
• *Duck in Two Courses (Duck Breasts Served in a Chinese Vinegar-and-Butter Sauce and Baked Duck Thighs and Legs)*
• *Green Salad with Duck Skin Crackling*
• *Lemon Cream Tart*

Duck is very popular in the East, especially in China, where by the second century B.C. it was already one of the primary food animals. Many Westerners are familiar with Peking duck, the ultimate duck and the centerpiece of the most glorious of the elaborate banquet dishes in Chinese cuisine. In China, ducks are specifically selected and raised for the Peking duck recipe. They are force-fed, and their movements are restricted in order to ensure tender and juicy flesh. But there is more than one way to enjoy this delicious bird, and it could make more frequent appearances on Western menus even if the Asian labor-intensive methods of raising the fowl were not adopted. Even a wild duck caught on the wing can be deliciously prepared.

In this menu, the sautéed duck livers are in the Western mode; liver is stir-fried or roasted on spits in the East. So prepared, duck livers approximate the French "foie gras" in texture and flavor. But the Chinese duck liver sausages are undeniably Eastern—spicy and delectable.

The two-course duck dish is a balanced and delicious combination of East and West. The duck breasts are marinated and quickly sautéed, then combined with a Chinese vinegar-and-butter sauce. The thighs and legs are grilled with soy sauce and rice wine. Just make your favorite green salad and substitute duck skin for chicken in the crackling recipe. Both the salad (with the crispy duck skin) and the lemon cream tart serve as counterpoints to the pronounced rich flavor of the duck: the light and the sweet balancing the substantial and the dominant tastes. This is a truly stimulating menu for lovers of duck.

*Wine Suggestion:* The first course of rich, almost sweet duck livers and sausages needs a sweet wine to stand up to it. This could be in the classic French tradition, a young Sauternes or Barsac served very chilled, or even an older, more aromatic wine, less sweet, such as a rich Madeira, a Bual, or a muscat such as Beaumes de Venise from southern France. It might sound strange, but the combination of rich dishes with sweet wines works well in the first course.

The reduction sauce of the first duck course needs a very full-bodied Chardonnay or white Burgundy. Here is a chance to star those rich, toasty, oily textured Chardonnay wines. This style could also continue through the second duck course, or a medium-bodied Pinot Noir or Burgundy- or Rhône-style red could accompany.

This is a rich meal. Dessert should stand alone. Perhaps just a touch of a fruit eau-de-vie or fruit liqueur served directly from the freezer could follow the Lemon Cream Tart.

## EASY BUT ELEGANT MENU

- *Goat Cheese Wonton Soup*
- *Steamed Fish with Tomatoes and Basil*
- *Roast Squab with Rice Wine-Butter Sauce*
- *Green Salad*
- *Fresh Fruit in Season*

In this menu, East and West blend nicely to our mutual pleasure and satisfaction. Steaming, an Eastern technique, is balanced by the Western method of roasting. Soups are almost always appropriate as long as they merely introduce the meal without overwhelming the appetite or palate. This spicy goat cheese wonton soup fits those criteria splendidly. The traditional Eastern wontons are stuffed not with the usual minced and flavored pork but with goat cheese. Tomatoes and basil, an uncommon combination in the East, enrich traditional steamed fish. Their distinctive flavors impart a necessary touch because, while steaming makes food succulent and tender, it also tends to render it rather tasteless. Similarly, the rice wine-and-butter sauce replaces the common Western deglazed sauce. Make your favorite green salad. The menu itself requires little effort. Many of the components can be prepared in advance: the squab, the chicken broth, and the stuffing of the wontons. The combinations underscore the elegance and sophistication of the menu with clean flavors characterizing each dish.

*Wine Suggestion:* Soup needs an accompanying full-bodied, full-flavored wine—that or nothing. If you want to accompany this soup with a wine, then a Sercial Madeira, Amontillado Sherry, or dry Marsala Vergine or Soleras would work well.

The steamed fish with tomatoes needs a full-bodied white wine to accompany the tomatoes but one not so full bodied that it overwhelms the fish: Chardonnay from California or France from good, not great vintages, with acidity and body; white Bordeaux, dry white Graves or Entre-Deux-Mers, 2 to 3 years old. Italian Pinot Grigio would support the tomato and enhance the fish.

I think roast chicken is splendid with fine claret or Bordeaux-style wine. If you have a good bottle of Bordeaux or California Cabernet, perhaps this is the dinner at which it should be served. The buttery, aromatic character of the chicken is enhanced by the cedary, berry character of Cabernet or Bordeaux. It should probably be 10 years or older.

The exotic aromas and flavors of these fruits are complemented by the rich, very aromatic late harvest wines from botrytised grapes, Riesling or Gewürztraminer from several different countries. These wines should also be several years old.

## AN IMPRESSIVE AND ELEGANT MENU

- *Broiled Oysters with Three Sauces*
- *Steamed Salmon in Chinese Cabbage*
- *Roast Pork with Chinese Spices*
- *Mango Ice Cream with Candied Ginger*

Oysters and pork are staple delicacies in both East and West, while salmon is distinctively Western, but here are all three. In many ways this combination of dishes illustrates the openness and cosmopolitan nature of American society. A bit of work is required here, but the results are well worth the effort. The broiled oysters and steamed salmon are cooked by Western and Eastern methods. The three colorful sauces—saffron, spinach, and tomato—are not only exotic in taste but reflect the Eastern tradition of delighting the eye as well as the palate. The scallion-ginger butter sauce combines elements of both East and West and makes exotic the traditional poached salmon dish.

Roast pork—a relatively simple food to prepare—is common to both East and West; the marinade of Chinese spices, however, makes this a distinctive dish. Chinese five-spice powder and orange zest impart a pronounced Eastern flavor to the roast pork, enhancing the taste and texture of the crisp skin and moist meat.

The ice cream—so Western—is transformed by the mango flavor and the candied ginger into a truly exotic and impressive finale to this menu.

*Wine Suggestion:* Grilled oysters need a sharp, incisive wine to accompany them and act as an aperitif. Champagne or méthode champenoise sparkling wine from California or elsewhere would be appropriate. There is no more elegant wine than Champagne.

The poached salmon needs a full but not ponderous wine. A *dry*, rather young Pinot Noir Blanc or a Rosé Champagne from France would be splendid. In fact, the Rosé Champagne might be the logical conclusion since a Blanc de Blancs could precede and then the rosé would follow the white with the salmon. A salmon-colored Blanc de Noir from California would also enhance the salmon.

The pork roast could be accompanied by a splendid opulent Burgundy or Pinot Noir to continue the pinot character of this dinner. A really fine Chianti Classico Riserva could also be used, and would be very traditional.

Again, ice cream does not meld well with wine. Since the menu is impressive, perhaps a fine old Cognac or domaine Armagnac should be served after the dessert. Failing this, service of a sweet liqueur, perhaps one based on fruit, could be used to great advantage.

---

## A SIMPLE AND LIGHT MENU

• *Steamed Scallops*
• *Vegetable Pasta*
• *Tomato Salad with Ginger-Scallion Vinaigrette*
• *Fresh Fruit in Season*

In this simple menu we blend East and West into what may be called cooking for today's lifestyle because it is so light and easy to make. The scallops, common to both cultures, are steamed in the Eastern fashion and lightly but distinctively enlivened with Chinese seasoned salt. The "pasta" in this menu is not of wheat but of vegetables properly shredded to look like strands of noodles, stir-fried with fresh herbs, and served with Parmesan cheese.

The scallops and pasta are set off by the salad: sliced fresh tomatoes in a ginger-scallion vinaigrette. The fresh fruit in season is a perfectly appropriate dessert.

*Wine Suggestion:* Simple food can take great wines. This menu might be just the thing to show off your cellar's finest wines. Perhaps only the finest white wines would be appropriate. Great Chardonnay or white Burgundy would be splendid with this menu, which sets off these wines with its direct simple

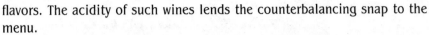

flavors. The acidity of such wines lends the counterbalancing snap to the menu.

Another choice would be to use only simple modest wines with soft, harmonious flavors. Jug wines that are not touched with sweetness would be a good and inexpensive choice. Light red wines could be used to advantage with the vegetable "pasta" course.

The fresh fruits are set off by rich, sweet, and liqueur-like dessert wines such as Sauternes/Barsac or the late harvest botrytised German-style wines. Nothing sets off these wines better than simple fresh fruit.

I would opt for the finest white wine combinations.

# EAST MEETS WEST
# IN PROFESSIONAL KITCHENS

East Meets West not only in the home but also in professional kitchens. In the past five years I have catered East-West dinners, taught East-West combinations, and cooked East-West menus with fellow chefs in restaurants. Here, I share some of my ideas and experiences.

One of the earliest supporters of the East-West concept was Belle Rhodes, a lovely and elegant woman who is extremely knowledgeable about food and wine. In 1980 she organized a series of classes at the Joseph Phelps Winery in St. Helena, California, where Jeremiah Tower and I joined forces for a number of cooking demonstrations celebrating East-West cuisines. There were no recipes; we concentrated on specific food themes and cooked away.

I later catered an extravagant dinner organized by Belle and her husband, Dr. Bernard Rhodes, for the delight of a number of their friends who love good food and wine, including some of the most famous California wine makers: Joseph Phelps, Joseph Heitz, and Jack Davis as well as well-known wine collectors Tawfig N. Khoury and Dr. Louis C. Skinner, Jr., and food writers William Rice and Jill Van Cleave.

The menu and wine were as follows:

---

*N.V. Domaine Chandon, Special Reserve, Magnums*
*1974 Schramsberg Blanc de Blancs, Reserve Cuvée*
- Pasta and California Goat Cheese Wonton Soup
- Dungeness Crab Soufflé in Taro Basket
  *1965 Stony Hill Vineyard Chardonnay*
- West Coast Shellfish and Fish Tart
  *1968 Beaulieu Vineyard Cabernet Sauvignon, Private Reserve*
  *1968 Heitz Wine Cellars Cabernet Sauvignon, Martha's Vineyard*
- Squab Marinated in Chinese Rice Wine. Roasted and Stuffed with

Chinese Duck Liver Sausages served on Cornmeal Crêpes
*1958 Beaulieu Vineyard Cabernet Sauvignon, Private Reserve*
· Cheese Savory
*1976 Joseph Phelps Vineyards Johannisberg Riesling, Select Late Harvest*
· Cold Coconut Cream with Fresh Fruit Compote
*1953 Ficklin Vineyards Tinta Madeira Port*
· Hot Pistachios

I was assisted throughout this dinner by Mark Dierkhising, Peter Hall, and Tom Worthington, all of them superb and imaginative chefs.

In November 1982, Peter Hall and I collaborated at his restaurant in Sacramento, The Fish Emporium. Over a three-day period we offered a series of special menus that included the following items:

---

· Stir-Fried Prawns in Rice Wine Reduction Sauce
· Gratin of Chinese Eggplants
· Grilled Ginger Lamb Chops
· Roasted Loin of Pork with Rice Wine-Butter Sauce

Earlier in the summer of 1981, at the suggestion of Ron Batori, then the dean at the California Culinary Academy, I directed my Academy students in eight weeks of East-West dinners, changing the menu every evening. The menus included such dishes as steamed duck consommé; fillet of pork seasoned with Chinese spices and served with a purée of fresh ginger and apples, Chinese plum sauce, and nectarine slices; and a true East-West vegetable course combining soy sauce and butter, with mushroom stock, over crisp snow peas and Chinese "tree ear" mushrooms. Patricia Unterman, a respected local restaurant critic, gave our efforts a warm review, writing that we had produced "some of the most remarkable, imaginative food in San Francisco." This well-received marathon of East-West cooking certainly encouraged me in my work.

More recently I participated as a member of a team of chefs in the preparation of an elaborate East-West banquet for over one hundred guests. The occasion was sponsored by the Christian Brothers winery to

celebrate its cellar-master's fifty years of service. For Brother Timothy, the venerable cellar-master, we worked together to bring off what Jim Wood, food editor of the *San Francisco Examiner,* described as "a perfect meal." The menu included such dishes as Chinese Greens Ravioli with Black Truffle Cream and Flowering Bok Choy, a real East-West treat. It was an experience enjoyed by both the guests and the kitchen staff. It showed me, once again, that in combining the best of East and West one may indeed achieve surprising and uncommon results.

# INDEX

 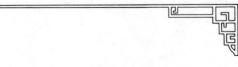

# ABOUT THE AUTHOR

Ken Hom is the author of *Chinese Technique* (Simon and Schuster) and *Ken Hom's Chinese Cookery* and the host of the popular public television series, "Ken Hom's Chinese Cookery." He also conducts a cultural/culinary tour of Hong Kong each Autumn. Ken Hom lives in Berkeley, California, and in Paris, France.